Primary Design and Technology

A Process for Learning

Second Edition

Ron Ritchie

David Fulton Publishers

London

David Fulton Publishers Ltd
Ormond House, 26–27 Boswell Street, London WC1N 3JZ

www.fultonpublishers.co.uk

First edition published in Great Britain by David Fulton Publishers 1995, reprinted 1998
Second edition published in 2001

Note: The right of Ron Ritchie to be identified as the author of this work has been asserted by him in accordance with the Copyright, Designs and Patents Act 1988.

Copyright © Ron Ritchie 2001

British Library Cataloguing in Publication Data
A catalogue record for this book is available from the British Library

ISBN 1–85346–737–5

All rights reserved. No part of this publication may be reproduced, stored in a retrieval system or transmitted, in any form, or by any means, electronic, mechanical, photocopying, recording or otherwise, without the prior permission of the publishers.

The publishers would like to thank Priscilla Sharland for copy-editing and Ray Jarman for proofreading this book.

375.5

Learning
Resource Centre
Stockton
Riverside College

Typeset by FiSH Books, London
Printed in Great Britain by The Cromwell Press Ltd, Trowbridge, Wilts.

Contents

Acknowledgements

This book is the result of my collaboration with primary teachers and other colleagues, some of whose work is included. They have all added to my understanding of design and technology. Like me, they share an enthusiasm for design and technology and have a commitment to constantly striving to improve the quality of children's learning through reflective practice. From my first tentative attempts to teach design and technology in the classroom to more recent work running in-service courses, I have benefited from discussion with other professionals.

In particular, I would like to thank Alan Howe for his contributions (especially to Chapter 7) and Dan Davies for his constructive comments on draft material. We all construct a unique understanding of the world; this text is an attempt to communicate my evolving understanding of design and technology. It is an understanding that is informed by the views of others, but I fully accept responsibility for any inadequacy or inaccuracies evident.

Finally, my thanks to Jill, Anna, Kate and Lucy for their continued support, reassurance and encouragement.

List of case studies

Preface

Design and technology has now been a statutory part of the primary curriculum for over a decade. The first edition of this book was published half-way through this period. It was based on the results of a time of considerable professional development for teachers who were involved in the demanding and challenging task of making the National Curriculum for Design and Technology work in the interests of their pupils. The last five years have been a stage of consolidation which have, in some ways, been a little less exciting for those of us involved in design and technology. The primary curriculum has been dominated by the core subjects, especially literacy and numeracy. In many schools design and technology has been put on the back burner. However, the introduction of National Curriculum 2000 (DfEE/QCA 1999) provided a new stimulus for promoting the importance of design and technology and improving the quality of teaching in order that children's potentials are fully realised. It was therefore timely to update this text in order to contribute to these endeavours. In many ways, the main ideas in the original are still relevant. Consequently I have retained that edition's overall structure. The changes in content are intended to ensure those ideas are explicitly related to the current educational context.

There are a number of themes that run through the book. The first relates to the parallels between the processes involved in design and technology, children's learning, teaching and professional development. Identifying needs and opportunities, planning, implementing and evaluating are common features of these processes. Another theme permeating the book concerns the nature of learning – individuals actively construct new understanding and develop new skills by building upon and modifying existing understanding and capability. This is true for children when tackling challenges and for teachers when improving their practice. Learning usually takes place in a social context, which affects how and what is learnt. Children work together and are supported by a teacher; teachers collaborate with their colleagues.

Over the next few years it is likely that the core curriculum will be less forcefully prioritised and that there will be a 'lighter touch' to inspection with greater reliance on school self-evaluation. This offers scope for further curriculum development in design and technology. I hope that this book will help teachers take up these opportunities as they seek to improve their practice and, consequently, the quality of children's learning.

Ron Ritchie
Bristol
June 2001

CHAPTER 1

The nature of design and technology

1. Introduction

From earliest times human beings have endeavoured to control the world around them in order to survive and to enhance the quality of their existence. For Stone Age hunters this meant making tools and weapons to improve the likelihood of a successful kill when hunting, or exploiting found materials to construct a shelter. Throughout history, humans have attempted to meet needs that they have identified for improving their environment and lives. They have done this by imagining new possibilities, putting their ideas into action and evaluating the outcome to decide whether the need has been met or further action is necessary. In this sense, the process which is the essence of design and technology in schools is one which has had a fundamental part to play in the development of human society. Obviously few of our early ancestors would have articulated their problem solving in these terms, but describing human achievements in this way provides a framework for understanding that development.

This book takes this process (or perhaps, more accurately, processes) as its key idea and explores its relevance and application to young children's education. The next section of this chapter outlines a more recent example of a human attempt to modify the environment in order to meet a perceived need and compares and contrasts this with an example of children's activity in school. This leads to a discussion about the nature of 'design and technology' in education and a rationale for its inclusion in the curriculum of primary schools. Throughout the book there are case studies of design and technology in action in primary school classrooms. To provide a framework for evaluating this work and relating it to your own practice, if you are a teacher, this chapter includes a section outlining the characteristics of quality in terms of learning and teaching, based upon Office for Standards in Education (OFSTED) requirements.

The chapter concludes by exploring how teaching and teachers' professional development parallels the processes involved in design and technology. Teaching involves identifying children's needs, planning a curriculum and learning activities to address those needs, putting those plans into action in the classroom and evaluating the success of the teaching in order to inform decisions about modifying future work. Teachers' professional development through action enquiry or action research can also be seen as a cycle that begins with needs identification, in this case the concerns teachers have about their practice and how it might be improved. The next step involves planning ways to address those concerns, implementing those plans (or changes to practice) and evaluating the effect of the changes. These parallels permeate later chapters. It is intended that teachers can take ideas and insights from the examples in this book and use them as a stimulus to improve the quality of children's learning in design and technology through engaging in action enquiries with their own classes.

2. Design and technology in the wider community and in schools

The label 'design and technology' is not used widely outside educational contexts but it covers the activities of a diverse range of individuals and groups from engineers to interior designers; from town planners to architects; from food technologists to fashion designers; and from graphic designers to furniture makers. The common feature of all of these people is the extent to which they engage in the activity of meeting perceived human needs (or perhaps, more accurately in many situations, *wants*). They are all professional 'problem solvers'. However, that label does not fully do justice to their activities since they are also 'problem seekers'. Part of their work involves looking for problems which they can then solve or opportunities for designing or making something. They are not always concerned with changing negative situations, as the word 'problem' might imply. Design and technology can involve looking for opportunities to improve the quality of lives where a problem is not necessarily perceived or experienced. Throughout this book the word 'problem' in the context of 'problem solving' is taken to include such opportunities. It would also be naïve to ignore the fact that some design and technology activity in the real world does not lead to improved quality of life and is motivated by commercial considerations and the desire for profit.

To understand more about design and technology let us consider an example in the wider community. Anyone crossing the River Severn between England and Wales recently will have benefited from the outcome of a major engineering project: the new Severn Bridge. This project, completed in the late nineties involved a large number of individuals and teams working together to meet a common goal. The perceived need for this enterprise arose from the demand on the existing river crossing and network of roads serving it. More and more people wanted to cross the river and local and national planners (from the local authorities on both sides of the river and from the Department of Transport) recognised that the existing bridge would not be adequate. A decision was taken to construct a new bridge. This decision was based upon information from a variety of sources, including geographers and social scientists who were able to predict population and demographic trends and future needs for travel between the Bristol area and Monmouthshire. Those with economic expertise analysed the financial viability of building a new bridge based on its potential returns from tolls and other economic considerations. The challenge of designing and constructing the bridge required different expertise. Geologists were needed to decide exactly where a bridge could be sited; structural engineers and designers produced ideas of what kind of bridge could be built; material scientists contributed understanding of the range of materials that could be used and in what ways. Those charged with generating ideas for the new bridge used their knowledge and understanding of bridge structures and their evaluation of existing bridges. At the design stage, when ideas were being generated, clarified, developed and communicated to interested parties, social and environmental issues were considered and a range of constraints that would apply to the project had to be identified. A considerable amount of time and expertise was necessary to refine ideas, produce more detailed designs and plan how such a major undertaking should be tackled. After several years and many thousands of hours of individual and collaborative activity it was time to implement the plans and begin the construction of the bridge and the infrastructure necessary to support its construction and operation. Construction involved the use of sophisticated skills and techniques as the workers used a variety of materials, tools and equipment. At each stage of construction new difficulties or problems arose and had to be solved. As during the earlier stages of development, evaluation of what was being done, and how, was ongoing. This evaluation provided insights into changes to designs, construction techniques and other aspects of the project that were needed to make necessary improvements. On completion of the bridge a more systematic evaluation took place including rigorous safety checks and an assessment of the structure's stability in different weather and under different traffic conditions. This confirmed that the new bridge could remain open in weather conditions that caused closure of the original bridge. Before it could be opened other designers and technologists had a part to play. For example, systems had to be devised to control traffic flow and organise the collection of tolls; the environment around the entry and exit points of the bridge had to be planned and constructed.

In simple terms, the construction of the second Severn crossing can be seen to involve aspects of researching and clarifying needs, generating ideas and designs, planning to implement a chosen design, implementing a design and producing an outcome and evaluation. These are the key elements of design and technology.

Such activity in the wider community can be compared with an example of classroom practice in design and technology. Figure 1.1 shows a group of children with whom I worked at Novers Lane Junior School, in South Bristol, who had also made a bridge. Tina, Philip, Kirsty and Sarah were 10- and 11-year-olds who had recently been on a class visit to London. Their parents had funded the trip and on return the class had decided to stage an exhibition to show their appreciation and illustrate what they had gained from the trip. The need for their design and technology activity was therefore identified. This small group decided, through discussion, to focus their part of the display upon the bridges they had seen. The bridge they designed and made is illustrated during a stage of construction. They had discussed the variety of bridges they had seen and decided to model Tower Bridge to illustrate the way it opens. The decision to make it from wood and card was based upon their previous, somewhat limited but successful, experience of working with wood. The children then produced designs: sketches, drawings and more detailed plans which were used to inform their making. The mechanism to raise the decks involved exploratory activities with construction kit components before they were satisfied with a method of using cotton reel pulley-wheels and a simple ratchet system. Kirsty decided that their bridge needed lights

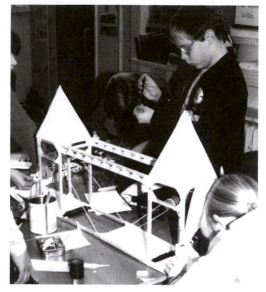

Figure 1.1 A model of Tower Bridge

like the real one and started work on simple circuits to provide illumination for the model. While doing this she had the idea of a warning system to show the bridge was being raised. Without help she invented a simple contact switch, using metal foil contacts on the tower structure and the deck to light a bulb on the bridge approach warning that it was opening. Individuals worked on specific aspects of the project, but the outcome was undoubtedly collaborative. It involved the children in developing their manipulative skills (for example in terms of accurate marking, measuring, cutting and joining) as well as applying and developing their knowledge and understanding (about structures and materials, simple electric circuits and mechanisms). The outcome was a working model, which functioned well (after considerable evaluation and modification) and was designed to look good. The finished model that was displayed, with other supporting material, made a valuable contribution to the exhibition and this gave its creators great satisfaction. Producing the outcome and the supporting material involved aspects of other curriculum areas, apart from the science already discussed. There were opportunities for work in geography (location and purpose of the bridge), history (when and why the bridge was built), art (aesthetic aspects of their model and representational painting of the bridge), maths (dimensions of the real and model bridges, scale, accurate measuring) and English (poetic and transactional writing about the visit and work).

What are the similarities between the two examples that might help us understand the nature of design and technology? Both cases:

- involved purposeful action in response to a perceived need or want;
- were concerned with what might be and in that sense were future orientated;
- required the individuals and groups to be creative in the generation of new ideas and finding solutions to a range of problem situations;

- were open-ended in that there was not one answer or solution to a problem. A variety of outcomes were possible and decisions had to be taken about the most suitable;
- involved learning through experience and quite often through trial and error;
- were concerned with aesthetics and function. Outcomes had to look good and work well;
- involved optimisation and value judgements. Decisions were taken based sometimes on incomplete data or had to be based upon the subjective views of certain individuals or groups;
- were cooperative ventures and involved working together collaboratively to achieve a common goal. They involved looking at what others had done and 'copying ideas' before developing them;
- were multi-disciplinary activities drawing upon concepts and information from a range of subjects.

These features of design and technology provide a starting point for understanding what it involves and why it has a part to play in education.

Of course, there are differences between the two examples given. One of the major differences between design and technology in schools and corresponding activities in the world beyond school is usually that of scale and the resources available, which is very evident in these examples! An even more significant one is the emphasis teachers place on the processes in which children engage and their potential for learning, as opposed to industry and commerce where the product or outcome is more important.

To return to the nature of design and technology beyond schools: such activity involves identifying, analysing and meeting human needs (and wants). These may be met by making some kind of product or outcome, for example: a chair; a system to control traffic around a city centre using traffic-lights; or an improved working space. It is a creative activity that requires the application of skills, resources and knowledge and understanding and making value judgements when designing and making these outcomes. As we have already noted, the term 'design and technology' encompasses a range of activities through which humans change the world around them. It is one of the means whereby we attempt to make progress and society develops. Crucially, it involves the ability to operate effectively in the made world.

Design and technology is treated as a unitary concept within the National Curriculum,

> Our use of design and technology as a unitary concept, to be spoken in one breath as it were, does not therefore embody redundancy. It is intended to emphasise the intimate connection between the two activities as well as to imply a concept which is broader than either design or technology individually and the whole of which we believe is educationally important.
>
> (DES/WO 1988, p. 2)

However, the two components make different contributions to activities. Good design, within design and technology, is a fusion of innovation, function, aesthetics, ergonomics (concerning the physical relationship between humans and machines), environmental considerations, communication and visual identity. It is more difficult to define the 'technology' component in design and technology. At this stage it is enough to regard technology as the science and art of getting things done through the application of knowledge. Technology is the means by which outcomes are made to work or function – it is the tools with which we design and make.

Effecting changes through design and technology involves engaging in a disciplined process (or processes) which I have simplified, so far, to identifying needs, generating ideas and designs, planning to implement those ideas, implementing and evaluating. However, it is important to recognise that design and technology is not concerned with a linear process, nor is it adequately described by the simple model outlined. It is usually cyclical and iterative; for example, it involves going back at each stage of the activity to plans, designs and original specifications in the light of new experiences. The cyclical nature of design and technology is also evident in situations where the evaluation of an existing product will lead to an identification of other needs or opportunities. The first stage is not always 'identifying needs'. The simple model is offered as no more than a guide; the elements described are more like 'staging posts' in an activity. It is not a set of hoops to go through in a particular order. What is essentially involved as an individual engages in this process is an interaction between thought and action: between cognitive and manipulative activity. The relationship between these activities is complex as illustrated in the case studies in this book.

Before finishing this discussion about the nature of design and technology, I would like to share with you a view that I originally heard in a talk by Ron Lewin (Technology Consultant in Berkshire). He described 'good' technologists (*sic*) as those who use their 'heads, hands and hearts'. He went on to cite, as an example, the flying buttresses that can be observed on some churches. The constructors of these had certainly used their 'heads' in terms of knowing that such an addition to the structure of the church would support the walls and make the building stronger (although they would not necessarily have understood why); they used their considerable craft skills to carve and construct the buttresses, and finally there was another dimension to their work that he described as the 'heart' – their belief in the power of the images carved into the structure to ward off evil spirits. Not all design and technology activities will involve 'heart' in quite this way, but it is an important reminder that feelings and value judgements have a significant part to play in design and technology alongside cognitive and manipulative activity. His example serves to remind us that design and technology are concerned with much more than 'high' technology. It is also timely, at this stage of our discussion, to remember that design and technology, as I have described it, is much more than applied science: it draws upon a range of subject disciplines.

3. A rationale for design and technology in the primary school

The above discussion runs the risk of implying that the purpose of design and technology in schools is to prepare children for similar activity in the wider community as adults: that design and technology is fundamentally a vocationally-based area of learning. This is far from the truth and although some children may go on to engage in design and technology as a part of their working lives, the rest of the school population also benefit from design and technology education, but in other ways.

Some of these benefits can be understood by considering the relationship of design and technology to children's development in their early years before schooling begins. Young children are curious and interested in the world around them. Almost from the first day of life children strive to control and change their immediate surroundings. They begin to realise that they can make choices and express preferences for certain conditions, food and toys. As they grow older they become more aware of their surroundings and the behaviour of others. They learn that decision making about options is an essential part of survival, of being happy and improving one's situation. Observing, helping and imitating adults and older children enable them to appreciate how others control and change the world. They learn that the 'right' material and 'right' tool are necessary for particular purposes. Through play children make full use of their imagination and begin to 'image', or to see in their minds' eyes, new possibilities. For example, the pile of bricks is imaged as a tower to be built. Play also helps children understand the relationship between people, places, objects and certain behaviours. The teddy bear can become a patient and a towel can become a bandage in order to role-play an experience of visiting the doctor. Children learn to represent the world through the medium of signs and symbols (such as images and words). They reorganise these mental pictures of the world through imaginative play, talking, questioning, listening and exploring. An awareness of the purposes of human behaviour develops through play; children become aware of the future dimension of their actions. Children's play provides firm foundations upon which design and technology builds. For the child and the designer knowledge of the past and present is used to speculate about the future. Both are 'building a mental bridge' outwards from what they know of the world as it is, towards what they believe might be made of it (Somerset LEA 1990a, p. 11). Children come to school already having learnt a great deal that is relevant to their design and technology work.

At another level, the links between design and technology and everyday life in the adult world are significant. There are many activities in which we engage as adults that have direct and indirect links with design and technology: redesigning a garden; planning a holiday; buying a house; decorating a room; planning a birthday party; making a cake for a special occasion; choosing and making clothes for an event; designing and making a toy for a present; organising a system for storing and retrieving CDs; putting up a display. All of these involve elements of designing, planning, making and evaluating.

Consequently, design and technology can be regarded as an area of experience in schools, which not only builds upon and is similar to children's development before they enter school, but also equips them to deal with everyday situations after they leave.

There are other aspects of our daily lives that are relevant as we consider the nature of design and technology and its place in education. We live in a 'technological society'. We use technology every day, from the moment the alarm wakes us in the morning to the moment we lay down our book and turn off the light at night. Technology has other, less direct or obvious influences upon our lives as well. The social and environmental effects of technological progress are well documented and awareness of these could be argued to be essential to informed and full participation in our democratic society (see Howe *et al.* 2001). Design and technology education is therefore contributing, or should be, to both of these dimensions: developing an individual's capability for using technology and developing awareness of technology and its effects. A personal anecdote can illustrate the importance of technological awareness. I joined the British Aircraft Corporation (now British Aerospace) when I left school and as an apprentice worked on the 'Concorde' project. I was impressed by the technological achievement of designing the plane, its aesthetic qualities and the sheer complexity of building it. However, I was also uncomfortable about why it was being built at all, particularly since it was likely to cause environmental damage if produced in large numbers. Where was the need? The opportunity to find out arose when the Managing Director addressed all of the apprentices. I naïvely asked the question, 'Why is BAC producing a supersonic passenger aircraft?' His answer was simple, direct and revealing, 'Because we can.' It confirmed, for me, that technological advance had a 'momentum' which is not necessarily in our collective best interests, nor always about meeting needs. The conclusion of this story of youthful idealism saw me at university, sponsored by BAC, writing a thesis evaluating the Concorde project and concluding that it should be cancelled. The aerospace industry and I parted company at that point and I resolved to become a teacher with the mission of producing more aware engineers for the future. As I write, Concorde has been grounded for technical rather than environmental reasons. It had been flying for 30 years, always looking spectacular, but constantly polluting the environment as it served the needs of a small minority. I still consider the conclusion of my thesis to have been sound! This book is, I hope, continuing evidence of my own perseverance towards my original 'mission'.

It is interesting that in our society it is generally acceptable to be technologically incompetent. Individuals even boast about not being capable of using products such as video recorders. Compare this with society's attitude to illiteracy and we see an aspect of our culture that appears to devalue technological activity and, perhaps by association, those who engage in it. C. P. Snow, back in the fifties, discussed what he called 'the two cultures': the science and literary communities in universities, their lack of common interest and – in some ways -contempt for each other (Snow 1959). The phrase has since become a cliché for wider divisions in contemporary western society between 'doers' and 'thinkers'; between vocational and academic interests. This is, of course, an oversimplified view, but design and technology education for all, as required by the National Curriculum, could be seen as playing a part in overcoming this divide.

Design and technology in schools has the potential to make a significant contribution to children's cultural knowledge and understanding. As I have written elsewhere (Howe *et al.* 2001), it is a myth that technology is a modern phenomenon that is associated with the industrial revolution, progress, development and firmly rooted in Western Europe. The fact is that various societies around the world were using 'technologies' long before the population of Britain benefited from them. For example, the Chinese were using sophisticated navigation techniques based on the compass; the Egyptians were using mechanisms to make work easier in order to construct pyramids; in India various innovative systems for cooling buildings, food and drinks were being used. Siraj-Blatchford (1996) highlights an interesting contrast between Pompeii, which was destroyed in 79 AD, where excavations indicate that the Romans had sophisticated technology related to plumbing and heating, and the fact that in 1951 over a third of houses in Britain lacked any form of fixed bath fitting (p. 5). He reminds us that 'cultural chauvinism runs deep'. He goes on to suggest that it is 'time we put technology in its place'. In other words, it is a responsibility of teachers to ensure the design and technology education they offer children is based on a sound and appropriate foundation regarding the history of technology, its global dimension and its impact on societies. Design and technology should have a multicultural dimension and make a contribution to anti-racist education – challenging such misconceptions as that discussed above.

The National Curriculum for design and technology (DfEE/QCA 1999), for the first time, provides a clear statement about the importance of Design and Technology which is worth quoting in full,

> Design and technology prepares pupils to participate in tomorrow's rapidly changing technologies. They learn to think and intervene creatively to improve quality of life. The subject calls for pupils to become autonomous and creative problem solvers, as individuals and members of a team. They must look for needs, wants and opportunities and respond to them by developing a range of ideas and making products and systems. They combine practical skills with an understanding of aesthetics, social and environmental issues, function and industrial practices. As they do so, they reflect on and evaluate present and past design and technology, its uses and effects. Through design and technology, all pupils can become discriminating and informed users of products, and become innovators.
>
> (p. 90)

Design and technology has been part of the statutory curriculum for every primary aged child in England and Wales for a decade, so it could be argued that it is not necessary to rehearse a rationale for design and technology: its inclusion in the National Curriculum makes that superfluous. This is not a view I share since primary teachers still have to make a professional commitment to making design and technology effective in their classrooms. Such a commitment deserves to be based upon a convincing case for its place in the curriculum. The discussion above and the National Curriculum statement offers the basis of that case.

The following summarises the reasons why it is worth putting effort and time into the development of design and technology in primary schools and classrooms.

- Children's learning is an active process: they learn through doing and talking about what they are doing (Ollerenshaw and Ritchie 1997). Design and technology activities provide ample opportunities for this since they involve children in producing practical solutions to problems. Such activities can develop cognitive and manipulative skills. They can help children develop an understanding of the world around them as well as learning how to work with tools and materials.
- Design and technology tasks provide scope for children working individually and collaboratively within groups. Most learning does not occur in isolation and the social

context in which learning takes place affects that learning. More than any other area of experience in the curriculum, design and technology should involve children working together, sharing ideas and developing group-work skills.

- Design and technology activities can foster personal qualities and attitudes such as curiosity, creativity, originality, self-reliance, cooperation, tolerance for others' views, respect for evidence and perseverance. Design and technology is not the only curriculum area to foster these, but it is one in which attitudes and personal qualities are particularly important and in some ways necessary for success.

- Design and technology provides potential for the use of problem solving skills and strategies and also, crucially, provides opportunities for 'problem creating'. Problem solving is a valuable approach to teaching and learning that can be applied in most areas of the primary curriculum. It is included in the National Curriculum key skills (DfEE/QCA 1999, p. 21).

- Design and technology can encourage children to tackle problems in contexts that are real, important and meaningful to them. These activities have an intrinsic appeal to children of all abilities and can enable them, within a stimulating and relevant learning situation, to experience excitement, a sense of achievement and the motivation to learn.

- Designing and making activities provide a context in which technological awareness and capability can be developed, thereby helping to equip pupils for living and working effectively and creatively in a technological society.

- Through design and technology work children learn about other times, other cultures and the world of work.

- Aspects of approaches and processes learnt in the early years are appropriate throughout schooling and beyond. Design and technology require a flexible approach and the ability of an individual to approach situations flexibly is a necessary life skill (at home, work and play).

- Design and technology provides rich opportunities for the development of a broad range of key skills including communication, application of number, information technology and working with others (DfEE/QCA 1999, p. 20).

- Design and technology develops planning skills, requiring children to organise themselves.

- Design and technology encourages children to look critically and appreciatively at the made world, the way it influences their lives and the values that they hold. Activities in these areas also encourage them to use their imagination to organise and improve the immediate environment.

- Design and technology can foster links between subjects and integrate rather than fragment the curriculum. In primary schools, this work may be planned as a part of topic approach.

- Design and technology can make a significant contribution to cultural understanding and the new curriculum area of 'citizenship' (Howe *et al.* 2001).

- Design and technology provides excellent opportunities for children to be innovative and demonstrate and develop their creativity.

4. The development of design and technology in primary schools

Long before the National Curriculum required teachers to teach design and technology, children had been offered experiences similar to those that we now call 'design and technology'. In the past a variety of labels have been used for this work. During the eighties 'problem solving' was a common way of describing such activities. In some of the literature and curriculum materials, as well as the approaches adopted by advisory staff, it was also common for science and technology to be seen as indistinguishable and appropriately (in the view of such advocates) covered by one umbrella term. These approaches fostered a narrow view in which design had little part to play and technology was seen simply as applied science. In other areas of the country, 'primary craft, design and technology' (CDT) became the way of describing work which was regarded as having a distinct role in the curriculum, separate from science. This approach suffered in some respects by seeing primary school work as a 'watered down' version of secondary CDT but at least recognised the importance of design. Such approaches focused upon the use of resistant materials such as card, wood and construction kits. They less frequently included work with textiles, food or graphic media.

In other publications and support material we find the following labels used to describe children's experiences in this area of the curriculum: 'technology'; 'design and make'; 'design-related activities'; 'primary engineering'; 'craft' and 'junk-modelling'. This proliferation of terms contributed to considerable confusion among teachers and a need for cohesion in the development of this curriculum area. In contrast to developments in areas such as art, maths, science or English there was little research into children's learning in design and technology and no real consensus about the subject. This confusion was even apparent in the development of the National Curriculum. Originally, in the primary phase, 'technology' was linked with science and the original report of the Science Working Group included proposals for primary technology (Science Working Group 1987). A year later this linkage was abandoned and primary design and technology became the responsibility of the Design and Technology Working Group (DES/WO 1988).

Despite the confusion with terminology, in primary design and technology the eighties and nineties were, in many ways, an exciting time of considerable development, if without clear direction. It is, however, possible to identify common features in all of the approaches advocated and the case studies reported by teachers during that period. The most obvious of these is the active involvement of children in practical activity and the emphasis placed on the processes in which the children were engaged. It was evident that, in general, children were, at some stage, involved in meeting needs or opportunities (their own or their teacher's); generating ideas (and sometimes designs); making plans; implementing those plans; and evaluating (their own or other people's) outcomes. The framework that subsequently became established in the original Design and Technology orders (DES/WO, 1990) reflected the best practice that already existed in some schools, although the National Curriculum was not intended simply to consolidate existing good practice but to structure and extend it. For other teachers, of course, the inclusion of design and technology in the National Curriculum came as a surprise and required them to introduce a completely new area into the curriculum. For the majority, successful implementation of the original National Curriculum in design and technology required changes to existing practice.

5. The National Curriculum requirements for design and technology

The original framework (DES/WO 1990), with its over-ambitious and complex programmes of study, was replaced by a simpler version five years later (DfE/WO 1995) and minor changes were subsequently introduced in September 2000 (DfEE/QCA 1999), on which this book is based. Davies (2000) provides a helpful account of the development of the National Curriculum and the implications of the three statutory versions. It is worth noting that consultation with teachers and professional associations prior to the introduction of Curriculum 2000 provided evidence of reasonable satisfaction with the post-Dearing (1995) version, which was regarded as workable.

The initial (1990) version conceptualised design and technology through the process introduced earlier in this chapter:

identifying needs and opportunities;
generating a design;
planning and making;
evaluating.

Although these elements were listed in a linear way (and were originally numbered as Attainment Targets 1 to 4), the Non-statutory Guidance (NCC 1991a) emphasised, as discussed above, that children's approach to design and technology was unlikely to be linear. The iterative/cyclical nature of the process and a view of the elements as 'staging posts' visited and revisited in a different order on different occasions outlined then is still sound and will be the basis of the analysis of later case studies. Teachers regarded the 1995 framework as much more manageable. It comprised two attainment targets (ATs) for assessing and reporting design and technology: Designing (AT1) and Making (AT2). There was a single, much briefer, programme of study (PoS) for each key stage and a clear articulation of the different types of activities involved in design and technology. The latest version (DfEE/QCA 1999) involves a reorganisation of the PoSs (with a slight reduction in content where there was overlap with other subjects, but more references to information and communication technology (ICT) and now requires assessment through one generic attainment target. The elements of identifying needs, designing, making and evaluating remain evident.

The Key Stage 1 PoS (DfEE/QCA 1999) states that,

pupils learn how to think imaginatively and talk about what they like and dislike when designing and making. They build on their early childhood experiences of investigating objects around them. They explore how familiar things work and talk about, draw and model their ideas. They learn how to design and make safely and could start to use ICT as part of their designing and making.

It is stressed that 'teaching should ensure that knowledge and understanding are applied when developing ideas, planning, making products and evaluating them' (DfEE/QCA 1999, p. 92).

What pupils should be taught is outlined under the following headings:

- Developing, planning and communicating ideas
- Working with tools, equipment, materials and components to make quality products
- Evaluating processes and products
- Knowledge and understanding of materials and components

The detail of these sections will be discussed in later chapters. Curiously, the term 'designing' has been removed and replaced by 'developing, planning and communicating ideas' as a heading. The range of activities to be provided are listed under 'Breadth of study' and comprise:

- investigating and evaluating a range of familiar products;
- focused practical tasks that develop a range of techniques, skills, processes and knowledge;
- design and make assignments using a range of materials, including food, items that can be put together to make products, and textiles.

These are almost identical to those listed in the previous version except that 'disassembling' has been removed from the list of activities.

The Key Stage 2 PoS states that,

during key stage 2 pupils work on their own and as part of a team on a range of designing and making activities. They think about what products are used for and the needs of the people who use them. They plan what has to be done and identify what works well and what could be improved in their own and other people's designs. They draw on knowledge and understanding from other areas of the curriculum and use computers in a range of ways.

(DfEE/QCA 1999, p. 94)

Identical headings are used to detail what should be taught. The major difference with regard to the activities described relates to the materials to be used, which at Key Stage 2 additionally includes electrical and mechanical components, mouldable materials, stiff and flexible sheet materials.

Statements about inclusion and health and safety in Design and Technology are included under 'General Teaching Requirements' (DfEE/QCA 1999, pp. 30–40) which cover both key stages.

Level descriptions of the attainment target are worded generally to allow teachers to judge a 'best fit' based on assessment of children's work throughout a key stage (discussed in Chapter 8). For example, Level 4 is described in these terms,

Pupils generate ideas by collecting and using information. They take users' views into account and produce step-by-step plans. They communicate alternative ideas using words, labelled sketches and models, showing that they are aware of constraints. They work with a variety of materials and components with some accuracy, paying attention to quality of finish and to function. They select and work with a range of tools and equipment. They reflect on their designs as they develop, bearing in mind the way the product will be used. They identify what is working well and what could be improved.

(DfEE/QCA 1999, p. 25)

In Wales a different framework exists (ACCAC 2000) which is simpler than the English version and structured under the following sections for each key stage: focus statement; knowledge and understanding; designing skills; and making skills. Interestingly, construction kits remain in the Welsh version as materials that pupils should use in both key stages whereas in England they are no longer explicitly included in Key Stage 2.

In September 2000, the Foundation Stage was introduced for children aged 3 to 6. Linked to this stage of children's development are the early learning goals (QCA/DfEE 2000a, p. 26). Appropriately, subject labels and divisions do not apply to such young children. However, there is ample evidence in the early learning goals of outcomes which have significant links to children's later learning in design and technology. For example the following are included in the goals for knowledge and understanding of the world.

By the end of the foundation stage, most children will be able to:

- build and construct with a wide range of objects, selecting appropriate resources, and adapting their work where necessary;
- select the tools and techniques they need to shape, assemble and join the materials they are using;
- find out about and identify the uses of everyday technology and use information and communication technology and programmable toys to support their learning.

(DfEE/QCA 2000a, pp. 86–99)

Goals for the other specified areas of learning (personal, social and emotional development; mathematical development; physical development; and creative development) all include outcomes that support later learning in design and technology. Consequently, design and technology experiences are now included in the statutory curriculum for all children from the age of 3 to 16.

The following section considers what good practice in design and technology might look like if the statutory requirements are being implemented.

6. Characteristics of quality in teaching and learning

At the present time, quality in schools is officially and publicly evaluated by OFSTED inspectors and so it is appropriate to start with their criteria from the current guidance for inspecting schools (OFSTED 1999a). Although couched in very general terms they do provide a useful agenda for evaluating later case studies. In determining their judgements, inspectors consider, among other criteria, the extent to which teachers:

- show good subject knowledge and understanding in the way they present and discuss their subject;
- plan effectively, setting clear objectives that pupils understand;
- challenge and inspire pupils, expecting the most of them, so as to deepen their knowledge and understanding;
- use methods which enable all pupils to learn effectively;
- manage pupils well and insist on high standards of behaviour;
- use time, support staff and other resources, especially information and communications technology effectively;
- assess pupils' work thoroughly and use assessments to help and encourage pupils to overcome difficulties.

(OFSTED 1999a, p. 46)

Inspectors also have Primary Subject Guidance (OFSTED 2000) which provides additional advice on design and technology. This details specific features of design and technology learning and teaching. OFSTED inspectors are required to evaluate standards, by judging pupils' ability to:

- investigate, develop, plan and communicate design ideas;
- know about and work with tools, equipment, materials and components in the making of products and systems;
- evaluate the processes they use and the products they make; and
- consider people's needs and wants and the opportunities of making products for them.

(OFSTED 2000, p. 60)

The Guidance asserts that where standards are high, pupils:

- creatively apply appropriate knowledge and skills;
- succeed in designing and making good-quality products from a range of materials and components;
- evaluate their work as they go along;
- test their products and carry out any necessary modifications to improve them;
- talk confidently about their technological ideas;
- present information and ideas by writing and drawing, including using ICT;
- work both independently and co-operatively.

(OFSTED 2000, p. 60)

To evaluate the quality of teaching, inspectors are expected to make judgements on:

- the frequency with which pupils are taught design and technology, and quality of planned progression in the scheme of work;
- whether teachers' lesson plans take adequate account of the length of time that activities are likely to take;
- how well teachers ask questions in order to elicit pupils' design ideas;
- teachers' confidence and understanding of the rationale for design and technology education;

- how well teachers organise the classroom, tools, equipment and materials;
- issues regarding the number of pupils involved in practical activities and other risk assessments;
- adequacy of space for pupils to work safely, for example has the teacher altered layout of tables, removed chairs etc. to give extra floor space?
- any concerns about classroom assistants or parents taking the lead;
- teachers' ability to demonstrate skills safely and effectively;
- the use of other pupils' work for exemplification;
- the use of pupils to demonstrate in order to consolidate and to check that pupils know exactly how to use equipment or tools;
- whether space is allocated for specific tasks such as drilling and gluing;
- availability of resources that may dictate numbers who can do practical work at any time; and
- if groups are engaged in different activities at any one time, is the teacher giving sufficient attention to design and technology or are pupils left to get on with it?

(OFSTED 2000, p. 60)

These criteria for quality are consistent with the nature of primary design and technology so far outlined and with the examples offered in this book. However, they cover only some aspects of design and technology and say nothing, for example, about technological awareness or the values involved. These aspects are, I consider, also important features of quality in design and technology.

A recent review of standards in primary design and technology (OFSTED 1999b), based on observations of 8,500 lessons over the previous 5 years, noted that,

> standards in D&T continue to improve in both Key Stages 1 and 2 although they remain lower than in most subjects. Standards in designing and making have risen markedly since . . . 1995 and are better than those in knowledge and understanding.

The quality of teaching in Key Stage 1 was judged to be better than that in Key Stage 2. Lack of subject expertise among teachers was a major concern of the review, which it was claimed adversely affected teachers' expectations of what pupils can achieve, the quality of the planning and preparation and assessment of pupils' attainment. The inspectors found that pupils' attitudes to work was almost always positive and design and technology made a very significant contribution to their overall personal development. They reported that pupils generally behaved well in design and technology, often working in groups as well as on their own. They showed interest and enthusiasm, enjoyed the practical work, usually persevered with problems and behaved sensibly with tools and materials. The review reported that standards were highest where teachers ensured that pupils: developed a simple specification, as part of designing, for what they were going to make, usually through lots of discussion about what the product would be like and what it had got to do; made products using a wide range of simple hand tools and materials; were given the chance, with guidance, to select these materials themselves; tested and evaluated products, including those they have made themselves. In the case of unsatisfactory work there was usually lack of clear, subject-specific learning objectives.

In order to further improve standards in design and technology, OFSTED recommend that schools should:

- develop and make the most of specialist expertise in design and technology and ensure that co-ordinators have the time and opportunity to monitor standards and progress in the school;
- check that design and technology work is progressively more demanding, building on previous experience. In particular, the generic skills of designing and making need to be advanced by each activity and not just repeated using a different material or process;
- encourage teachers to use the full range of interdependent activities identified in the National Curriculum (designing and making assignments; focused practical tasks; investigation and evaluation);
- check that pupils have access to an adequate range of materials, tools and equipment when they are designing and making.

(OFSTED 2000, p. 63)

The Chief Inspector's most recent annual report (OFSTED 2001) highlights that pupils' achievements in design and technology (and geography) are lower than other subjects and that pupils continue to be better at making than designing (para. 13). This report also indicates that able pupils are often set insufficiently challenging work (para. 23). The loss of time for design and technology in some schools is associated with loss of depth and breadth of the curriculum (para. 29). These reports provide the challenge for primary teachers in the next period of development of design and technology. It is a purpose of this book to help teachers meet this challenge.

7. Improving the quality of design and technology teaching

Teaching involves a process which parallels that outlined as describing design and technology. Teachers aim to meet children's needs by generating ideas for learning experiences that can be provided. Selecting starting points and contexts for activities and identifying opportunities for learning requires creative thinking and imagination on the part of teachers. Teaching involves 'designing' the curriculum, planning – often in some detail – how activities will be introduced to the children and developed. Teachers then put their plans into action in the classroom and collect evidence to help them monitor and evaluate how successful their teaching has been in providing experiences that have led to children learning. This evidence will come from their assessments of individual children, their perception of how well things worked and from the children's responses.

A key question which this book aims to help teachers address is, 'How can I improve the quality of my teaching in design and technology?' However, no amount of reading of case studies describing and analysing other teachers' classroom work will, on its own, change what goes on in another teacher's classroom. Changes to teachers' practice require them to make a commitment to change and become actively involved in making changes.

Constructive and effective changes are likely to be based upon an honest and analytical examination of what they currently do. This will enable them to construct an understanding of their practice and recognise the professional dilemmas faced every time they teach. Those of us involved in teaching hold a set of educational values (what we believe about teaching and learning and the way children should be taught). Often these are implicit but they inform decisions we take. Unfortunately the reality of our classrooms is inevitably such that we are not always able to put our educational values into action. Whitehead (1989) claims they are, in effect, often 'denied in action'. Changes in practice will potentially lead to teachers' educational values being more fully lived out in their day to day work. How then might a teacher go about making changes to practice?

Consider the following statements from Whitehead (1989):

- I experience a problem when my educational values are denied in practice;
- I imagine ways of overcoming my problems;
- I act on a chosen solution;
- I evaluate the outcomes of my action;
- I modify my problems, ideas and actions in the light of my evaluations.

Following these steps involves teachers carrying out 'action enquiries' into their practice. It is a sequence which again parallels the simplified design and technology process discussed above. Identification of needs is now replaced by identification of a concern; generating a design and planning to implement it is replaced by imagining new ways of working and planning to implement a chosen way forward; making a product is replaced by implementing a new approach and collecting evidence of its effectiveness; evaluation of outcome is there in both processes. Like design and technology activities, action enquiries can be most successful when they are approached systematically; when collaboration is involved and when evaluative decisions are based upon the best available evidence. Engaging in action enquiries (that, it should be stressed, are not limited only to situations were values are 'denied in action') is one way in which several of the teachers who have contributed case studies to this book have attempted to improve their practice. Their approach is discussed in Chapter 9. It has been introduced at this stage to inform decisions about your own professional development and ways in which you might choose to use this book. Consideration of the case studies and related discussion may help you clarify the nature of your educational values related to design and technology. If you are a teacher, it may help you to reflect upon your current practice. Some aspects of what you read will no doubt act to reinforce and consolidate what you already do: the values involved will be congruent with your own. In other examples you may gain a new awareness and recognise ways in which your practice could be improved. The examples and/or related discussion may then offer pointers to the nature of changes you could make. However, ownership of those changes remains absolutely with you. Nothing I write can directly make any difference in your classroom. You are the only one who can do that. At times, of course, you may find your values are not reconcilable with a centralised curriculum and pedagogic control – but that's the subject of another book!

8. The content of other chapters

The rest of the book is structured around ways in which design and technology contribute to children's learning. The next chapter, 'Children's learning in design and technology', considers the skills, knowledge and understanding, values and personal qualities/attitudes used and developed during design and technology activities. Providing design and technology activities for children does not guarantee individual children will necessarily engage with the task in a way that leads to learning. Similarly, it cannot be assumed that children asked to solve problems will actually be using problem solving skills, they may simply be repeating a previous task or activity. The role of the teacher is therefore vital, and the ways in which teachers facilitate the whole range of children's learning at different stages of design and technology is analysed.

The significance of context in design and technology activities is the starting point for Chapter 3, 'Opportunities for design and technology', which also focuses on identifying needs. The chapter treats, in parallel, opportunities for design and technology across the curriculum and the importance of context when planning and implementing classroom work. The relationship between design and technology and other areas of the curriculum is analysed.

Chapter 4, 'Designing', explores the place of imaging and concrete modelling at this stage of design and technology activities. The use of a variety of media, and techniques for generating, developing and communicating ideas are outlined. The way in which children can be helped to design effectively is explored.

The following two chapters deal with making aspects of design and technology. Chapter 5, 'Making – using construction kits', introduces this phase of the process and the opportunities it provides for the assessment of children's skills, knowledge and understanding and attitudes. The rest of this chapter focuses upon the use of construction kits and the learning potential they offer. Chapter 6, 'Making – using everyday and other materials', includes case study material illustrating children working with a variety of media including resistant materials (everyday materials and wood), clay, textiles and food. The skills and techniques used to work with them are introduced.

'Evaluation', is the theme of Chapter 7. It is evident throughout the earlier chapters as an aspect of design and technology that is used at each stage of the process. However, this chapter looks at evaluation in more detail and explores evaluation of outcomes and of the process involved in producing these. There is an analysis of the assessment opportunities that are linked to evaluation and the way in which the review phase of classroom work can be used for assessment purposes.

Chapter 8, 'Planning for learning', considers short-, medium- and long-term planning of design and technology and the significance of planning work for the individual child, the class and throughout the school. Different approaches to planning design and technology are compared. The need for whole-school planning and schemes of work is another area covered by this chapter. The QCA Scheme of Work (SoW) for Design and Technology (QCA/DfEE 1998 and updated in QCA/DfEE 2000b) is outlined and ways in which it can be used by schools explored. There is also a section drawing together issues related to assessment and record-keeping.

Chapter 9, 'Professional development', returns to the relationship between design and technology and action enquiry (in terms of the processes involved). Different routes to professional development and the value of collaboration are emphasised. The key strands of the book are brought together and the issue of how children can best be prepared for life in the twenty-first century is examined. This section considers the extent to which current educational practices and the National Curriculum are an adequate preparation for adult life in a fast changing world in which technology will play an increasingly important part. The conclusion re-emphasises the need for technological capability as a life skill and technological awareness as an essential element of full participation in a democratic society.

9. Conclusion

This chapter has attempted to clarify what is meant by design and technology and why such work should be treated as essential and important elements of the primary curriculum. Teachers of children at Key Stages 1 and 2 have a daunting task in finding time, enthusiasm and expertise for delivering all of the requirements of the National Curriculum, even in the slimmed down form that applies from September 2000. Therefore it is important for teachers to be clear about the nature of design and technology, understand what children can gain from such experiences, and how design and technology experiences can benefit learning in other areas of the curriculum. It is the one area of the curriculum that is genuinely futures orientated (Howe *et al.* 2001). For creative teachers, work related to design and technology is not an additional burden. At times, design and technology can be central to the curriculum they plan for children, providing them with the means of offering children purposeful activities that they can enjoy and from which they can learn.

CHAPTER 2

Children's learning in design and technology

1. Introduction

Every teacher holds certain beliefs about the way children learn and these beliefs, whether they are explicit or implicit, inform the decisions a teacher takes every day about how to teach. The decisions may involve what to do with the children (within the statutory frameworks), how to organise it and what role to adopt.

There are four key features of children's learning that inform my approach to design and technology, based on my personal experience, reading and research. Firstly, children learn from experience and practical activity has a vital part to play in providing that experience. Secondly, learning is an active process which involves learners in constructing their unique understanding of the world and this understanding will be significantly influenced by what they already think. Thirdly, learning normally takes place in a social context and that context, similarly, influences learning. Finally, different children learn in different ways. The first part of this chapter discusses these points.

In terms of learning in design and technology, it is helpful to distinguish between the skills and processes, knowledge and understanding, personal qualities/attitudes and values that are involved. These are addressed in separate sections of the chapter. Later sections deal with the development of collaborative group-work skills, progression, and differentiating to meet children's individual needs. The chapter concludes by considering the role of the teacher in facilitating children's learning at different stages of design and technology activities.

2. How do children learn?

The first premise outlined above was that children learn from practical experience. It is, of course, not the only way they learn, but it certainly plays an important part, especially in design and technology. Most design and technology projects or activities result in some form of practical activity. That practical experience will not necessarily lead to learning but within it it has that potential. The origins of a view of learning centred on practical experiences goes back long before the beginning of this century, but it was the work of Piaget (1929) that provided a firm research base for such views. Most teachers have at some time in their professional lives come across the saying, 'I'm told and I forget; I see and I remember; I do and I understand.' While making an important point, this glib phrase rather oversimplifies the nature of learning. Perhaps it would be more accurate to say, 'I do and I talk about it and I begin to understand.' Talk is just as important as practical activity for learning and in this book is regarded as an important aspect of the experience from which children learn. Piaget and many who developed his ideas placed less emphasis on this aspect and the associated social context of learning. His work, particularly those features of it which led to notions of 'readiness', i.e. the concept that children can only achieve certain things at particular ages (or stages), has been heavily criticised and some of his claims have been challenged (for example, Donaldson 1978; Wood 1988). Despite this, his work continues to be influential and informs one strand of the view of learning underpinning this book. He recognised the extent to which children's interactions with the world around them contributes to their learning. A view of learning which recognises the active part that an individual learner has to play if learning is to be effective is 'constructivist' (von Glaserfeld 1989). It is a view that sees the learner as actively constructing new understanding. But it goes further and recognises that new learning is the result of the existing ideas and skills that the learner brings to a learning situation as well as the experience and 'evidence' resulting from that situation. This may be practical experience or ideas provided by others. A constructivist view of learning can be summarised in the following way (based on Ollerenshaw and Ritchie 1997, p. 6):

- what is already in a learner's mind and what a learner can already do matters;
- individuals construct their own, often unique, meanings;
- the construction of meaning and the development of practical capability is a continuous and active process;
- learning may, but does not always, involve conceptual change;
- the construction of meaning does not always lead to belief;
- certain constructed meanings, which do not correspond to conventional understanding, are common in children.

Such a view has implications for how we teach. For example, a teacher who accepts this view of learning recognises the significance of a child's existing ideas and skills to future learning and will want to spend time *eliciting* those ideas and assessing practical capability in order that decisions can be taken about the most appropriate form of teacher intervention. This phase of work will also involve the teacher in helping the learners to become more aware of what they already know, think and can do. The teacher will help children *structure* and express existing ideas in order to clarify, develop and communicate those ideas. The 'constructivist' teacher will plan interventions which are intended to help learners *restructure* their current understanding, if this is necessary, and develop their skills. This will often involve encouraging the learner to test out ideas in order to extend, develop and replace them. It will also involve introducing learners to new ways of doing things and inviting them to use new materials and techniques. It may involve challenging the practicality of design and construction ideas. As children design and make they are also building cognitive structures by replacing, extending and enhancing existing ones (Bentley and Watts 1994, p. 10). Learners need to be made aware of any changes that result from a learning episode and therefore there is a need to encourage learners to *review* their learning: to clarify changes in their thinking and new skills and insights into the design and technology process that they have gained. Finally, a constructivist teacher will seek to encourage learners to *apply* new ideas and skills and integrate them into everyday thinking and activity.

Learning nearly always takes place in a social context and another essential foundation for the view of social constructivism underpinning this book is the work of Vygotsky (1962) who, unlike Piaget, gave more attention to the social dimension of learning. His work explored the ways in which an individual's learning is influenced by the social context in which it takes place. He took into account the relationship of learners to their peers and the effect of that on learning, as well as the role of adults, as more knowledgeable and experienced participants, in the social context of learning. Vygotsky introduced a concept which is helpful to our understanding of children's learning, especially in design and technology. This is what he termed the 'zone of proximal development'. It is the difference between the level of problem difficulty a child can engage in independently and the level that can be achieved with adult support. Learning takes place in this zone and the role of adult intervention and the nature of the 'scaffolding' provided by an adult to enable the building of extended and enhanced cognitive structures are therefore crucial to learning. The adult's role may involve breaking a problem or learning experience down into more manageable bits for the learner and deciding on a sequence of steps for a learning route. Consequently, the view of learning outlined in this book is one that recognises the importance of individuals as active constructors of their own knowledge and understanding as well as the significance of the social dimension of such learning.

The final strand of this brief discussion about children's learning relates to the differing ways in which children learn. Our understanding of this has been much improved in recent years by research into the way the brain works (Greenfield 1998) and work on learning styles (Smith 1996), multiple intelligences (Gardner 1993) and the emotional dimension of learning (Goleman 1996). There is increasing evidence about the significance of children having different preferred learning styles and the need for teachers to identify these and work with them. In classrooms, according to Smith (1996, p. 34) it is likely that about a third of learners will have preferences for using the following senses: hearing (34%); sight (29%); and feeling (37%) (audible, visual and kinaesthetic learning). Gardner (1993) identifies seven 'intelligences' that learners have to differing degrees: linguistic; mathematical and logical; visual and spatial; musical; interpersonal; intrapersonal; and kinaesthetic. In subsequent work he and others have added others to this indicative rather than comprehensive list. All of these 'intelligences' have relevance to learning in design and technology. Increasingly educationalists are looking at how children's learning can be fostered, valued and enhanced through adapting approaches to support learners in all these domains (Smith, 1996, pp. 51–64). The purpose of this is twofold: firstly to enable appropriate differentiation – different approaches to meet the differing needs of pupils; and secondly to help children to broaden their styles of learning so that they are not always dependent on their preferred ones. An effective teacher will identify and work with a range of learning styles in any one topic and design and technology activities lend themselves particularly well to supporting such preferences, for example, in the way children are supported in generating ideas or communicating them to others (see Chapter 4).

The promoters of 'emotional' intelligence (for example, Goleman 1996) emphasise the affective domain of learning – how children feel about learning will affect how well they learn. Emotions have the power to aid or disrupt thinking. There is strong evidence that it is biologically difficult for children who are worried, distressed or feel unsafe to learn. It is vital that teachers provide a 'non-threatening learning environment' – children cannot learn effectively without this. The 'feel good' factor, by contrast can enhance learning – and through design and technology, with its potential for motivation and enjoyment, teachers can exploit this feature of the human brain.

A final thought in this general discussion about how children learn comes from the work of Guy Claxton, who in his book *Hare Brain, Tortoise Mind* (1997) argues that in schools we ask children to think too quickly in too narrow ways. As his book title implies, time to think around and to mull over is not time wasted, but a route to more effective learning. For example, taking children back to their initial ideas for an outcome a day or two after they have been generated may lead to them offering new insights or ideas not initially provided. Design and technology activities offer particular potential for encouraging a more productive way of learning for children – work is often spread over a longer period encouraging lateral and diverse thinking.

Learning in design and technology involves the development of skills and processes, of knowledge and understanding and the fostering of personal qualities, attitudes and values. The following sections address each of these strands. They have been separated to provide a framework for analysing teaching and learning in design and technology. However, they are inextricably linked and together they provide an holistic view of learning which is more than the constituent parts.

3. Development of skills and processes

When children engage in design and technology activities they are using and developing skills. However, categorising or listing those skills is not easy and considerable confusion tends to exist about the relationship between skills, processes and concepts. For example, observation might be considered a skill (looking closely and observing fine detail) or a process (drawing upon existing knowledge and understanding in order to make decisions about what to observe, deciding how to observe and whether to use an observation aid, and making sense of what is seen) and there is a concept labelled 'observation' which refers to the use of all the senses to gather evidence. For the purposes of this section, skills will be taken to be specific behaviours which are used during design and technology activities. A combination of skills are needed to engage in a process, which is a way of describing how something is achieved, for example, how a problem is solved.

The current statutory orders (DfEE/QCA 1999) identify the framework for skills and processes in Figure 2.1.

Area	Key Stage 1 Pupils should be taught to:	Key Stage 2 Pupils should be taught to:
1. Developing, planning and communicating ideas	(a) generate ideas by drawing on their own and other people's experiences (b) develop ideas by shaping materials and putting together components (c) talk about their ideas (d) plan by suggesting what to do next as their ideas develop (e) communicate their ideas using a variety of methods, including drawing and making models.	(a) generate ideas for products after thinking about who will use them and what they will be used for, using information from a number of sources, including ICT-based sources (b) develop ideas and explain them clearly, putting together a list of what they want their design to achieve (c) plan what they have to do, suggesting a sequence of actions and alternatives, if needed (d) communicate design ideas in different ways as these develop, bearing in mind aesthetic qualities, and the uses and purposes for which the product is intended.
2. Working with tools, equipment, materials and components to make quality products	(a) select tools, techniques and materials for making their product from a range suggested by the teacher (b) explore the sensory qualities of materials (c) measure, mark out, cut and shape a range of materials (d) assemble, join and combine materials and components (e) use simple finishing techniques to improve the appearance of their product, using a range of equipment (f) follow safe procedures for food safety and hygiene.	(a) select appropriate tools and techniques for making their product (b) suggest alternative ways of making their product, if first attempts fail (c) explore the sensory qualities of materials and how to use materials and processes (d) measure, mark out, cut and shape a range of materials, and assemble, join and combine components and materials accurately (e) use finishing techniques to strengthen and improve the appearance of their product, using a range of equipment including ICT (f) follow safe procedures for food safety and hygiene.
3. Evaluating processes and products	(a) talk about their ideas, saying what they like and dislike (b) identify what they could have done differently or how they could improve their work in the future.	(a) reflect on the progress of their work as they design and make, identifying ways they could improve their products (b) carry out appropriate tests before making any improvements (c) recognise that the quality of a product depends on how well it is made and how well it meets its intended purpose.

Figure 2.1 Programme of Study: design and technology (DfEE/QCA, 1999)

This is a mixture of cognitive (e.g. generate ideas), communicative (e.g. talk) and manipulative skills (measure, mark and cut) and processes (follow procedures) which needs amplification to be useful for planning classroom work. It is an attempt to break down design and technological capability into three areas (designing, making and evaluating) and within those identifying specific skills. It is inevitably an incomplete analysis of all the skills needed, but includes nothing which might be considered inappropriate. Further reference and discussion of these will be included in later chapters (for example, Chapter 4 will address the first area, 'developing, planning and communicating ideas' in detail).

The National Curriculum also identifies 'key skills' to be promoted across the curriculum (DfEE/QCA 1999, p. 20) which are grouped under: communication, application of number, information technology, working with others, improving own learning and performance, problem solving and thinking skills (information processing, reasoning, enquiry, creative and evaluation). Again, no distinction between different types of skills and processes is made, although the recognition of the importance of these to learning is welcomed. Most of the key skills can clearly be developed in the context of design and technology. There will be further discussion of this in the later chapters.

The early learning goals for the Foundation Stage (QCA/DfEE 2000a) include reference to skills development in several areas, including physical development, where reference is made to children's ability to handle tools, objects, construction and malleable materials safely and with increasing control (p. 114).

As stated in Chapter 1, design and technology capability involves the complex interaction of thought and action and whatever skill teachers attempt to develop in children it is necessary that they recognise both dimensions are involved. In some skills, such as 'cutting', the action dimension is emphasised; in others, such as 'evaluating', the cognitive dimension is more evident. The important point to make at this stage of our discussion is that learning in design and technology involves the development of certain skills, some specific to design and technology, but many that are generic. The role of the teacher is to plan learning experiences for children which lead to the development of these skills.

Processes require learners to use a range of skills, and draw upon existing knowledge and understanding, in order to achieve a particular purpose. Throughout this book I have referred to the design and technology process as one way of understanding what it means to achieve a successful outcome and meet a particular purpose. However, the attempt to reduce a complex set of human behaviours to a basic process which can be simply described is fraught with difficulty and unlikely to do justice to the behaviours involved. Chidgey (1994) provides a critique of attempts to use a simplified process model to structure and assess learning in design and technology. His perspective, as a practising teacher, is congruent with the findings of more extensive research in the secondary field (APU 1987, 1991). Learning is more complex than such process models suggest (Johnsey 1995, 1998). However, identifying key elements involved in design and technology activities provides a framework that can help us with decisions related to teaching. As long as teachers do not allow the framework to become a strait-jacket that restricts the opportunities they provide learners with, or narrows their perspective when it comes to assessing children's achievements, it remains a useful means of analysing teaching and learning.

A key question remains to be answered – what can and do children learn about these processes? In much that is written about design and technology, the benefits of developing transferable skills and processes, both for work within design and technology and for work in other curriculum areas, are articulated (for example, Sellwood 1990). Research evidence suggests that this is not as straightforward as some might imagine and it is certainly not enough for teachers to assume that such transfer will automatically occur. Hennessy and McCormick (1994) claim that during design and technology activities in secondary schools 'pupils may merely try to accommodate teachers' aims through superficially and mechanically following the procedures prescribed (by teachers), whilst simultaneously adhering to their own product-orientated agendas, thus creating a "veneer of accomplishment"' (p. 100). If children are going to develop problem solving skills during their design and technology work, and become aware of how they can be applied in different situations, teachers will have to support this learning and teach strategies and approaches that can be used.

The relationship between the processes of 'problem solving' and 'design and technology' is important. Problem solving can be seen as a generic process that is applicable within many curriculum areas or everyday situations. The National Curriculum includes it as a key skill and describes it as: identifying and understanding a problem; planning ways to solve a problem, monitoring progress in tackling a problem and reviewing solutions to problems (DfEE/QCA 1999, p. 21). It is also included within the early learning goals as an element of personal, social and emotional development (QCA/DfEE 2000a, p. 28).

In the past problem solving has been described in many ways (County of Avon 1985; Fisher 1987; Johnsey 1986; Watts 1991). However, in all cases, it is seen to involve elements of identifying and clarifying a problem; having ideas and selecting one to implement; planning; implementing; evaluating. It has obvious similarities with design and technology. Crucially, it is, like design and technology, cyclical and involves revisiting stages in the light of new experiences. It is usually open-ended, without one right answer. Most design and technology activities (particularly design and make assignments (DMAs)) will offer the potential to involve learners in problem solving, although problem solving skills will not necessarily be used to produce successful outcomes: learners may be simply repeating something they have done previously. Problem solving does not always involve design and technology nor involve a made outcome; the National Curriculum reminds teachers that all subjects provide opportunities for it (DfEE/QCA 1999, p. 21). The generic process can be applied to composing music, making art and writing stories. Of course, simplifying problem solving in the way outlined above leads to the same criticisms as those levelled at a simplified design and technology process. Some research (Glaser 1992) indicates that expert problem solvers rarely follow a generalised decontextualised process such as that described. It is evident that problem solvers, be they novice or expert, use a range of approaches that are dependent upon the circumstances of the problem solving situation. Since learners, as novice problem solvers, are often working in unfamiliar situations they are in need of adult support, or 'scaffolding', to recognise the nature of their problem solving and the extent to which they have engaged in a recognisable process. Roden (1997, 1999) provides valuable insights into the nature of young children's problem solving and strategies that can be used by teachers to support children including: personalisation; practice; negotiation and reposing the task; focusing down; identifying specific difficulties; talking themselves through sub-tasks; tackling obstacles; praise, encouragement and providing reassurance; sharing and cooperating; pretend panic and persistence. This book is based upon the premise that the development of problem solving skills, the use of the 'process' of problem solving, its transferability within design and technology and from design and technology to other curriculum and everyday situations, are problematic, but nonetheless important.

The significant message is that children use 'processes' when engaging in design and technology; that these processes need to be made explicit to them; that they need to be taught how to engage in processes and, crucially, taught to apply processes from one situation to another.

4. Knowledge and understanding in design and technology

When children are using skills or engaging in processes in design and technology they will draw upon knowledge and understanding. The programmes of study (PoS) for design and technology include the statement that 'Teaching should ensure that knowledge and understanding are applied when developing ideas, planning, making products and evaluating them' (DfEE/QCA 1999, p. 94). Design and technology does not have an easily defined knowledge base such as that of more traditional subjects, for example mathematics and science. The knowledge and understanding described in the design and technology PoS is much more limited than earlier versions and only covers materials and mechanisms at Key Stage 1 and materials, mechanisms and electric circuits at Key Stage 2.

This limited knowledge base, identified in the National Curriculum, clearly has close links with science. For example, in terms of materials, it includes knowledge and understanding concerning the working characteristics of materials used to make something. Depending on the type of project or activity, children may also need knowledge of forces, structures and energy, not explicitly included in the Design and Technology Curriculum. 'Control' is another concept area about which children can develop understanding through their activities. It is the means by which we can make things do what we want them to do. It can be mechanical (levers, pulleys, gears), pneumatic, hydraulic, or electrical (switches, computers). During design and technology activities children will often be applying knowledge and understanding of a scientific nature, but also, significantly, developing that knowledge and understanding further.

Before moving on, it is worth noting that knowing how to use or apply something does not necessarily require an understanding of how or why it works. The Chinese were using technologies many centuries before science provided sophisticated explanations of why they worked. Many modern designers use 'black-boxes' in their outcomes, without needing to fully understand the inner workings of these devices. In other words, although design and technology may provide opportunities for learning in science, or for children to apply learning from science, it is not always necessary for these to be seen as aims of such work.

Successful design and technology outcomes can be produced in school and beyond without the creators having an understanding of the science involved.

Design and technology also draws upon knowledge and understanding from other subjects, especially art and mathematics. The concepts of *colour, shape* and *form* are often essential for developing the aesthetic aspects of design and technology outcomes. Mathematical concepts related to *geometry, shape, symmetry, numeracy, measurement, pictorial representation, probability* have a potential contribution to make to design and technology activities. Economics, although not a subject usually associated with the primary curriculum, may have a part to play in areas such as *consumer demand, costs, availability of materials, marketing*. Such concepts provide a link with the National Curriculum through the cross-curricular themes of 'financial capability' and 'enterprise education' (DfEE/QCA 1999, p. 22). The humanities add to the knowledge base on which children will draw if they are offered a broad and balanced design and technology curriculum. For example, evaluating outcomes from other times and places is one aspect of design and technology experience for children in which concepts and knowledge from history and geography become important. In terms of the discussion about values and personal qualities below, understanding of concepts from religious and moral education contribute.

Knowledge and understanding for the Foundation Stage is included as an area in the early learning goals (QCA/DfEE 2000a). As indicated in Chapter 1, these specify what most children should be able to do by the end of the Foundation Stage, including the following, which can be related to design and technology:

- investigate objects and materials by using all of their senses as appropriate;
- find out about, and identify some features of, living things, objects and events they observe;
- look closely at similarities, differences, patterns and change;
- ask questions about why things happen and how things work;
- build and construct with a wide range of objects, selecting appropriate resources, and adapting their work where necessary;
- select the tools and techniques they need to shape, assemble and join the materials they are using;
- find out about and identify the uses of everyday technology and use information and communication technology and programmable toys to support their learning;
- find out about past and present events in their own lives, and in those of their families and other people they know;
- observe, find out about, and identify features in the place they live and the natural world;
- begin to know about their own cultures and beliefs and those of other people;
- find out about their environment, and talk about those features they like and dislike.

(QCA/DfEE 2000a, pp. 86–98)

In many ways this is a confusing list to define as 'knowledge and understanding' as clearly some of these, for example, selecting tools, overlap with skills and processes as described in the National Curriculum PoS and the last one, in particular, relates to young learners' values (see below).

To return to the earlier discussion about how children develop new understanding, it is worth reflecting a little more on the provisional nature of children's developing concepts. Research findings provide evidence of the extent to which children's mental models are flexible and context-specific (Hennessy and McCormick 1994). Over the last few years a wealth of research has documented the nature of children's alternative frameworks (Willig 1990), especially in the area of science (Ollerenshaw and Ritchie 1997). If design and technology involve learners drawing upon existing knowledge from other areas of the curriculum, it is possible, indeed very likely, that these alternative frameworks may influence design and technology outcomes. They will need to be elicited and challenged by teachers in the context in which they are being used. For example, alternative ideas pupils hold about series and parallel circuits will impact on their designs for a lighting system in a model house. The expectation that children will be able to draw on knowledge from other subjects in an unproblematic way during design and technology work is unrealistic.

5. Attitudes and personal qualities

Primary school teachers have always attached importance to personal attitudes and qualities. These cover aspects such as curiosity, inventiveness, perseverance, determination, enterprise, resourcefulness, open-mindedness, originality, independent thinking, self-discipline, willingness to accept uncertainty, willingness to use and appraise evidence and enthusiasm. Social attitudes include cooperation, tolerance of others' views and respect for others, which link closely with the National Curriculum key skill area of 'working with others' (DfEE/QCA 1999, p. 21) and the early learning goals related to personal, social and emotional development (QCA/DfEE 2000a). There are also attitudes a learner has towards the subject or activities. Successful design and technology work demands children demonstrate such attitudes and therefore fostering them becomes an important task for teachers. Attitudes and personal qualities do not appear explicitly in the programmes of study within the National Curriculum orders for the reason that they are regarded as difficult, if not impossible, to assess. Furthermore, attitudes can be very context bound, for example, a child can be extremely curious in one context and uninterested in another. Planning to foster particular attitudes is not easy, although social attitudes, such as cooperation, can be fostered through specific approaches to group work. Attitudes demonstrated by children are influenced by the ethos of a classroom which results from the teacher's attitudes and behaviours. If a teacher values children's ideas, they are more likely to be curious and open-minded. If a teacher is interested in children's differing opinions, children are more likely to be tolerant of others' opinions. In other words, the teacher's attitudes have a direct effect upon children's attitudes.

In the last section the inextricable links between skills, knowledge and understanding were established. Now that we have added attitudes and personal qualities to the equation we need to recognise that these three strands of children's learning are intertwined. However, the picture is not quite complete, because learning in design and technology has a fourth strand: related to value judgements.

6. Values in design and technology

Design and technology, like teaching, involves value judgements that have a subjective dimension. Design and technology in school and in the wider community take place within a cultural context which means those involved are operating within particular value systems which affect behaviours and decisions. Every individual adult and child also has a personal value system – what they consider important about the nature of people and things. Children can begin to be made aware of these systems and recognise their significance, especially within Key Stage 2, but certainly not exclusively as Allison's work illustrates (1999). Values judgements related to design and technology might concern economic, aesthetic, environmental, technical or social matters (Benson 1992; Layton 1992; Siraj-Blatchford 1996). Values and beliefs vary from one culture to another, even from one community to another. Indeed, the value systems children meet in school may be at odds with the ones they experience at home or in the park with their friends. Decisions taken related to design and technology activities are often value-laden and children should be aware of the implications of their own values and those of others whose needs they might be considering. The constraints involved in a particular project often mean that the outcome created is not congruent with the values of the creator. In the wider community, the designer of a car, whose values might include the belief that cars should be as safe as possible, designs a car with less safety features than ideal because of constraints concerning selling price. In the classroom very young children's value judgements may be about personal likes and dislikes and it is up to the teacher to help them recognise the basis for preferences expressed in order to help them become more open-minded. They should be made aware of the preferences of others and recognise they may be different to their own. Older children can be invited to deal with more sophisticated questions that involve value judgements. For example, a problem regarding litter could be solved by designing and making litter bins or educating others not to drop litter. The decision is a value-laden one that requires children to consider their own and other people's attitudes.

For the Foundation Stage, attitudes and values are covered by the early learning goals related to personal, social and emotional development (QCA/DfEE 2000a p. 28) which have been generally welcomed although regarded by some as somewhat ambitious. These state, for example, that by the end of the Foundation Stage, most children will:

- be confident to try new activities, initiate ideas and speak in a familiar group;
- have a developing awareness of their own needs, views and feelings and be sensitive to the needs, views and feelings of others;
- have a developing respect for their own cultures and beliefs and those of other people;
- work as part of a group or class, taking turns and sharing fairly;
- select and use activities and resources independently;
- understand that people have different needs, views, cultures and beliefs, which need to be treated with respect.

(QCA/DfEE 2000a, pp. 32–42)

The National Curriculum document (DfEE/QCA 1999, p. 147) includes, for the first time, a general statement about values, listing them in categories of: self, relationships, society and the environment. The document claims that they can be regarded as a concensus view which teachers could confidently use as the basis of their teaching. For a more thorough discussion of values and their contribution to design and technology see Howe *et al.* (2001).

Learning in design and technology involves a combination of skills and processes, knowledge and understanding, attitudes and value judgements. Teachers need to hold all of these in mind when planning design and technology, when interacting with children in the classroom, when assessing design and technology learning and when evaluating the success of their teaching.

7. Developing collaborative group-work skills

As discussed above, learning takes place in a social context and design and technology are areas of experience that should involve children working collaboratively. This is specified explicitly in the Key Stage 2 PoS (DfEE/QCA, 1999, p. 94) which states 'During key stage 2 pupils work on their own or as part of a team'. The quality of children's learning will be dependent upon the way in which they operate collaboratively within social contexts. Sitting children in groups is no guarantee of collaborative work nor of the development of group-work skills. It is necessary for a teacher to make a deliberate attempt to develop those skills in children.

One way of doing this is to introduce children to a systematic approach to collaborative group work, such as that used in the SACLA (Systematic and Cooperative Learning Approach) project, which was based in Oxford and Avon (*Times Educational Supplement* 1989). The aims of the project included: helping children work with others, developing children's self-esteem and their awareness of their own strengths and skills, increasing children's ownership of their learning and commitment to it. The framework adopted by this project was used successfully, in a number of pilot primary schools, to structure groups' approaches to collaborative tasks through cycles of preparation, action and review and has since become a common way of working in some schools. The approach becomes known by the children as the 'Systematic Approach'. In groups, they are trained to work through the following sequence (or a simplified version), discussing and coming to an agreement at each stage:

1. Planning
   - Why are we doing a particular task or activity – what is it for?
   - What do we want to end up with?
   - How can we measure our success?
   - What ideas and relevant information do we have, do we need and can we obtain?
   - What jobs/activities have to be done?
   - Who is going to do what – how and when?
2. Implementing plans
3. Reviewing the successes and difficulties experienced – identifying the causes in order to make plans to improve in the future.

Teachers have found that use of this method encourages children to become more aware of the processes of their learning; improving their capacity to cooperate effectively. Such approaches therefore not only support children's learning in the key skill area of 'working with others', but also in 'improving own learning and performance' (DfEE/QCA 1999, p. 21). When introducing their children to such an approach teachers sometimes allocate specific roles to individuals in a group (such as scribe, timer, chairperson, spokesperson, resource-collector/allocator) or identify the roles and ask the group to 'appoint' someone to each job.

Children can be taught group skills such as active listening, negotiating, questioning, clarifying, seeking help, telling, respecting others and cooperating, through the use of these structured steps. This approach encourages children to become more aware of the way they are tackling a problem and helps them to learn how to learn from experience.

8. Capturing progression

How can a teacher ensure a child's learning develops progressively? Identifying the nature of progression in well-established subjects such as mathematics and science is difficult, but the problems are even greater in design and technology. The National Curriculum orders, through the programmes of study and level descriptors, provide one way of looking at progression, although the lack of detail in the revised orders does not offer the teacher much guidance (DfEE/QCA 1999). The QCA Scheme of Work (SoW) is a little more helpful in identifying progression in terms of what children should be able to do 'at the early stages', 'as they make progress' and 'as they make further progress' (QCA/DfEE 1998, p. 21, and reproduced in Chapter 8, p. 142) but again there is little detail provided. A much more practical guide is provided in *Expectations in Design and Technology* (QCA 1997a). Although based on the earlier version of the National Curriculum, it still remains useful in identifying what can be expected by pupils at the end of years 2, 4 and 6. These expectations are well illustrated by examples of children's work. Others have sought to provide guidance for teachers in 'capturing' progression in design and technology. Bold's (1999) thorough treatment is highly recommended as are the very accessible 'ladders' of progression included in Stein and Poole's (1997) practical guide. They provide an analysis of progression in many aspects of design and technology related skills and knowledge and understanding.

A different approach is to see progression in children's learning as a continuum involving a number of different axes which relate to the activity and to the skills, knowledge, understanding, attitudes and values used during the activity. Figure 2.2 illustrates some of these. Progress can take place on different axes and at different rates in any particular activity. These, together with analyses of progression in particular skills and areas of knowledge and understanding, can be used to help a teacher plan for progression in children's learning. For example, a teacher could plan to focus upon a particular axis when planning an activity or series of activities. However, the more difficult issue is related to supporting progressive learning for an individual learner during an open-ended design and technology task.

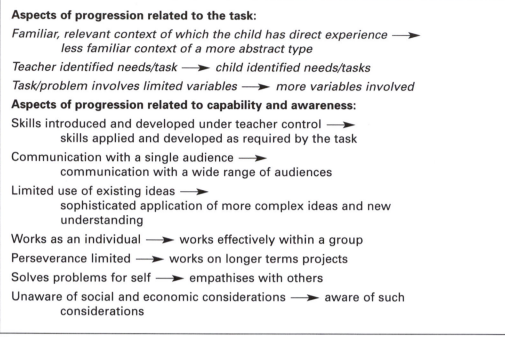

Aspects of progression related to the task:

Familiar, relevant context of which the child has direct experience ——➤
less familiar context of a more abstract type

Teacher identified needs/task ——➤ *child identified needs/tasks*

Task/problem involves limited variables ——➤ *more variables involved*

Aspects of progression related to capability and awareness:

Skills introduced and developed under teacher control ——➤
skills applied and developed as required by the task

Communication with a single audience ——➤
communication with a wide range of audiences

Limited use of existing ideas ——➤
sophisticated application of more complex ideas and new
understanding

Works as an individual ——➤ works effectively within a group

Perseverance limited ——➤ works on longer terms projects

Solves problems for self ——➤ empathises with others

Unaware of social and economic considerations ——➤ aware of such
considerations

Figure 2.2 Progression in design and technology

Learning in design and technology does not follow a linear path, which creates a difficulty for the frameworks discussed above. An individual's route to particular skills or knowledge and understanding will be unique, not simply a matter of progressing from one predefined step to the next. Teachers' decisions about individual children will need to be flexible and the important evidence to inform decisions is from assessments of what the children can already do or understand. A teacher must then plan appropriate steps, which may not necessarily be to a higher level; consolidation or revisiting more basic ideas or skills may be necessary. There are as many routes to understanding as there are learners; the teacher's role is to know the conceptual and procedural landscape well enough to direct individual learners towards their goals from wherever they may find themselves.

9. Meeting individual needs

It will be evident that it is my view that children must, as far as possible, be treated as individual learners since they are all actively constructing unique understanding and practical capabilities through their experiences. Consequently, effective teaching will need to allow a teacher to respond to each child's needs. However, the reality of classrooms means a compromise is often needed and the child's needs are addressed through group or whole-class teaching. This is where differentiation becomes important within planning and classroom interventions. Two obvious ways to differentiate are by task or by outcome.

In the first, different children or groups would be set different tasks. For example different focused practical tasks on cutting and joining wood might be planned for 2 or 3 groups of children in the class or an evaluation task, such as looking at a collection of shoes, would be planned to involve different methods of recording for different groups. In the second they would tackle a similar task, but the teacher would anticipate a range of outcomes. The latter is more common in design and technology, but not always easy as Deacon discusses (1996). An example of differentiation by task might involve the whole class making pop-up cards. Individual children, or small groups, are supported by their teacher to produce outcomes that involve the use of different levels of capability and knowledge and understanding. This might involve the teacher grouping the children according to the predicted level of success. In either scenario, the teacher's task, through ongoing formative assessment, is to make appropriate interventions which provide 'scaffolding' for the child's learning. This, as with so much in the classroom, is no easy matter. We will return to the implications of planning for differentiation in Chapter 8. Evidence of teachers scaffolding children's learning can be found in many case studies (e.g. Case Studies 9 and 10).

The practical basis of design and technology makes it a subject which has particular potential for children with special educational needs (SEN) in so-called more academic subjects. In my discussions with teachers about their work in design and technology they often mention how surprised they have been by the achievements of children who do not normally have a great deal of success in the classroom. Early in my teaching career an episode occurred which I have never forgotten. At the beginning of a new school year with a Y3 class one of the children, Andrew, brought into school a complex *Technical Lego* model of a car with working suspension, steering and engine components. I knew little of Andrew apart from class records that indicated he had considerable learning difficulties and was apparently an isolated child who lacked self-confidence. One indicator of his 'ability' was a reading age two years below his chronological age. I was, however, impressed by the model and I initially assumed it had been made by a parent or older sibling. Andrew soon made it obvious that I was wrong. I showed interest in its mechanics and he became animated and explained how each component worked. It was evident that it was his own work, and not even a model copied from an instruction card. I decided to try and capitalise upon this capability and self-confidence. I intended to make use of the basic *Technical Lego* kits I had in the class and set out to use Andrew's expertise. Over the first few weeks of term he spent time working with other members of the class on a one-to-one basis, teaching them how to assemble parts and make models. He did relatively little written work in those first few weeks but what he did do had surprising impact on his learning. His social standing with his peer group was enhanced and his confidence 'blossomed'. Perhaps for the first time in his school career something that he was good at was valued within the school context. In a class in which practical designing and making work was as important as other activities Andrew experienced a level of success that was new to him. This had knock-on effects to his learning in other areas. During the year he was with me Andrew's reading improved, until his reading age exceeded his chronological age. This was not a result of my teaching of reading, but of his own belief in himself as a learner. Design and technology activities provide those opportunities that allow certain children, who have experienced difficulties and perhaps failure, to succeed. Cullingford Agnew (1996) provides evidence of its benefits to children with severe learning difficulties. The benefits for pupils with behavior difficuties (in this case, Y6 boys) is demonstrated by Linton (1998).

This is not, of course, to suggest that design and technology is a panacea for solving the problems of all children with learning difficulties. Nor will the experiences be accessible to children with specific educational needs without the teacher taking those needs into account when planning and implementing work. The National Curriculum includes a section on inclusion and providing effective learning opportunities for all pupils (DfEE/QCA 1999, pp. 30–37) and guidance from ACCAC (1998) is particularly helpful in this area. Examples will again be found in later case studies, including the one later in this chapter

Design and technology activities can be equally stimulating and made demanding for children at the other end of the so-called ability spectrum. It would be very wrong to consider design and technology as somehow less academic than other subjects. The needs of 'high-fliers' must be addressed as well as the needs of those with learning difficulties (see Lewin (1994) for further discussion). The quality of some of the work included in case studies will show this in action (Case Study 14 provides an excellent example).

It is a common feature of many of the case studies in this book that the teachers involved made explicit mention of the fact that they and their children enjoyed the work. This sense of enjoyment and involvement of teachers in classroom work is something which I believe children sense and respond to in a positive way.

10. The role of the teacher

The case studies selected for this book provide evidence of the diverse roles that a successful teacher needs to adopt: coordinating, motivating, supporting, responding, facilitating, directing, informing. A constructivist teacher will draw upon a range of teaching strategies and approaches to ensure the learners' needs are met in the most appropriate way. There will be times when the teacher will be working with the whole class: setting a context for work, giving information, eliciting ideas through brainstorming, giving instructions, demonstrating safe use of tools and techniques, 'chairing' discussions, reviews and evaluation sessions. There will be other occasions when the teacher will be working with groups: facilitating discussion, encouraging collaborative work, challenging ideas and approaches to develop the children's thinking and awareness, suggesting new ideas and perspectives to keep the work going, introducing other ways of working and extending the range of resources available, advising, motivating, helping them work together, encouraging a systematic approach, listening to plans, focusing the group on specific difficulties or issues, helping them come to decisions. There will also be a need for a teacher to interact effectively with individual children: asking the right question at the right time, encouraging the child to explore ideas further and clarify existing ideas, making appropriate interventions to challenge existing ideas. The level and nature of teacher intervention will vary at different phases of the work and it is common for teachers whose classes are experienced in design and technology work to find that at certain times the need to intervene is limited and they can focus on monitoring and assessing children. As children become more independent they make less demands on their teachers who can then be more selective about the nature of interventions. In some situations the most effective strategy might be not to intervene so that a child or group is left to work things out for themselves.

The following case study of a design and technology project in a reception class illustrates some aspects of the teacher's role, and also provides an example of a class with a number of children who have learning difficulties.

CASE STUDY

1: Our neighbourhood

Inge Fey was teaching a reception class at Embleton Infants' School in Southmead, Bristol. In this case study, her class of 26 children have all experienced at least a year in a nursery school. The classroom is spacious and has various areas including a home corner, book, computer, art, mathematics, water and sand areas which the children know will be designated 'open' or 'closed' at various times during the day. She also has the benefit of a full-time general assistant and during the project had a trainee nursery nurse in the classroom. This case study is based upon work she did in the spring term just after she returned to school from maternity leave. Consequently, this was the first major project she had tackled with the class.

Inge is very clear about her own values as far as design and technology education is concerned. In her words,

> Many of the children in my class have considerable learning difficulties and some of these are severe. I regard design and technology as an area of the curriculum where children who are experiencing difficulties with more academic subjects (*sic*) can succeed. For me, design and technology provide a way of increasing the children's self-esteem. I want the children to appreciate their self-worth. I want them to be comfortable with designing and making and I always try and give them positive encouragement. However, it's important that the children do things for themselves. I want them to choose what to use and make; do the making, only coming to me for help when it's really necessary; and explain to me afterwards what they have done. I think it is important to find the time to talk to children individually and value their contributions. The children and I enjoy design and technology work and I spend quite a lot of time on it because I can see the spin-offs. It's important in its own right but there is also lots of maths and language . . . and that is how I justify the time I give to it.

She had planned a topic on 'Our Neighbourhood' during which the children had heard the story *On the Way to School* and talked about the routes they take and what they see. Inge used this to set the scene for the children's design and technology, although as we will see, the emphasis was on planning, making and evaluating as opposed to designing. Inge intended to introduce more structured 'designing' later in the year. She decided to set aside two full days for the work and intended to organise it so that all the children were engaged in a practical making activity at the same time. Her rationale for this 'short/sharp' approach was to ensure that the children retained interest in the work throughout. She was keen for the children to use a range of everyday and reclaimed materials and gain experience in how to cut and join them. On her return to school, in January, she had set up a design and technology area in the classroom where materials were stored in a way that allowed the children to collect them when needed. Small items such as bottle tops, straws, corks, pipe-cleaners, cotton wool, were stored in labelled ice-cream tubs on the surface of a large low-level storage unit. Larger items were also sorted and stored in boxes. This acted as a central classroom resource for use during the project.

The project began with a whole-class discussion at the start of the first day. Before the children had come in Inge and her adult helpers had covered the tables with newspaper and placed a pot of glue and spreaders on each. When the children were on the carpet, Inge, having dealt with the day's administrative tasks, explained that she wanted them to make a model of a neighbourhood, 'Let's make a model of where we would like to live.' (She subsequently regretted the use of the word model because some confused it with 'muddle' and proudly reported to visitors, 'We're making a muddle!') Inge then asked, 'What can we put on our model?' Their ideas were listed on a long sheet of paper which was put up on the wall. Early suggestions included: people, grass, trees, cars, pond. Inge then asked them to think about what they see on the way to school. Further suggestions were: houses, shops. Inge made another intervention, 'What else would you like that you don't see?' which elicited the idea of, 'a park' from Kimberley. The next stage was to remind the children what was available to make their models. This was done by asking them to think about this for themselves, 'What do we need to make a model?' The new list was recorded: Lego, plasticine, paint, glue-gun, paper, glue, straws, boxes, lids, cardboard. The children then talked in more detail about what they could make. The discussion with the whole class lasted about 40 minutes and Inge was pleased by their concentration for this length of time. Before setting them off, Inge said,

> Now *you* can choose what to make for our model from the list we have made. Remember, if you want to do something else whilst you're waiting for things to dry or want a change for a while, the computer, the sand area, book and home corner are open.

The children went to a table in friendship groups to start their making which was tackled individually.

Inge and the learning support assistant supported two groups each. The helpers had planned the project in collaboration with Inge and she had reminded them that their role was to support the children and not to do the making for them or telling them how to do it.

The children decided what to make and started work. Most of the children on one table Inge was supporting decided to make cars or lorries. Boxes were used to make the body of each outcome and these were adorned with various features. The children were competent with scissors and gluing seats, doors, windows, steering wheels and decoration on to the box was not problematic. Inge had to help Steven who wanted to cut some fur fabric for a seat. He tried with small scissors unsuccessfully. Inge said, 'I'll do it, but you must show me just where to cut.' Problems also arose when it came to fitting wheels. PVA glue was spread too thickly and cardboard or lid-top wheels would not stick. Andrew remembered the glue-gun and asked Inge to help. The wheels were stuck straight on, but of course would not turn. One of the other children, Darren, said to Andrew 'But your car doesn't work 'cos the wheels don't turn'. Andrew had been quite happy with this until it was pointed out to him. The consequence was to cause Andrew to start again.

On another table, boxes formed the basis for house and shop structures. Abigail was the first to evaluate her model critically and express her concern that all the writing on the box could be seen, 'I don't like the numbers on it.' Her solution, arrived at without adult intervention, was to cover it with plain paper. This technique was subsequently copied by others in the group. Abigail's house had other features which were added one by one, including a door and windows. In this sense the outcomes, whether they were vehicles or buildings, involved a similar approach and skills. Inge showed both her groups how they could make people out of twisting pipe-cleaners. Ryan had an idea of using 'lolly sticks' with drawn faces. The final outcomes provided evidence of Ryan's suggestion being most commonly used. This pleased Inge since it showed that the children were not relying on her alone for ideas and nor were they simply trying to please her by doing what they thought she wanted. They were making decisions independently based upon their particular preferences.

The production of the 'park' proved interesting. This was the part of the work where Inge assessed that some children were identifying needs, which she had not anticipated happening. Kimberley decided to make seats 'in case the grown ups want a tea party'. Others made a climbing frame and a roundabout. Kelly was determined to have a separated area 'for cats and dogs to play'. Even at this young age it is evident that other human (and animal) needs feature in children's thinking and 'values' are emerging.

The making phase of the work dominated the rest of day one and for some children all of the morning of the following day. At the beginning of the second day Inge chose four children to assemble the final model. It was to be displayed on another low-level storage system with a large surface area. The base for the display was made of sugar paper and a road was painted on this by the 'assembly' group. During this Ryan insisted they had a pavement, which he made out of stickle bricks. He commented that this was needed for 'safety' and provided more evidence of a child identifying a need.

Before contributing their parts to the display the children were asked to get into pairs and tell each other about their models. Some found this very difficult. Andrew admitted, 'I want to tell everyone about mine but I don't really want to listen!' Great excitement surrounded the addition of all the component parts, carefully labelled with the maker's name. Decisions about where each was to go was discussed by the team of four and this was the first time in the project that collaboration had been explicitly encouraged by Inge. The model was assembled by lunchtime and everyone went off to eat feeling satisfied with their work.

The afternoon began with the class sitting around the model and Inge asked them, 'What do you think about our model?' This evaluative question was not intended to elicit detailed comment since much of that had been picked up informally by the adults as they had worked with the children. Inge wanted to establish the idea that everyone's views about it were being sought and valued. Again the responses were written down to add to the display. Tara thought it was 'wonderful'; Lisa said, 'I like it'; Ryan said, 'It's really nice.' Kelly topped these with, 'It's absolutely fabulous.' Mrs Fey's contribution was 'It's the best!'

Overall, Inge was very pleased with the project. In particular, the children who, she considered, often showed poor concentration and listening skills were involved throughout and were obviously motivated. There were few examples of behavioural difficulties during the project although Jason got cross when told by another child on his table that 'You're not doing it right.' In terms of her own role, she found it difficult, as she had in the past, not to give the children her suggestions. She felt the best interventions she made were when asking questions in order to focus the children's thinking and help them plan and make more carefully.

The key features of this work related to the teacher's role include:

- a well-organised classroom in which resources are readily available and labelled;
- the classroom prepared before the children arrived;
- emphasis given to the safe use of tools and adequate adult supervision;
- other adult helpers well-briefed about their role and involved in collaborative planning;
- strategies (such as listing contributions) to reinforce to the children that their ideas are valued;
- interventions to encourage children to generate and develop their own ideas;
- interventions intended to improve children's self-esteem and confidence;
- emphasis upon asking questions as opposed to giving too many ideas and suggestions.

This teacher had decided to concentrate the work into two intensive days rather than spread it over a longer period. Later case studies will illustrate different approaches. This project illustrates pupils working towards many of the early learning goals specified for the Foundation Stage (QCA/DfEE 2000a). Go back to those listed earlier in this chapter (pages 29, 31) and evaluate which goals you consider to be potentially covered.

The quality of children's learning in any design and technology project will be dependent upon the quality of teacher intervention. Teachers approaching their role with a constructivist view of learning will recognise the extent to which that role requires them to engage in an active process of constructing understanding about individual children's learning and the common needs evident within groups or the whole class. To make appropriate interventions requires teachers to assess children's current understanding and skills and to make decisions about how best to move learners forward in terms of developing their practical or cognitive skills, in developing their knowledge and understanding, in fostering particular attitudes and personal qualities. These interventions are the way the teacher provides the 'scaffolding' that will enable the learner to build new and improved cognitive structures in order to better understand and operate in the world. In design and technology, teacher intervention may involve: asking a focused question, giving information, making a suggestion, encouraging or facilitating peer discussion, pointing out how others are tackling similar problems, demonstrating new ways of doing something, using an analogy to illustrate a similar problem and its solution, encouraging further exploration/research or reminding the child of previous learning in related areas. A teacher's skills in making the right intervention at the right time, whether it is with an individual or with a group or whole class, will come from experience and a reflective approach to professional activity.

11. Conclusion

This chapter has outlined a constructivist view of learning in design and technology, in which learners are recognised as the active constructors of their own knowledge and understanding. However, this view does not regard learning as something that an individual does in isolation; the social context and the role of peers and adults is vital. Learning has been discussed through the skills, processes, knowledge and understanding, personal qualities and attitudes and values which are involved. The intention has been to highlight key aspects of learning and explore some of the difficulties any teacher faces when seeking to be an effective teacher of design and technology.

The emphasis has been upon the child as a learner, but implicit reference has also been made to the teacher as a 'learner'. Like children, adult learners must actively construct understanding through interaction with others and the world around them. In the context of teaching design and technology there are several aspects to this knowledge and understanding: subject knowledge – understanding more about design and technology and its knowledge-base (the conceptual and procedural landscape); professional knowledge – understanding more about how children learn and the role of the teacher in that process; understanding of the needs of children and their existing capabilities. Like younger learners, adults come to learning with existing ideas and new understanding will result from a process of clarifying their existing understanding and, if appropriate or necessary, restructuring that understanding. In all of these cases of adult learning, a constructivist view of learning can be applied.

CHAPTER 3

Opportunities for design and technology

1. Introduction

This chapter deals with opportunities for design and technology within the primary curriculum and the nature and importance of context in terms of planning and implementing classroom work. The relationship between design and technology and other areas of the curriculum is analysed, particularly with regard to science, art, literacy and numeracy. Starting points for design and technology are offered and the role of teacher creativity in identifying these is emphasised. Examples of teacher and child identified needs and opportunities are discussed. The chapter illustrates a range of different outcomes resulting from work within a variety of contexts.

2. The importance of context

To make design and technology activities relevant to children they need to be set in contexts which children can understand and to which they can relate. It is the context which often provides the motivation for successful work. Contexts can be connected to home, school, community, recreation, business and industry situations. These were made explicit in the previous version of the National Curriculum (DfE/WO 1995) and are implicit in the current one (DfEE/QCA 1999). Younger children will find it much easier to relate to the more immediate contexts of home and school, but there is no reason why, as they get older, the other contexts should not be exploited. A context which is also common in primary school design and technology is that concerned with imaginative or fantasy situations. This might involve basing children's designing and making in the context of a story, meeting the needs of imaginary characters or, perhaps, designing and making a small- or large-scale fantasy environment. The choice of context for this kind of work is usually made by the teacher and within the context the particular need or opportunity for a project may be identified by the children or again by the teacher. These decisions are significant ones and it is at the stage of identifying and planning a context for the work that teacher creativity (Howe *et al.* 2001) is most needed.

As well as selecting a context for design and technology and planning the work, a teacher also has to decide how to fit the work into the rest of the curriculum in organisational terms. In the current situation where literacy and numeracy dominate and often account for the use of time before lunch, this is a major challenge. There are two distinctly different approaches here. Teachers can either plan design and technology activities as stand alone projects that are organised alongside other curriculum work, with their own allocation of time; or they can plan design and technology activities or projects as part of cross-curricular topics, or linked with a particular curriculum area, sharing an allocation of time. The first approach is the focus of the next section. A later section will consider design and technology within or linked to other curriculum work, especially English, mathematics, science and ICT. The implications for planning of these different approaches will be explored further in Chapter 8. Of course, because of its nature, approaching design and technology as discrete activities will also involve learning and spin-offs in other curriculum areas.

As outlined in Chapter 1, the National Curriculum categorises design and technology activities as design and make assignments (DMAs), focused practical tasks (FPTs) and investigation/evaluation activities (IEAs) (DfEE/QCA, 1999). The assignments, often referred to as projects in this book, are holistic activities which are most like many of those featured in this chapter, although in most case studies aspects of all three National Curriculum categories are covered, as appropriate.

3. Identifying opportunities for design and technology

Children's lives in and out of school provide countless starting points for design and technology projects which can be exploited by the creative teacher. This section begins with an account of a teacher who decided to turn a very common school activity – producing greetings cards for special occasions – into a design and technology project with genuine opportunities for learning. In most infant, and many junior classrooms, teachers ask children to produce greetings cards to take home, perhaps at Diwali, Christmas, Easter and Mothering Sunday. Often such work is seen purely as an art/craft activity and sometimes every child produces an identical card based upon a teacher design or template. As the activities frequently take place at the end of terms, teachers sometimes use such work as a time-filling activity with limited educational potential. The teacher whose work is described below, intended the work with her class to have a different emphasis. It is set in a familiar context for the children related to 'home'.

CASE STUDY

2: Greetings cards
Marie Harris taught at Two Mile Hill Infants' School in Bristol where she had a class of 33 Y1/Y2 children when this work was done.

During a topic on 'Celebrations' the previous term, the children had evaluated examples of greetings cards that would be given for different reasons, e.g. Birthday, Christmas, Get Well, Diwali. Marie began the design and technology project, which is the focus of this case study, by reminding the children about that work. She organised a brief class discussion about why cards get sent, what they are made of and which cards are liked or not. Marie then asked the children to complete simple evaluation sheets while looking at a collection of birthday cards she had put together. The sheets asked the children to say why they liked certain cards and not others. Some of these were filled in with pictures drawn by the children and the teacher scribing while others were completed entirely by the children. As Mothers' Day and Easter were approaching Marie planned for the class to make cards to give their families. She decided that if she repeated a similar task within a few weeks (both involving designing, making and evaluating cards) there should be some opportunities to address progression in terms of the skills, knowledge and understanding and attitudes used by the children as they tackled the tasks.

The work was planned in the following way:

Week 1
    Reminder of last term's work on Celebrations
    Evaluation of birthday cards (whole class)
    Identify needs for sending Mothers' Day cards (whole class)
    Brainstorm ideas for cards (whole class)
    Introduction to pop-up techniques (whole class)
    Design card (individually, during group time)
    Make card (individually with help as needed, during group time)
    Brief discussion about own card (individually with an adult helper or teacher, during
       group time)

Week 3
    Identify need for Easter cards (whole class)
    Brainstorm ideas about Easter (whole class)
    Design Easter card (individually)
    Make card (individually with help as needed during whole-class time)
    Evaluate own card (and a friend's) (in pairs during whole-class time)
    Evaluate own and others' cards (whole class)

Marie felt it was important for the children to be involved in identifying the need for individual cards and had no intention of 33 identical cards being produced, based on a teacher template. The initial discussion was focused upon Mothers' Day and how children might show their appreciation for their mothers or someone else special who cares for them. During the discussion, which was wide-ranging and included ideas such as 'being good' and 'helping' as well as the idea of 'sending a card', Marie focused their attention on the latter. Marie had identified a context for the work focusing upon the children's experience of 'home' and specifically related to 'showing appreciation for mothers' and within that context the need for a greetings card had been identified through discussion.

After evaluating the cards, which included pop-up examples, and the decision to make their own cards, Marie demonstrated to the children some simple techniques for making pop-up cards. She anticipated the children might then wish to use the ideas in their designs. The children had previous experience of designing before making. She provided a 'design sheet' to aid this part of the process. Prior to making an actual card, Marie recognised some children would need practice at making pop-up mechanisms. A few children, in fact, decided this for themselves during the design activity and Marie encouraged others to do the same. She did this by questioning them during the designing stage about how they were going to make their cards work. This led to her organising a focused practical task. After this, one group at a time made their cards in the art/technology area she had set up in the classroom. At this stage, to aid her assessment of the children, she had listed the skills that would be needed. These were: *manipulative* – writing, gluing, folding, cutting, sellotaping, stapling, measuring, painting, drawing, making pop-up mechanisms; *cognitive* – observing, imaging, estimating, creativity; *social* – sharing materials, cooperating, tidying up, considering others' needs for space and tools.

The outcomes from the making sessions were original and most had been produced with limited adult help. After talking about their outcomes with an adult the cards and designs were displayed for the rest of the class to see, prior to being taken home and given to the recipient whose response added to the evaluation evidence!

The Easter card work developed in a similar way, with Marie intervening to develop children's skills and understanding. For example, during this task she pushed some children to make their designs clearer, such as adding labels to their sketches and specifying colours to be used. She recognised, however, that her professional decision about which children to treat in this way was an important one. 'For some children it would have dramatically lowered their motivation to ask them to go back and add more to their designs.' She was aiming to achieve a balance between developing their skills and understanding and fostering their confidence, motivation, perseverance and independence. The making session for the Easter cards was organised as a whole-class activity to further develop the social skills listed above. Unlike the Mothers' Day cards, the Easter cards were evaluated more systematically. Marie asked the children to explain what their cards were like and how they differed or were similar to their original designs. She asked them what they had found easy and what they had found hard about making the card; whether they liked their cards and why; how they could make them better if they made them again.

Marie analysed the learning involved for individual children. For example she wrote about George, a six-year-old, Y2 child:

George's design for his Mothers' Day card was triangular and he had difficulty explaining how it would stand up so he decided to make a 'practice card'. He discussed his ideas for an Easter card with another child. His design shows a chick in a broken egg. What is not clear from his drawing is that the card had a movable top part of the egg that flapped open to reveal the chick. However, his design-related drawing skills have developed since the first card and he now uses arrows to help annotate his sketch. He was able to identify what was easy and hard about making his card, 'The difficult bit was putting the shell on the chick to get them to slot together, so I needed an extra bit of cardboard.' Neil asked him, during the class discussion, 'Did you and Paul do the same design?' At this point he showed his design to the class so that they could see the similarities and differences in both the designs and the cards. George developed his manipulative and problem solving skills when he fixed the egg and shell in position. He was aware of his own preferences and those of his mother. She obviously liked the flower on the front of the Mothers' Day card as he chose to use a similar design on the Easter card (the chick was on the back!). He made the Easter card without any adult intervention and worked more independently than on the Mothers' Day card.

This project involved a product which every child in the class had experience of making and a task which had relevance to each child because of the familiar context in which the task was set. There is evidence of the children engaging in all three types of National Curriculum activity (DfEE/QCA 1999): the overall project was their 'assignment' (DMA); they had time for focused practical tasks (FPTs) during which they developed and practised their skills concerning pop-up mechanisms; the project began with investigative/evaluative activity (IEA). Of course, there is an issue concerning the choice of context and the need for sensitivity towards those children who do not celebrate Easter or who do not live with a mother. However, such a 'personal' theme meant the children's values were being made explicit and explored. They were also thinking about others and their preferences. Planning for a topic on greetings cards can be based on the QCA Scheme of Work (SoW) (QCA/DfEE 1998) which has a unit on Moving pictures (1A) for pupils of this age. The use of the QCA units will be discussed more fully in Chapter 8. Mechanisms that can be used in greetings cards include sliders, levers, rotating wheels and floating planes. Useful background knowledge for teachers about some of these mechanisms can be found in the Teacher Training Agency (TTA) materials, *Assessing your needs in Design and Technology* (TTA 1998a).

School provides another immediate context for design and technology projects of which all children have direct experience. The following are some opportunities this context offers: redesigning and organising a part of the classroom – wet area, computer area, book corner, display areas, storage facilities; designing and making temporary homes for minibeasts, wildlife area or pond; designing and modelling playground equipment; designing and making a guide for new pupils, parents, and visitors to the school. Others will be illustrated in later case studies.

The following case study illustrates a successful design and technology project focused upon a 'school' context. It is based upon the work of Alan Howe when he was teaching at Batheaston Primary School.

CASE STUDY

3: The library

Alan was teaching a Y4 class and planned a project focusing on making improvements to the school library. It began with a discussion with the whole class about the school library and what the children thought about it. He posed the question, 'How can we improve our library?' and the class then took responsibility, with his support and guidance, for addressing the concern.

The initial class discussion highlighted a number of criticisms that the children had, but they were also aware that others used the library and they soon suggested a questionnaire to elicit the views of children of other ages. This stage involved a group of four, including Sally (who had first suggested asking others), in constructing a simple set of questions. These were word-processed and photocopied. The resulting questionnaire was tried out by classmates and revised to make the questions clearer and to give more space for responses. It was also decided, after Sally had tried it out on her little brother, that younger children should be interviewed and not given the sheet to fill in.

The outcomes of this research phase indicated a number of common concerns from children throughout the school: the area was considered dark and gloomy, it was often untidy, some shelves were too high for users to reach, there were too many old and 'boring' books. The latter finding led to another group setting out to find out more about what kinds of books the children wanted in their library (and excellent links were made with literacy work).

From this information collecting period the children were identifying a range of needs within the main concern of 'improving the library'. In terms of the design and technology process, the class were evaluating an existing space in order to identify needs which they could realistically meet.

The next phase involved decisions about how the library area could be improved, based upon evidence from users. Groups focused upon different aspects and generated designs and plans for their particular focus. Several groups, set out to brighten up the library area by designing new curtains, cushions for the floor and murals for the walls. The textile work involved children generating designs on paper, evaluating those designs and getting evaluative comment from others before the design was implemented using iron-on transfers. The murals were designed on squared paper and once approved by the class were turned into wall murals through a process of enlarging each square. Some parental help was available during this stage of the work.

Another interesting challenge that Alan set the whole class during this project came from a particular suggestion that one child, David, had made during a discussion about how the library could be improved. He described the way book stands were used in his local library to display books. Alan logged this idea on a flip-chart of possible ways of improving the library (which he built up during the class discussion) and went back to it in the fourth week of the work. The children were invited, in pairs, to design and make a bookstand. They had available a range of everyday materials, wood, corriflute and construction kits. This mini-project, again within the overall theme, involved the whole-class in work with resistant materials and allowed them experience of working through the design and technology process. A whole class evaluation of these outcomes led to the selection of several which were agreed to be durable and attractive enough for library use. Several of these were then manufactured.

At the end of the period a major class review took place to which the head teacher was invited. During this, each change was considered and discussed in terms of the children's, Alan's and the head teacher's views.

Like the first case study in this chapter, the teacher here had exploited an opportunity and planned the subsequent work in a thorough and professional manner and in both cases, although the projects were specifically planned as design and technology, there was considerable learning related to other curriculum areas.

Contexts beyond school may require more background information and more organisation in advance if the children are to explore and investigate the issues involved thoroughly. However, such work can have considerable potential for design and technology projects for all primary children, but especially those at Key Stage 2. The following are some examples: design and modelling a new housing or shopping development; addressing local problems such as litter, car parking, poor signing; designing and making aids for the elderly or people with disabilities.

Design and technology projects aimed at developing 'financial capability' and 'enterprise education' (DfEE/QCA 1999, p. 22) include mini-enterprise projects which are increasingly common in primary schools. These involve children engaging in projects in school that have parallels in business and industry. For example, children may set up their own 'company' to produce and sell products such as badges, stationery sets or kites.

The following case study illustrates one such initiative that has become an annual event at Crossways Junior School in Thornbury involving all classes.

CASE STUDY

4: The autumn fair

At Crossways Junior School the autumn fair is an opportunity for every class in the school to get involved in a mini-enterprise project. The parents' association provides each class with £15 to fund the projects and the challenge is to make as much money as possible by selling items at the school fair. Two examples follow.

Vanessa Wrench's class of Y3 children brainstormed products they could make and decided to produce 'refrigerator magnets'. They agreed to make them from *Fimo* and attach clothes pegs so that notes could be held in the peg. They spent their money purchasing the modelling material, pegs and small magnets (bought through the school's design and technology subject leader). The production workshop was then set up and all the children made 'magnets' to their own designs. Further discussion led to an agreed price. The idea proved a success and the stock sold out, although rumour has it that most were purchased by the producer (or her/his parent)!

The Y6 class, with their teacher Myra Ginns, adopted a more systematic approach to market research, production and marketing. They researched, by asking other children, parents and teachers what they would actually buy at the fair. From this they discovered that Christmas tree decorations would be popular. They then brainstormed different types and how they could be made. After much discussion and practical exploration they decided that they could make them from: a flour and water mixture, baked and varnished; origami; and everyday materials. The advantage, readily appreciated by the entrepreneurs in the class, was that none of these materials would cost much, and most could be obtained for no cost! Having agreed to concentrate on stars, miniature parcels and origami Santas they conducted some research to find out how much people would pay for these products. They then organised production lines to maximise efficiency. The next phase involved decisions about marketing. A stall was designed around a Christmas tree and signs and price tags made (some of the original money was spent on advertising and promotion). Overproduction meant that towards the end of the fair 'final reductions' were made to offload stock. Once the final budget had been calculated by the class accountants a profit of over £50 was announced, much to everybody's satisfaction. The children were later invited to make suggestions about how the contribution to the school's funds could be best used.

Evaluation of the products of business and industry can provide a profitable starting point for the children's own designing and making. School–Industry links, such as those encouraged by the Engineering Council (such as the Neighbourhood Engineers' Scheme), can lead to exciting and innovative projects which help increase children's awareness of industry and also increase their own capabilities (see Bowen 1996; Jacobs 1994). Gardner (1996) discusses a project involving a link with 'Body Shop' which led to her Y5 children producing 'green' tee-shirts. Another example of work in a very different context is provided by Helean Hughes, from Wellesley Primary School in South Gloucestershire (see Iredale and Price 1999 for this and other examples of primary schools linking with manufacturing industries). Her Y6 pupils linked with British Aerospace and investigated the fabrics used in aircraft seating prior to designing their own ideal seats. Their link gave them valuable insights into the use of ICT in industry which they could compare and contrast with their classroom use of ICT.

Another way into design and technology for young children is through the use of imaginative and fantasy contexts. In Chapter 1, we explored the way in which children's play provides the foundation for school design and technology. This can be built upon in the early years of school. Figure 3.1 illustrates an example of my own daughter's design and technological capability at three and a half-years-old. Lucy had been to a christening for the first time and observed carefully what took place. She obviously put herself in the position of the recipient and when she got home, unprompted or helped by an adult (apart from providing some biscuits), she made a 'christening machine' using *Big Builda*. Her outcome took into account the baby's comfort and needs (a toy for entertainment, a drink and food). She also considered the needs of the vicar and thoughtfully provided water and a musical instrument to accompany the imaginary 'service'. In Lucy's imaginative world she had identified a need and 'designed' and made something to meet that need. Reception-aged children can often be observed producing similar outcomes when they use the available construction kits in their exploratory and imaginative play.

Figure 3.1 Lucy's christening machine

Stables (1992) reminds us about the relationship between fantasy and reality in early years design and technology,

> The ability to handle both fantasy and reality simultaneously could be argued to be of fundamental importance to the design and technologist (*sic*) – to be able to conceive ideas that push out the boundaries of the possible, while mediating these ideas through a grip on reality.

> (p. 111).

Lucy was managing to hold both fantasy and reality in mind as she made and played with her invention and research would suggest young children do not find this difficult (Stables 1992). It is a key role of the teacher to encourage this ability, without letting the 'flight of fancy' lead to the child losing touch with reality. There is also a risk that projects such as 'homes for people in rainforests' end up being treated as a fantasy context producing ideas which show no awareness of the needs of real people with real concerns and their own culture.

In school, stories are used to stimulate the children's imagination and introduce them to a world beyond their own direct experience. The use of children's fiction, poems and songs is a rich vein for teachers to exploit when looking for starting points and contexts for design and technology. Some stories provide, as part of the story line, a problem or challenge which the children can meet in their own way, even if a solution is suggested in the book (see Case Study 9: A house for mice). Teachers can read the part of the story which sets up the need, invite the children to identify and explore that need and then get them to design and make a solution. As part of the evaluative phase of the work the end of the story can be read, in order that the children can compare and contrast their solutions with that of the author. Another approach to children's literature is to use the story as a context and then invite the children, perhaps as a brainstorming exercise, to identify needs and opportunities for design and technology projects (see Lewisham LEA 1999). Teachers can, if necessary, do this themselves and then invite the children to work on teacher-identified projects related to a story.

4. Design and technology across the curriculum

Links between design and technology and other subjects are emphasised in the current National Curriculum Orders (DfEE/QCA 1999). There are explicit links identified between the design and technology PoS and those for English, ICT, mathematics and science. These are further amplified in the QCA SoW (QCA/DfEE 1998, p. 32 and individual units) which also provides examples of links with other subjects.

This section begins by examining the relationship between design and technology and science, introduced in the last chapter. In the primary school context, science and technology can sometimes be treated holistically within the curriculum and children may not be aware of which subject is being experienced at any particular time or stage of the work. However, teachers need to be able to identify the elements that reflect the distinct nature of each subject, and recognise that not all design and technology work is related to science. Much has been written about the links between science and design and technology, at both primary and secondary level (see Bentley and Watts 1994; Davies 1997; Howe *et al.* 2001; Layton 1993). There are obvious dangers in oversimplifying the issues involved. However, I regard the difference between the two areas relatively easy to understand if the purpose, the nature of the processes involved and the outcomes are compared. Science has the purpose of improving our understanding of how the world works; whereas design and technology is about creating an outcome in order to change the world in some way. Scientific enquiry is a process that can begin with a question and through hypothesis, experiment, analysis and evaluation, lead to a changed (and preferably improved) understanding. Design and technology, by contrast, can begin with a need and through a process of planning, making and evaluating lead to an outcome. Of course, during design and technology activities, children may well be improving their scientific understanding. For example, a design and technology task concerning the production of a waterproof hat may well involve children in finding out more about waterproof materials, perhaps through some investigative work. However, children do not need to understand why some fabrics are waterproof in order to meet the design and technology challenge.

Despite the differences, design and technology and science can be taught appropriately in an integrated or interactive way in the primary sector (Howe *et al.* 2001). The processes involved have obvious similarities and the skills used are often common to both. Design and technology can provide excellent ways of helping children to apply scientific knowledge and understanding. Design and technology activities are 'resourced' by such knowledge and understanding and therefore, on some occasions, success in design and technology is dependent upon the child having an adequate scientific knowledge base to draw upon. Conversely, design and technology activities may provide a concrete context through which children develop an abstract scientific idea, such as buoyancy during a boat-making task. The integrated approach is problematic if design and technology becomes the poor relation, and children are designing and making purely to improve their learning in science. The following example of classroom work illustrates design and technology and science working well together, in a context drawn from yet another curriculum area, history.

CASE STUDY

5: Air-raid shelters

Richard Brice was a teacher at Christchurch Primary School in Bradford-on-Avon, Wiltshire. The following case study covers his work with a class of 35 of Y6 children who were engaging in a design and technology project linked to a topic on the Second World War.

The design and technology project was planned by Richard with the following purposes:

- to encourage the children to produce 'quality' design and technology outcomes and evaluate their function systematically;
- to encourage the children to produce accuratly drawn designs of an outcome before making it. Richard considered the class had had limited experience of, or indeed opportunities for, producing accurate designs. He coined the phrase with them – WYSIWYSG (what you see is what you should get!);
- to encourage the children to apply ideas about the strength of materials developed during the previous term's science topic;
- to encourage the children to apply ideas from their history studies related to the Second World War to a practical design and make task;
- to provide opportunities for children to develop their skills in conducting fair tests (linked to the PoS for Science 1).

With such a large class, in a relatively small classroom, and with limited resources on hand, he decided to organise the work in a way which was manageable for him, but allowed the children to work independently on their own ideas. Consequently, he decided to have the whole class working on the project in friendship pairs, and to set a challenge which required minimal resourcing. He challenged the class, several weeks into the topic, to design a strong model air-raid shelter using only four sheets of A4 paper. There were other constraints: it should stand at least 8 cm high and 15 cm long and have an entrance. This could be criticised as a rather limited problem solving exercise, but his approach ensured it provided considerable potential to develop children's learning in design and technology.

The children had already seen shelters in a television programme and in books. Richard asked each pair to draw their designs as carefully and as accurately as possible. They were encouraged to produce scale drawings of their ideas on isometric paper. They had sheets of scrap paper for trying things out and modelling at this stage of the process. As an example, Figure 3.2 shows Adam's design. This phase of the work lasted for about an hour and involved plenty of discussion within pairs. Table arrangements also meant that pairs could compare ideas with at least two other pairs during a review period at the end of this session.

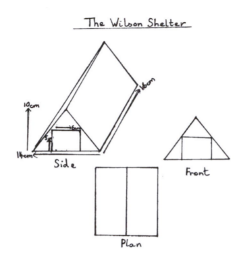

Figure 3.2 A design for an air-raid shelter

The making phase took place at various times over the next few days. Richard set a time limit on this and provided opportunities for the work on a group and whole-class basis. However, several children got so involved in constructing their shelters that they asked to take them home to finish, which was allowed. He was pleased to get feedback from parents that some children were so motivated by the task that they made others at home using different materials. One child was even reported to have been found testing an outcome in the kitchen with potato 'bombs'! Some children discovered relations and neighbours who remembered using shelters and could offer useful advice. On the day of the deadline for completion every pair had successfully made and 'finished' their outcomes. This, in itself, was a pleasing achievement and the quality of most of them impressed Richard. There was an interesting variety of outcomes, based upon tent-like structures, arch structures, domes and even a teepee. Some had not given sufficient attention to the purpose of the shelter, providing limited space, in some cases, for occupants and in one case failing to provide an entrance! However, all of them were carefully made with good evidence of measuring, marking, cutting and joining skills. In most cases the outcomes were very similar to the designs although appropriately, in some cases, modifications had been agreed during the making phase. For example, Adam and his partner included a central square-sectioned column in the middle of their 'tent' and a square-sectioned 'girder' as a ridge, which was not in their drawing. The 'A' frames at each end were also accurately constructed out of square-sectioned struts (Figure 3.3).

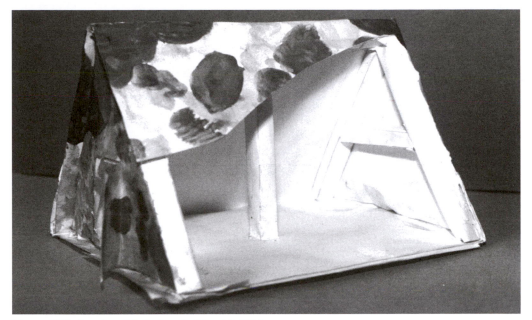

Figure 3.3 An air-raid shelter built with 'A' frames

Adam provided Richard with clear evidence of applying learning from the earlier topic since his notes on the design stated, 'We remembered the triangle was the strongest shape, that's why it's like a tent with A's at each end'. The model was beautifully finished in camouflage colours. During the making phase Richard ensured, by his actions, that the children were aware of his interest in their work and his enthusiasm for the project. Some of his comments were made in a role appropriate to the context, for example, talking about 'a major bombing raid is forecast in the near future'. The size of the class limited the extent to which he could find time to work with each pair but the engagement of the children with the activity was such that, at this stage, he was not really needed. They had the necessary construction skills and few problems resulted from access to tools and materials. PVA glue and paints were readily available and scissors were the only tools needed. Richard did not allow the children to use sellotape on this task as he regards it as 'a low skill material'. A wet area outside the classroom was used for painting at the latter stage of construction.

Richard's role was significant when it came to evaluation. Again, he decided to organise this with the whole class. He recognised this would limit his interaction with particular groups, but considered that the activity would be disruptive if tackled during group time when other 'quiet' activities were also going on. He had told the children at the outset that they were going to 'test' their outcomes in order to evaluate their effectiveness. When the shelters were assembled he set the scene with, 'The planes are on their way to bomb Bradford-on-Avon!' He asked the children to think about how they could test their models. After ten minutes of initial discussion in pairs he brought them together and described a science 'test' he had seen children in another class carry out recently, which was related to friction investigations rather than the strength of materials. It was by no means a 'fair' test. He asked his children to comment upon what the others had done and used this to focus their thinking upon the way in which they could test their shelters. They returned to devising a fair test. He had decided to structure the testing groups (of four children), based on the nature of the outcomes, so that the results would allow each group to compare different structures, for example an arch and a cuboid. He organised these groups and asked them to share ideas for a test and agree on which one, of the two, to use, or to devise a modified one based upon both ideas. The testing got underway after a discussion about safety aspects. One group asked Richard to be the 'bomber' to increase the fairness of their test (see Figure 3.4). The following is Adam's account of his group's test:

> To test we got the two shelters. With a metre stick we dropped 50 g weights on them from 40 cm, then 50 cm and every 10 cm. Once we got to the top of the metre we changed the weight to 100 g. Both of the shelters were strong and I thought it would be a draw. We gave up after 200 g from 1 m. Our shelter was a bit stronger because ours was a triangle and Ben's was an arch. Ben's was more damaged but the bomb had not broken through!

Figure 3.4 Testing an air-raid shelter

The tests reinforced the links Richard wished to make between the children's work in design and technology and science. The design and make task had required the children to apply knowledge and understanding from science, history and art. The evaluation phase involved application of children's scientific process skills and led to a further development of those skills. The discussion of the results and reasons for the different performance of different structures also had potential for further developing the children's scientific knowledge and understanding. There were other aspects to the topic which involved other curriculum areas. These experiences for the children informed and were informed by their design and technology work. Drama work during the same week involved role play activities about what it would be like waiting in the shelters for the enemy planes. The design and technology project had been about the structure itself, not what might be needed inside the shelter. The consideration of needs related to time spent in the shelter was a further development of children's design and technology capabilities. A music session included songs that might have been sung in the shelter to pass the time and a task during English work involved each child writing a letter to a relative 'from the shelter' describing what it felt like. These experiences helped reinforce the purpose and nature of the real shelters which they had been modelling. It also involved developing cultural understanding (see Howe *et al.* 2001, Section 2).

In summary, this project was positively evaluated by Richard (and other teachers with whom he shared it as part of an INSET activity). He was pleased by the quality of the children's design and technology work and the learning which resulted; he considered the task motivating and relevant and was encouraged by the way in which all of the children stayed on task throughout the work; he considered the cross-curricular links to be genuine and not contrived; links between school and home were fostered as a result of the children's level of interest in the work and desire to do things at home. His concerns about the work related to the organisation of the task for the whole class, and the extent to which that limited his opportunities for assessing individual children's learning during the designing and making phases. He was also a little disappointed by the similarity of all their tests, which he recognised was fairly inevitable considering the nature of the shelters' function. An advantage from working with the whole class was the fact that he could focus all his attention on the one activity. He commented, 'I get the best results from the children from activities in which the children see I get totally immersed. They see my interest, commitment and enthusiasm for the activity and respond to it likewise'. He also considered his input to the class could be made in the most efficient way and he did not have to keep repeating himself with instructions and advice.

This case study illustrates the successful use of a historical context. It also provides a good example of design and technology and science being taught in an interactive way – the design and technology was planned, in part, to encourage children to apply knowledge and understanding from science. The design and technology outcome was then used to further develop children's learning related to fair testing in science as well as reinforcing the importance of systematic approaches to evaluating products. This case study provides a good example for applying the OFSTED criteria for quality teaching and learning outlined in Chapter 1. You will find evidence that many are met. It links with the QCA SoW unit on Shelters (6A) intended for this age group (QCA/DfEE 1998).

Links with history can also be developed in design and technology by asking children to evaluate outcomes from other times and places as part of their work and using such evaluations to inform their own designing and making. Historical contexts for design and technology can be used by teachers in other ways. Projects on particular periods can be a stimulus for modelling artefacts and outcomes of that period (cooking utensils, costumes, storage methods, carrying devices, writing implements). Outcomes can be models of buildings or other large-scale pieces of historical evidence. An example of this is given in Chapter 6 and involves children modelling a ship as part of an Exploration topic (Case Study 13: A new ship for Columbus). A role play, based in the historical period being studied, can provide a purpose for design and technology activities. In my own teaching two examples spring to mind. During a project with a Y4 class on the Romans, the children planned and implemented a Roman feast with appropriate foods (although demands for roast dormouse were rejected on health and safety grounds!), costumes, table decorations, entertainment and rituals. I can still vividly remember Ian and Paul acting out a gladiators' fight for the entertainment of the guests (which included parents and head teacher) and unbeknown to me releasing fake blood after a particularly realistic blow had been struck. The shock took a little while to wear off! Information informing their work on this project came from a variety of sources including television, books and a visit to the Roman Baths in Bath. A similar project with a younger class involved planning and organising Greek games as part of a project on that era. That year, the Greek games replaced the traditional sports' day for my class and the events and organisation were informed by the work they did related to the project. Hards (1998) outlines a project on Ancient Egypt involving Y4–Y6 pupils with a strong design and technology dimension which led to an exhibition of the children's outcomes that was opened to the general public.

Geography and geographical topics can provide other starting points and a context for design and technology. The following case study involved a class working on a topic about other European countries and offers another example of a link with 'business' and of food being used as a medium for design and technology (as in the Roman feast).

CASE STUDY

6: An Italian restaurant

As part of a project on Italy at Batheaston Primary School, Alan Howe and the class of Y1/Y2 children he was teaching planned and implemented a special lunch-hour which involved transforming the dining hall into an Italian restaurant serving a range of appropriate foods.

Alan intended to provide the class with some experience of using food as a medium for design and technology work, recognising the constraints imposed by practical and health and safety issues. His solution was to involve the school cook in the class work linked to their half-term project on Italy, planned as part of a whole-school theme on European awareness.

The children began their involvement through a discussion with the school cook about meals and foods that could be part of an Italian menu. This was three weeks before the arranged day. The cook talked to them about healthy eating and the constraints she was under in terms of what she was allowed to provide. For example, the children were surprised that pasta and chips were an unacceptable combination for a main meal! As a result of the first discussion it was agreed that the children from Alan's class would: help select a menu, act as waiters and waitresses on the day, find out more about pasta and design a pasta salad to be on the menu, design an ice-cream sundae and be actively involved in the assembling of it on the day. The menu was agreed and included pizza as a main course, with a salad option.

Alan arranged for a parent to visit the class with a pasta making machine and this led on to investigating different kinds of pasta and designing a salad with different vegetables and the class's own 'Italian' dressing, much influenced by a recipe provided by Lucy's father, who was Italian. Various salads were made by groups in the food activities area, under parental supervision one afternoon, and evaluated by the class before a decision was taken about the most suitable. The design for the salad and the recipe were passed on to the cook for approval and action.

On another day, each child was invited by Alan to design an ice-cream sundae. They presented their ideas to each other and with Alan's help decided on the best features to put into the final design. It wasn't hard to get agreement that three coloured ice-creams (red, white and green) should form the basis of the 'treat'. Chocolate sprinkles were also regarded as essential and David's idea of a small Italian flag on a cocktail stick was chosen as appropriate decoration. The agreed design was redrawn and coloured for presentation to the cook. The production of lots of small flags posed another interesting challenge for these Y2 children.

Other design and technology tasks involved in this short-term project included the table layouts (not a minor problem for some children in this class); invitations to staff and other classes; menus on each table; a publicity board outside the dining hall. Alan also identified speaking and listening skills as significant to the table-waiting role and practice on asking polite questions was needed.

This work raises issues about whether a project like this encourages children to adopt stereotypical images of other cultures. However, Alan was sensitive to this and found little evidence that it was happening. He also recognised the considerable potential that a link with an Italian school would offer for work such as this. For example, the children could have written to a linked class to find out what they actually eat in school and at home and even ask the Italian class to 'evaluate' their proposals for the menu. Such links require considerable development work. Visits outside school can be valuable and in this project a visit to a restaurant would have been another way of increasing the children's background knowledge and understanding.

Pupils from St Peter and St Paul RC Primary school in Bristol also learnt about making pizzas. Their experiences were linked to the school's education business partnership and involved a visit to a local branch of Pizza Express. There they were taught about food hygiene, teamwork and health and safety by their teacher and restaurant staff. They made pizzas, got to eat the results and thoroughly enjoyed themselves. This approach had the advantage of avoiding restrictions that now apply to school meals production.

History and geography related design and technology projects can lead to an increased awareness of other times, places, cultures and needs. These subject areas can be a source of inspiration and opportunity as well as a means to challenge racist and ethnocentric stereotypes. 'Intermediate Technology' (IT) (see Hammond 1997) is an international development agency that produces materials for teachers that are very useful in supporting the latter goal. They are also intended to help raise children's global awareness and introduce them to the resourcefulness and inventiveness that exists all over the world. The use of these materials and other examples of multicultural and antiracist approaches to design and technology can be found in Howe *et al.* (2001, Section 2). That book also deals in depth with the ways in which design and technology can support children's learning in the area of citizenship (Section 3), which is not strictly a curriculum subject, but is likely to become a political priority for primary education in the next period. This is discussed further in Chapter 9.

Art and design clearly has a special relationship with design and technology, not only as they have the label 'design' in common. For example, both are concerned with shape and space, colour, texture, line and visual communication. 'Art' activities can often be approached through design and technology as well as children being asked to apply skills, techniques and understanding from their art studies to their design and technology projects. The Art and Design SoW (QCA/DfEE 2000c) covers activities which parallel IEAs, FPTs and DMAs and includes several units which can be used to develop appropriate links between design and technology and art and design. For example there is a unit on textiles (1B) which could involve looking at technologies in other cultures. Unit 5B on containers could be easily linked with design and technology tasks. Other units which would link well with design and technology include 1C, 2C, 3C, 4B and 5C. Chapter 4 considers the links between art and designing in more detail.

Other 'arts', such as music, drama and dance, provide potential for links such as designing and making instruments (for example, those used in other times, cultures and places), puppets and puppet-theatres (see Case Study 8: Puppets; and Williams 1994), props and sets for class and school productions, costumes and special effects (see Howe *et al.* 2001, Section 2). Carnivals can provide good opportunities for bringing these together. For example, my own children went to an inner-city school, Sefton Park Junior School in Bristol, and each year they took part in a Caribbean-style parade in St Pauls in Bristol. At school, they designed and made their own costumes on the theme of the carnival and choreographed movement routines accompanied by rhythms played on whistles.

5. Links between design and technology, literacy, numeracy and ICT

The literacy and numeracy strategies have had a major impact on developments in primary schools over the last few years and remain at the top of the political agenda. There is evidence that the emphasis placed in schools on these core subjects has been at the expense of foundation subjects such as design and technology. It is therefore appropriate to look at ways in which links can be made between these subjects. Such links should benefit pupils' learning in both areas.

The Library case study (Case Study 3) provides an example of how a project can have a strong language element – the class also wrote and made books during the project. The potential of design and technology for developing speaking and listening skills is self-evident. Using fiction to promote design and technology and provide a context has been discussed earlier in the chapter. Stories or factual text concerning design and technology can be used during literacy lessons and followed up in a later practical sessions focused on design and technology. Literacy work focused on word, sentence or text levels can obviously be based on design and technology themes and can provide a good way of introducing children to specific vocabulary (see DATA 1995c; QCA/DfEE 1998, p. 17-18; SCAA/QCA 1997). Word games, perhaps focused on themes such as 'tools and uses', 'materials and properties' and 'mechanisms and types of movement' could be devised. Non-fiction texts with a design and technology content can be used in a variety of ways, perhaps comparing style and structure in advertisements with that used in consumer reports. Texts could be used to explore, introduce or reinforce knowledge and understanding related to previous design and technology work or to that planned for the future.

Writing tasks (for example, sequencing or writing instructions) used within the guided-group element of the literacy lesson can be based on design and technology outcomes or intended design and technology activities. Design and technology activities can lead to a variety of writing styles for different audiences (for example procedural, report or explanatory writing). They can provide opportunities for children to be introduced to and use a range of 'writing frames' (for example, *What I am going to make, What I need, What I did, What I like about it, What I would change*). Outcomes can also provide a stimulus to creative writing (as mentioned in Case Study 5: Air-raid shelters in this chapter). Other ways in which design and technology can be linked explicitly with the Literacy Hour are outlined in a useful DATA publication, *Developing Language through Design and Technology* (DATA 1999b). Another useful publication is one that focuses on links between science and literacy (Cork and Vernon 2000) which includes a wealth of material that can also be adapted to design and technology.

The Library case study (Case Study 3) provides a good example of how a project can have a strong language element. The potential of design and technology for developing speaking and listening skills is self-evident. Mathematics skills and knowledge are used in many design and technology projects, again as a 'resource' for the work. An obvious example is the use of measuring and understanding of shape, area and angles during designing and making activities (DfEE/QCA 1999, pp. 71–72). Work on gears has potential for developing understanding of ratios. The Teacher's Guide accompanying the QCA SoW for design and technology includes further examples (QCA/DfEE 1998, p. 19). There are other ways, however, in which the curriculum links between these areas can be strengthened. For example, maths games are increasingly used in schools, and older children can be challenged to design and make a maths game for a younger age group based upon a particular skill, concept area or mathematical problem solving activity.

ICT provides further opportunities for close ties with design and technology which have been recognised and advocated since the introduction of the National Curriculum (DATA 1995b; Davies, L. *et al.* 2000; NCET 1989, 1993; Ritchie 1989; Ritchie and Smith 1987b; Smith 1999). However, evidence would suggest they are still not being fully exploited by primary teachers (OFSTED 1996, Pritchard 1997, p. 116). Used well, ICT can enhance and enrich children's learning in design and technology. Some of the ways this can be done are included in the National Curriculum (DfEE/QCA 1999) that emphasises the use of ICT more strongly than previous versions. Excellent material is also available from the TTA (1999) that is aimed at supporting teachers in training, but will support any teacher seeking to include more ICT in their design and technology teaching. Internet links related to design and technology can be found on DATA's excellent website (http://www.data.org.uk). ICT can be used in design and technology as a resource, a tool or a component, for example:

- as a source of information or stimulus for projects and activities (this includes the internet as well as CD-ROMs and other computer-based databases);
- to generate and develop design ideas, using drawing, paint or net-generating software (3A);
- to collect, store, analyse and retrieve information using a database or spreadsheet;
- to model or simulate situations using specific software such as that which allows room layouts to be explored, the nutritional content of different foods to be analysed (5B and 5D) or aircraft to be flown;
- to monitor using sensors and datalogging equipment to investigate design contexts such as traffic noise in a classroom, the effectiveness of sun-glasses or the temperature in an animal cage overnight;
- to communicate with designers and manufacturers through email;
- to communicate and display design ideas, reports and promotion materials using desktop publishing (DTP) software;
- to plan and sequence events using software to produce flow charts;
- to record the process involved and evaluations using word-processing software and/or digital cameras, video or audio recordings;
- to produce finishing effects, such as wallpaper for a model room, using scanned images, clip art, image-processing or pattern-generating software;
- to control products, such as a model roundabout (6C) or alarm system (4D and 4E), using control hardware and software or a floor turtle/robotic toy (3C).

(relevant QCA/DfEE SoW (1998) units are in brackets):

This discussion has emphasised links between design and technology and particular subjects. However, the integrated nature of many of the examples reminds us that teachers in primary schools, despite the National Curriculum and its subject-based framework, often plan and implement classroom work in an integrated cross-curricular way (see DATA 1999a for more examples).

6. Conclusion

This chapter has illustrated a variety of starting points for design and technology. Design and technology involves children in generating ideas through creative thinking to meet needs identified by them or their teachers. A parallel, evident in this chapter, is the way in which teachers plan curriculum activities to meet children's needs. Again creative thinking is involved, not to generate ideas for their own making, but to generate starting points, contexts and opportunities for children to design and make. For design and make projects to work in classroom settings it is important that both teacher and children are motivated. This means choosing starting points and contexts that interest the teacher, are relevant to the children and fit in with whole-school planning (see Chapter 8). Children need to recognise the purposes of their work. Children are very sensitive to teachers' attitudes towards classroom work. Successful design and technology will require commitment and involvement from teachers and children alike.

Creative and innovative thinking on the part of teachers is a theme that will be picked up again in Chapter 9, when teachers' professional development is addressed. Teachers who engage in action enquiries to improve their practice need to identify concerns and starting points for their enquiries. These may relate to classroom organisation and management, the use of particular resources, aspects of children's learning or the teacher's role. Identifying them can be compared to the identification of needs and opportunities as discussed in this chapter. For these enquiries to be successful teachers must again be motivated and committed.

CHAPTER 4

Designing

1. Introduction

This chapter explores the nature of designing and how we can encourage children to engage in 'designerly behaviours'. Designing is the means by which children can make a response to the challenge of a project and it can be an important step towards producing an outcome. The chapter is structured around the themes of generating, developing and communicating ideas. Designing involves thinking creatively and begins with hazy, speculative ideas that become clearer and more tightly formulated as they are refined and shared with others. Teaching strategies that facilitate lateral and creative thinking are aspects addressed in this chapter. Designing involves 'imaging' or seeing in the mind's eye and then being able to model these images in a concrete way.

Designing is much more than simply drawing something you are intending to make before construction. It is the means of ensuring an outcome combines both functional and aesthetic elements: that it works well, does what it is supposed to do, and that it looks good. Designing and producing art are related: both involve compromise – between what individuals want to do and what the medium, technology and other constraints will allow them to do. Design may lead to compromise because different people want different things and because technical and aesthetic requirements can be in conflict.

Despite appearances from the order of chapters, designing does not always come before making and evaluation. The links between evaluation and the identification of needs have already been discussed (for example, Case Study 2: Greetings Cards): one often leads to the other. Similarly, evaluation of the natural and made world plays a vital part in the generation of ideas and designs. The relationship between designing and making is complex and in many situations (including those in the world beyond school) designing is ongoing throughout making.

2. What is designing?

Designing requires children to be reflective about their ideas and those of others, apply their previous experience and knowledge and suggest achievable ways forward. It involves the use of oral, graphic and other communication skills; talking, drawing and manipulation of materials are equally important. Children's designerly behaviours include explaining and clarifying ideas through discussion with each other and their teacher. This will lead them to refine their ideas.

A simple definition of designing is difficult since the term is used in different situations to mean different things. In the context of design and technology work it is probably most usefully understood as the process of generating, developing and communicating ideas related to outcomes which may be made. In doing this factors such as function, aesthetics and economics must be considered. The Design and Technology in Education (DATE) Project (1990) described designing as the conception and resolution of the future configurations of environments, products and communication. The term 'configurations' refers to the arrangements of parts or elements, the shape or form of the outcome. Design is therefore used to indicate the qualities that result from it having been 'designed' rather than it happening by chance, good luck or natural forces!

The key to successful designing is the ability of a designer (child or adult) to think creatively. Creativity is 'imaginative activity fashioned so as to produce outcomes that are both original and of value' (NACCCE 1999, p. 29). According to the excellent report from which this definition is taken, creativity is a capability that we all share. In this democratic view, 'being original' can refer to work that is original in relation to previous work of that person or relative to that person's peer group as well as encompassing work that is historically unique. However, Shepard (1990) reminds us that creativity can be repressed, inhibited or, at least, under-used in some individuals, including children. Creative thinking involves a disposition of mind that is experimental, open and engaged. A creative thinker is prepared to replace preconceptions with new ways of seeing or to combine old ones in new ways. A creative thinker is innovative, prepared to take risks and constantly searching for different ways of seeing a problem or situation; looking at the common and familiar and seeing or applying it in new ways (Bishop 1991; Howe et al. 2001).

Without venturing too deeply into the psychology of creative thinking, it is generally accepted by neuroscientists that the left and right hemispheres of the brain control different aspects of our cognition. The left side largely controls rational, analytical thinking and is used when dealing with language, mathematical operations and logical processes such as sequencing. The right side is more concerned with creative thinking: intuition, spatial orientation, crafts, skills, expression and emotions. Both hemispheres play a part in design and technology work. At some stages of their work designers may be investigating and analysing the world as it is in a logical and rational way. At other times designing is much more concerned with how things might be and designers draw upon creative talents. It is wrong, in some respects to try and separate these since in a 'good' designer they will be integrated: design and technology brings the arts and sciences together.

Teaching design-based activities is difficult (Anning 1997). There is evidence (Chalkley and Shield 1996) that teachers are less skilful in deconstructing designing, into elements that can be taught progressively, than motor skills and knowledge aspects of design and technology. This makes it much more difficult to plan for progression and scaffold children's learning in design-related activities. So how can teachers foster designing skills in children? Simply asking children to draw something before they make it is not enough.

While many designers do produce drawings, there is more to effective design than the working drawing. Indeed, asking young children to draw something before they make it may inhibit their designerly behaviours. Design involves skills such as researching, imaging, representing and communicating. It can involve the use of a range of media and means of communication as we will see later in this chapter. Designing requires children to clarify their ideas and often to share ideas they have with others. Clarifying ideas requires learners to structure, and perhaps, restructure their cognitive frameworks. Sketching, drawing or painting can provide a practical means of doing this. However, ideas can also be generated, developed and communicated through the manipulation of materials such as construction kits, clay, everyday materials, or from the use of ICT.

3. Encouraging children to generate ideas in the context of design and technology

> Wonderful ideas do not spring out of nothing. They build on a foundation of other ideas . . . The more we help children to have their wonderful ideas and to feel good about themselves for having them, the more likely it is that they will some day happen upon ideas which no one else has happened upon before.   (Duckworth 1987, p. 14)

The key to getting children to have 'wonderful' ideas is ensuring that they engage with the challenge they are facing. This, as we have seen in Chapter 3, is related to the way children are orientated to the work and the context in which it is set. If the children have been involved in the identification of needs and opportunities they are more likely to look for creative and lateral solutions to these. The ethos of a classroom also plays an important part. If the children are used to working in a very structured way on tasks which have right answers, usually right answers that they know the teacher already knows, they are less likely to demonstrate the qualities of creative thinking. If the ethos of the classroom is such that children's ideas are valued, and they are encouraged to be innovative in other areas of the curriculum, then they are more likely to respond to a design and technology task in a creative way. For example, children whose experience of mathematics includes open-ended investigations and problem solving, will already be used to working in situations where the answer, or outcome, depends on their thinking, not the teacher's or the back of the book. The generation of ideas requires a stimulus and it is the teacher's responsibility to provide this in order to trigger ideas in the children. These triggers can come from a variety of sources: evaluation of the made world and other people's designs, discussion, books, stories, magazines, pictures, video, TV, computer simulations or databases, visits, visitors, exploring the natural world, exploring and investigating collections of artefacts/materials, a display. The teacher is 'designing' a learning environment in which these starting points are provided. For the children to make the most of such stimuli requires them to be taught the skills of locating, selecting and retrieving information – another vital aspect of designing (Anning 1997, p. 51).

There are strategies which a teacher can use to encourage children to be creative in their thinking, for example, the use of uncritical sharing of ideas as a group or whole-class activity. Establishing ground rules which mean contributions cannot be challenged when first offered ensures a range of ideas are offered and unexpected links may be made by the children in a way not anticipated by the teacher. De Bono (1970) said of 'brainstorming' (a term which some find problematic because of its connotations with epilepsy),

> In a brainstorming session one gives out stimulation to others and one receives it from others. Because the different people taking part each tend to follow their own lines of thought there is less danger of getting stuck with a particular way of looking at a situation.

Sharing ideas in this way, is a practical strategy for getting children to think laterally, although that one which needs to be used appropriately. Joyce *et al.* (1998) caution that it can be a restrictive technique especially if used in isolation from other approaches. It is desirable to ensure that children do not always settle on their first idea as the one to develop. A Nobel prizewinner, Linus Pauling is said to have claimed 'the best way to have a good idea is to have lots of ideas'. Time at the early stages of design is time well spent. Too often in the classroom, children's first good ideas are developed without them first spending time thinking about other good ideas. Children should be provided with systematic ways of comparing a range of ideas in order to decide which has the most potential and is most worth further effort.

Analogies provide another strategy that can be used to trigger children's creative thinking. The teacher can ask them to think about other similar, but different, situations which might provide a new perspective on how to solve a problem or meet a challenge. For example, the children in the last chapter who were designing air-raid shelters (Case Study 5) were asked to think about tent structures, they could have been asked to think about shells or nuts; the children redesigning their library (Case Study 3) could have been asked to think about features of a room where they enjoy relaxing at home or another place where they like reading. Talk is, again, the essential vehicle here, and getting children to think aloud and around a problem can lead the individual involved and others to make links and come up with new possibilities.

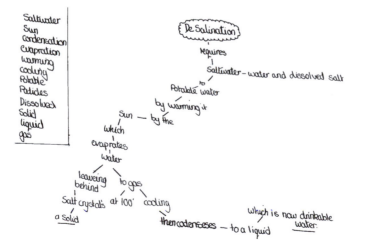

Figure 4.1 Nicola's concept map

Concept-mapping (Brodie 1994; Novak and Gowin 1984) is an under-exploited strategy for helping children organise their ideas about a particular project and allow a teacher access to those ideas. Figure 4.1 illustrates an example. Nicola was a Y6 child in Richard Brice's class at Christchurch Primary School, Bradford-on-Avon. During a topic called 'Survivors', based around the theme of being marooned on a desert island, she was attempting to design and make a small desalinator. She produced the concept map, based upon words her group brainstormed, to help her clarify her ideas and provide evidence for her teacher of her current thinking. The illustrated version is a second draft, after discussion within her group based upon their first attempts.

Manipulation of materials can provide another way of stimulating ideas for young and old alike. While some people can visualise possibilities easily and have the spatial awareness to manipulate these images in their heads, others prefer to work immediately in the concrete world. These people will have their best ideas when handling materials: 'tinkering', fitting things together, moving parts relative to each other, dismantling, viewing things from different angles. This can be especially true of young learners who might have limited experience of a range of materials and their properties. In some ways designing literally involves 'playing' with ideas and materials. Indeed, Hope (2000) claims that 'those children who have rich imaginative play are better at visualisation and hence design tasks' (p. 112). Play has a significant contribution to make to designing and the generation of ideas. It offers a context in which children can share and explore ideas in an unthreatening way that is conducive to them having original and innovative ideas. Davies (1996) investigated the designerly behaviours of young children when they were working with a professional designer. He provides evidence of the crucial role that 'play' performs in developing children's inventiveness (and ability to solve problems). He found that 'through playing and using their narrative language to describe their actions, children are learning to interpret their own mental images'. He suggests that 'by comparison with some of the rigid models of "the design process" described in schools, designers and children have more in common that we realise' (p. 45). Asking children to explain what they are doing or making and why is an important role for the teacher if this route to 'designing' is taken. Fisher (1990), in his excellent book, *Teaching Children to Think*, provides a range of other strategies for encouraging creative thinking.

Another aspect of the cognitive activity used in designing is imaging (Davies 1996, p. 52). We all have the ability to see in our mind's eye. This skill is vital to designing and is one that is often not developed in classroom situations. Seeing in the mind's eye is not simply about seeing mental pictures; most people can 'image' smells, tastes and tactile sensations. Try it now – close your eyes, relax and 'image' a beach you know well. Can you see the detail of pebbles; can you smell the fresh air, taste the salt on your lips and feel the sun on your face? In a designing context imaging has to go further and the images of the world as it is are manipulated to allow us to see new possibilities. Imagination and imaging are different. Our imagination allows us to think about ideas, situations and events which are not real; imaging is the way we 'experience' known or new possibilities, in our minds. Structured activities can be used to encourage children to develop these skills and use them for design and technology. Imaging is a way of generating new ideas and possibilities but it is also a means of developing and improving an idea. In other words, imaging is not something that children should only do at the start of the design stage, it can be used throughout designing and making. If children are able to hold an image they can be invited to compare drawings, models and outcomes with that image at each stage of the work, including evaluation, to compare them. Changes along the way will be necessary (and desirable), but a return to the original image can remind children of the nature of the changes and why they have been made. Indeed, re-imaging might be appropriate if a change of direction is necessary: a new idea needs more time spent imaging and analysing its features.

As children get older and more experienced in design and technology, their ideas for meeting a challenge should increasingly involve them in taking into account the views and preferences of others, including those for whom they are designing. They should also be taking more account of the materials and components they might use. Reflection upon ideas, in terms of the purposes of the outcome, becomes increasingly important; the children should be able to establish criteria for their designs in terms of what the outcomes will do: how they will work and how practicable they will be to make.

The ideas children have for solving a problem or challenge will usually need expressing in some concrete form before they can be developed further. This is when cognitive modelling is turned into concrete modelling. The Assessment of Performance Unit (APU) (Kimbell *et al.* 1991) produced a classic model of this relationship between mind and hand, thought and action. Ideas are externalised in order to modify and develop them. Concrete modelling is the process of making ideas visible and open to criticism, by the originator and by others. It can involve a wide range of outcomes: drawings, paintings, annotated drawings, posters, plans, models, sketches, role play, story boards, computer simulations, written accounts. All provide a means of communicating ideas so that they can be shared, explored and developed. A good designer will use the most suitable method of modelling at the appropriate time and focus upon the modelling being a means towards an effective outcome. The meaning of modelling, in this context, is broader than simply the production of a smaller-scale 'model' of a large object.

The following discussion resulted from work with a group of Somerset teachers working on an INSET course. It provides some interesting insights into the nature of children's imaging and modelling. The course involved participants in working collaboratively in pairs with groups of children during school-based sessions. The following is based upon evidence collected from some of these sessions.

CASE STUDY

7: Play areas

A key concern that arose during the first term of the course was how to support children in generating ideas and designs. The teachers were provided with opportunities during a centre-based session to develop their own imaging skills and use them in the context of generating designs. For many, it was the first time that they had been asked to acknowledge and use their capabilities to image and manipulate images. Few found it difficult. As a result of this experience they were invited, in pairs, to plan work for a small group of children that would involve them in generating designs for play areas. The teachers worked with three age groups (R, Y2 and Y5) and selected a medium to use with the children (graphics, clay or everyday materials). The work was aimed at providing some insights into progression in generating designs and into the advantages and disadvantages of different media. Each pair worked with the same group of four children for two sessions (45 minutes and an hour) with a playtime in between to allow the children's responses to be analysed and the teachers' plans to be modified. One course member worked with the children while the other observed and collected evidence for later analysis. They swapped roles for the second session.

The first session concentrated on orientating the children to the task and on encouraging them to image possibilities through structured exercises. They were then introduced to the specific media and supported in their attempts to develop their ideas. The children were restricted to one medium to provide the teachers with an opportunity to reflect on the appropriateness of each. The pairs were asked to analyse the data they collected in terms of: the nature of the children's imaging, the children's response to the medium used, the nature of outcomes of design generation, and issues concerning the social context. This analysis and the resulting discussions provided some fascinating insights and raised some interesting issues. The following draws particularly on work done with the Y2 age range, but refers to work with the other two age ranges.

Some children found imaging and articulating their 'images' difficult and needed the teachers' reassurance that it was acceptable to have unusual ideas. Several children were strongly influenced by television images. These TV-based images tended to be very clear and resistant to change when teachers asked them to consider the practicality of their ideas or ways in which their ideas might be improved. They also led to some designs for play areas that had story lines and these sometimes involved the children being part of the plot. These children seemed to find it harder to separate themselves from the outcome they were designing. A positive aspect of these images was that they tended to be holistic and did not lead to disjointed elements in their designs.

Indeed, a general point that arose during the teachers' discussions was the importance of encouraging children to image in a more holistic way and then encourage them to focus in on more specific aspects as they worked on their designs. Linked to this is the need to encourage children to image throughout design generation. It became clear that successful design generation occurred when children were encouraged, sometimes quite systematically, to revisit their images and articulate how they had developed or changed their ideas.

A surprising element of children's imaging was the significance of smell. A Y2 child designed a 'mint' playground which gave off strong smells as equipment was used. Natasha (Y2) imaged a pink swing that gave off 'a fresh smell like clean washing'. Children's images were often strongly influenced by colour; there was a 'multicoloured play park' and a 'magic park' that included areas of particular colours. This aspect was best developed by children who used graphic media and even the younger children's designs often used colour effectively and occasionally in an abstract way to convey feelings (as in a violent element of a 'Fun House' design).

Those children who used graphic media produced outcomes that could be grouped in the following way:

(a) drawing or painting that includes the designer;
(b) drawing of the whole design without the designer included;
(c) drawing of disjointed elements;
(d) diagram (more stylised than a drawing);
(e) annotated diagram.

There were some interesting aspects of these features. Younger children more often included themselves in their pictures. Some very young children produced designs that were simple, but included novel and unusual elements. Natasha (Y2) produced a pencil drawing of herself on the swing. Initially she was reluctant to erase a part of the drawing she did not like and had to be reassured that changes were acceptable and indeed desirable. She used colour with purpose for the swing frame, but then started to colour in the sky and grass. This happened in a number of cases where simple designs were involved and suggests that the children had forgotten the purpose of the work and did not understand the distinct nature of designing by drawing. They were producing finished pieces of art, rather than designs. There were also several examples where the children were not generating designs but making art representations of known play areas.

The more sophisticated the design, the less likely it is to include the designer and diagrams rarely included the designer. Those children who described a clear initial image tended to produce more holistic designs. However, those who did not have a clear image of the whole design at the outset tended to illustrate some elements of a design, usually along the bottom of the paper. As they were encouraged to develop their ideas as a result of teacher intervention they tended to add new, but often unrelated elements, to the picture, at the top of the sheet of paper and so they ended up with a picture consisting of several separate elements.

Children radically changed their initial images when they were asked to use reclaimed materials to model their ideas and they needed to be encouraged to re-image possibilities after they had had time to explore the materials available. It was still, however, felt desirable to encourage imaging without thinking about the constraints imposed by the medium used. Clay and graphic media led to children being less likely to change their initial ideas significantly. Reclaimed/everyday materials and clay also avoided the inclusion of self in the design. Clay was found to be an excellent medium for design generation and did not lead to the frustrations some teachers anticipated in terms of children not being able to realise drawn complex ideas in a concrete way – the transfer of ideas from 2D to 3D was redundant. It had numerous advantages including allowing texture to play an important part in the design.

There was some evidence of gender related differences to outcomes. With the Y2 age group the girls produced more traditional playgrounds and parks with a variety of different play equipment. It was the boys who produced play areas with themes. The boys also included more technical elements in their designs, such as pumps for a whirlpool, a computer to control a spaceship simulator and robot turtle playmates. The boys' graphic designs were more often diagrammatic whereas nearly all the girls in the Y2 class produced pictures (of which only a few included labels). Only the boys included any 'violent' elements in their designs.

With all age groups and with every media, the teachers involved in this case study felt that the quality of imaging and design generation was affected by their teaching skills. Asking the right question at the right time, providing space and time for children to think and to explore and creating an atmosphere in which the children can feel confident enough to express tentative and very personal ideas are all crucial for successful design generation.

4. Developing ideas

The development of ideas requires time and needs to be valued by teachers if children are to be successful in their design and technology. The desirability of encouraging children to come up with more than one idea has already been stressed (although sometimes, of course, one really good idea is enough). The next stage in effective design involves supporting children in looking critically at their own ideas in order to identify strengths and weaknesses, to highlight inappropriateness, to explore aspects of the designs in more detail. Cushing (1994) cites an example of inappropriate design which was submitted in the final stages of a competition for young designers. A design for an expanding tool to enable a person with disabilities to pick up milk bottles from the step was highly refined and reached the final of the competition before a judge asked why the designer had not thought of building a shelf at the right height upon which the milkman could place the bottles. Developing good ideas is fine: developing poor ideas less useful! This stage of designing involves children in evaluating their ideas and clarifying what the final outcome will be like and how it will be produced. If they are not supported at this stage there is a likelihood that outcomes will end up stereotypical, impractical or limited in terms of how they work or look. Developing ideas involves 'thinking around' the problem and teachers' interventions can be crucial. Teachers should not be attempting to influence the children by imposing adult ideas upon their designs. They should be focusing the children's thinking on the detail of their proposals, perhaps against the design brief which they have produced (which should include criteria by which the success of the product can be judged). The teacher needs to get the children to confront the practical reality of their ideas. This needs tackling sensitively, especially with young children, since it can be threatening for the learner and the last thing a teacher wants to do at this stage is inhibit creativity. Developing ideas is another stage where information gathering and handling skills are needed by children – using secondary sources (including ICT and the internet) to provide information relevant to the ideas being developed is increasingly important as children get older. There is a danger that developing ideas systematically can become formulaic and demotivate children. A variety of approaches used selectively are needed.

5. Communicating design ideas through drawings

When children reach the stage of communicating their ideas, the links between art and design become most obvious. Through art, children learn to use drawing and other means of communication for a range of purposes: recording from observation, exploring ideas and responses, visualising, generating and refining ideas in visual form. All of these aspects of art education are important to children's design and technology. The ability of children to develop their ideas through drawing needs to be developed throughout the curriculum from an early age so that 'drawing an idea' becomes second nature (Weston 1991). This needs to begin by helping young children (from the time they start school) appreciate that a drawing can, in fact, convey information about an object or idea. As children make progress in drawing, there is a danger that they, and their teachers, place too much emphasis upon the quality of the drawing in the context of designing, rather than the quality of the idea. Rough, quick 'idea' sketches have just as much value at the early stages of design (although not necessarily for the purpose of communicating to others) as the more polished drawings displayed for parents or others. Perhaps, teachers should more often display and value children's early 'back of an envelope' sketches. The same is, incidentally, true for other means of modelling ideas. Crucially, teachers should look at the value of the modelling a child uses in terms of how it has helped develop the individual's thinking and reward that rather than the attractiveness of the model.

The 'aesthetic' dimension of design and technology is concerned with much more than embellishment and decoration to make something look good. It is a more fundamental aspect of a design related to individuals' subjective and emotional responses to an outcome. Art is about such personal, emotional, imaginative and affective responses and therefore has a vital contribution to make to design and technology.

6. Developing children's drawing skills

Young children find it very hard to draw something before they make it and I have already stressed that this is certainly not always desirable. However, developing children's skills in this area is important and one that OFSTED continue to highlight as a weakness in primary schools (OFSTED 1999b). Hope (2000) provides a useful discussion of the relationship between drawing and designing. She stresses the value of drawing as a tool for thought rather than just a recording medium. She and others (Baynes, 1998) are critical of the National Curriculum for Design and Technology which they regard as undermining the contribution of drawing by giving it a role it cannot fulfil – they suggest that producing a design drawing and then carrying it out is a 'peculiar' approach rarely used by designers (p. 108). Hope claims that in her research with young children (aged 5–9) drawing ahead of a task can appropriately support idea generation, but not detailed construction techniques. Garvey and Quinlan (1997) support this with their finding that primary-aged children in their study did not make significant use of their drawings once they had started making unless prompted to do so by their teachers.

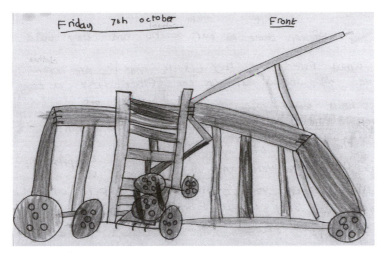

Figure 4.2 *Reoclick* fire-engine

How can teachers improve children's understanding of the purposes of drawing and develop the skills they need? One approach is to encourage young children to draw an outcome when they have made it, perhaps with the purpose of showing others how to make it or to retain when the outcome is dismantled (in the case of construction kits). Figure 4.2 shows a Y2 child's drawing of a *Reoclick* fire-engine she made with a similar purpose. The children can then be asked to compare their outcomes with the drawings and the link between the two made explicit. A next step could be to ask the children to draw their ideas in advance, develop and make the outcomes, draw the finished products and compare the drawings. Essentially the teacher is helping children understand the purposes of the first drawings as directly linked with the making phase. With experience children will then become more competent in communicating ideas through drawing. Figure 4.3 illustrates an example of a Y6 child's annotated and 'exploded' drawing of a cardboard toy that she intended to make and shows more advanced drawing skills.

The following case study illustrates how a reception class teacher, Sue Leah, introduced her class to designing during a half-term topic on 'Toys'. Sue teaches at Broadway Infants' School in Yate. The case study describes several aspects of the children's design and technology activities in order that the 'designing' work can be seen in relation to the whole topic.

CASE STUDY

8: Puppets

Sue planned during the topic to provide opportunities for designing and making moving toys and puppets. She left her plans fairly open to allow her to pick up the children's interests and develop specific projects based upon these. The class of five-year-old children had been in school for a term and this was to be their first structured design and technology experience, although they had had numerous experiences of art, craft and other practical making activities.

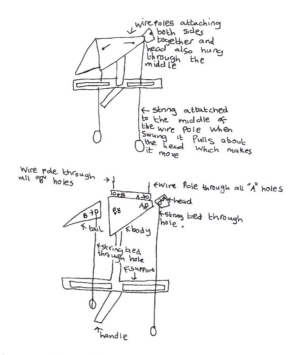

Figure 4.3 Design for a cardboard toy

The project began just after Christmas when presents were still being talked about and the children were bringing in new toys to show each other. Sue put together a collection of moving toys as a stimulus for some evaluative work which she hoped would lead on to a making activity. Sue manages her class in groups and ensures the nature of activities for each group allows her time to concentrate on a target group during any one session. She also had a general assistant in the class during much of this work and regularly has parents working alongside her in the classroom. During the first week the toys collection was a target activity for her attention. Children were invited to explore the collection, in friendship groups, and talk about what they liked and disliked. Among the toys was a wooden *jack-in-the-box*. Emma, aged five, was particularly taken by this and produced a beautiful picture showing considerable detail. Sue then asked Emma to tell her about the toy and she noted Emma's words under the picture,

> You undo the hook on the box to make him jump up. You push him down to close the lid. The box is made of wood and *Jack's* face is made of wood. He has a hat and some eyes and some hair and a smiling mouth. I like the surprise you have when you open him.

At the end of this activity there was a review time which is a common feature of Sue's classroom management. Emma's group talked enthusiastically about the toys and showed their drawings. As they were finishing Emma said 'I want to make one.' This provided Sue with the hook for the following day's work for Emma's group and in some respects can be seen as Emma identifying her own need (or want). It certainly provided Sue with the opportunity she was looking for to modify her plans for the following day to exploit the group's interest and motivation.

The classroom is organised so that the children have access to materials and tools as they are required and there is an expectation that they will return things to the appropriate place when they have finished with them. Sue has a 'design and technology' area which includes a wooden bench, open shelves for equipment and small items, which are labelled (words and pictures), and a cardboard box storage system for larger everyday materials. This unit allows reclaimed materials to be sorted for easy retrieval (small boxes, large boxes, cylinders, pots, etc.). Each compartment is labelled with a word and picture of what can be found in that particular box. A taped flap at the front of each box ensures things cannot fall out and the compartments (cardboard boxes) are taped together for stability. This organisation of resources meant that the following day, when Emma and her friends set out to make working models of *jack-in-the-box*, they already knew what was available and where to find it. Sue reminded them of the previous day's work and left them to explore the materials and work out a way of making their own toys. The children worked independently but remained aware of what others were doing and they talked as they explored. Emma was the first to hit on the idea of using a piece of dowel, from underneath, to push her *Jack* out of the top of a box. Her 'generation of an idea' resulted from manipulating the materials available and trying things out. Once the others saw this idea in action they soon used a similar mechanism. There was no attempt by Sue to get the children to produce a design on paper. However, once they had made their outcomes, to their own satisfaction, she invited them to draw what they had made and talk to her about their work. This was to get them to reflect upon the materials used, the sequence involved in making the outcome and to elicit evaluative comments. The children's words were written below their pictures. Emma said,

> I made a *jack-in-the-box*. I used a toothpaste box and put silver paper on it. I used glue and paint. I had a stick to push it up and down. I made a hole in the bottom to put the stick through. I drew his face with felt tip pens.

When Emma's group showed the rest of the class their outcomes it provided a stimulus for further groups to design and make other toys that moved.

A couple of weeks later the class did work on 'dolls'. Sue's design and technology planning at this stage focused upon the movement of limbs and how the children could make pivoting joints (a FPT). She planned specific skills training on the use of a particular form of fixing at this stage of the work. There was, of course, a variety of other work going on linked with the 'dolls' theme during this week. However, Sue anticipated the work on making parts move might prove useful later when she had planned to make puppets with the children. During this third week every child in the class was given the task involving the use of split pins to make arms and legs move on a cardboard doll that they drew on card and then cut out. They were asked to mark on their drawings where each split pin would be used to join parts.

Week 4 was the stage when the class was introduced to the challenge of making puppets for use in an assembly that would be used to share their work on toys with the rest of the school. Sue read her class the story of Pinnochio at the beginning of the week and provided the children, in groups again, with a collection of puppets and pictures of puppets. There were examples of glove and finger puppets, push-up puppets (the type which pop up from an inverted cone on a stick) and pictures of string-operated puppets. Each group was invited to make the puppets move; think about how they work; think about how they are made and which ones they like.

sticks

strings

My puppet is Pinnochio. He will have sticks and strings. Shoes made of wood and face made of Wood. His jumper is material.

My design, Tomas

Figure 4.4 A design for a Pinnochio puppet

They were then asked to draw a picture showing a puppet they would like to make, which Sue introduced to them as 'your design drawing'. This was the first time Sue had used the term 'design' and the drawings produced were the children's first attempts to put ideas on to paper before actually making the outcomes from other materials. Sue was pleased by the variety of ideas they had and, in most cases, the fact that they were practical to make. She had asked them to think about what materials they would use and she labelled their drawings according to their instructions, using their words. Tomas, decided to make a Pinnochio puppet (see Figure 4.4). He described his puppet to Sue, 'My puppet will have sticks and strings. Shoes made of wood and face made of wood. His jumper is material.' The following day Tomas had a session during which to make his puppet. Like Emma, he found and collected what he needed and began constructing a puppet to his design. His first problem was that he could find no wood suitable for the face. Although there were pieces of appropriate size he realised, in discussion with Sue, it would be too difficult to cut. He therefore revised his ideas and decided to use cardboard. Another problem with construction resulted, as it often does with young children, from trying to join thin 'limbs' to a body. Sue hoped he might remember the split pin FPT but he decided to have the limbs stapled on. When the puppet was finished Sue asked him, and others in his group, to draw what they had made to compare with their designs. She also wrote down their evaluative comments. Tomas said, 'I tried to glue the arms but they kept falling off so I asked Mrs Leah to use staples. He only has one stick. His shoes are tissue because wood was too difficult. His face is cardboard.'

Figure 4.5 Sally and Emma with their puppets

Emma decided to make a 'panda' hand puppet using fabrics (see Figure 4.5). Her evaluation went one stage further than Tomas. Although, like him, she wrote about her outcome in comparison to her design she came into school the following day with improvements in mind, 'I was thinking last night, my panda hasn't got enough spots.' She asked Sue if she could work on it again, a request to which she happily acquiesced. Sally, also from Emma's group, had considerable difficulties making her idea for a finger puppet. Her plans were articulated as,

My puppet is going to be a finger puppet. I need sellotape, paper, scissors and felt tips. I will draw the lines before I cut it out. You put your finger inside and the puppet will move about. My puppet is going to be a mouse.

However, considerable perseverance was necessary which is hinted at in her later evaluative comments, 'I tried paper but it came too small so I want to make a cotton one instead.' What she had done was cut off the triangular finger shape (based upon what the mouse puppet looked like drawn in two dimensions) and found it could not be wrapped around her finger. She found some fabric and managed to cut out a shape which could be wrapped around a finger but the next problem concerned joining the fabric, 'The sellotape has dried out. I need to put more sellotape on.' This was solved by wrapping the sellotape so that it stuck to itself, but other challenges lay in store,

> He hasn't got any whiskers. They just fell off because they were wet. I put too much glue on. Next time I would put a little bit of glue on. I sewed the ears on with a bit of cotton. A grown up helped me sew it. I made my mouse red because I couldn't find any pink.

In the end Sally's mouse finger puppet (also see Figure 4.5) ended up looking very similar to her design with the one or two changes mentioned. The most significant aspect of the evaluation was probably summed up in her own words, 'I love it'. Sally and Emma were not alone in feeling proud of their work. Sue was encouraged by the way all of the children wanted to play with their puppets. For several days the puppets became the focus of role play and activity in the home corner. This was in itself an important preparation for the final stage of the project: the production of a puppet play.

The comparison between design and outcome provided a successful means of helping the children evaluate their finished puppets and the process involved in producing it. It should also help them with future design-related activities in terms of recognising, at the designing stage, some of the difficulties that might be involved in turning their ideas into reality. This is a key issue when working with such young children. It is also evident that these young learners were evaluating at each stage of their work, and that often this evaluation, as in the cases of Emma and Sally, was self-motivated. However, evaluation can be facilitated by the teacher through her one-to-one interactions with each child at significant points in the process and through whole-class reviews of the outcomes. Sue was prioritising the first strategy in particular with her class at this time. She was using key questions when talking to individuals after they had made a puppet such as: Did you change anything as you made it? Did you have any problems? Did you use different things from those you planned to use? Are you happy with it? What would you change now?

These young children are already actively involved in the processes of design and technology. They have been introduced to the concept of designing and have begun to appreciate the way in which a drawing can be used as a means of having an idea and turning it into a tangible outcome.

The following example illustrates design-related skills being developed in slightly older (Y2) children. In this case study, I was teaching the group of children at Elm Park Primary School near Bristol, although the approach could be easily adapted for work with a whole class.

CASE STUDY

9: A house for mice

The children that I have focused on in the account were Christopher, Matthew, Nicole and Jenny. They had had a story read to them about a family of mice who need a new house because they are being troubled by a cat. The story is illustrated and includes examples of plans and drawings used by the mice. In the story the father mouse invites the family and friends to offer ideas and plans and then puts together the best ideas in the plan used to build a new house. This strategy was discussed with the children and their attention drawn to the detail of illustrations from the story.

This starting point had a number of advantages: there were several jumping off points from the story which had potential for design and technology activity; the notion of needs were explicit in the story; the story made the generation of a variety of design options and the selection of one explicit; the story posed a problem (designing and making a new house) that the children could tackle.

During the initial story reading and discussion the children were hooked and very interested in the story line. The children offered lots of ideas about what the mice might need in their new home which I listed on a large sheet of paper.

The next stage of the work was planned to develop the children's understanding of plans. They had had some difficulties with the birds' eye views illustrated in the story, especially of a bedroom in the mice house. I asked the children to think about their own bedrooms and list what was in them. I (Teacher) then modelled the process for them:

Teacher:	I'll tell you about my room. I'm going to draw it (*on a large sheet of sugar paper – draws rectangular outline*). What do we call these (*points to outlines*)?
Christopher:	Walls.
Teacher:	(*marks an open door and window*) What have I shown already?
Matthew:	Window and door.
Teacher:	My window looks out on the street. Where is the street? (*Matthew and Christopher point correctly*)
Teacher:	(*draws rectangular shape 'in street'*) That's my car. My room is next to my daughter's, Anna's. Where is her room? (*Christopher points*) The bathroom is on the other side. (*Christopher points correctly again*) (*Teacher takes a small rectangular piece of paper*) This is my bed.
Christopher:	No, it's too small!
Teacher:	(*choosing a bigger shape*) I'll take this one then.
Christopher:	That's it. It should be wide.
Teacher:	From my bed I can see the door and out of the window. Where is it? (*gives it to Nicole*)
Nicole:	There. (*on the same wall as the door*)
Christopher:	No, it's there (*on a wall opposite to the door*) 'cos he can see the door.
Teacher:	That's right. The wardrobe is in a corner near the window. Where is it Jenny?

Jenny:	(*points to a corner behind the bed*)
Nicole:	No, I think that's wrong.
Teacher:	Where is it then?
Nicole:	(*points to a correct position*)
Teacher:	I've got a dressing table. Where would you like that to be?

This 'game' continued for another few minutes and the concept of changing the room by moving the parts around on the plan was explored. Small elements, like an alarm clock, were added and a suitable position chosen for them by Christopher (*on a small table next to the bed so that it can be easily reached*). I then opened the story book to the page showing plans of top and side elevations.

Teacher:	What is the difference between these? These look from the side. (*points to side elevation*) How are we looking at these (*top elevations*)?
Christopher:	It's a bird view. (*'flies' his hand over the plan*)
Teacher:	Do the rest of you understand that – What's a 'bird view'?
Christopher:	This bird (*hand held above the page*), its eyes are looking down from the top.
Teacher:	We could imagine one of the mice going up in a balloon and looking down on their house.

I asked the children individually to try and make plans of their own bedrooms. Cut-out shapes of different sizes to represent furniture were put on the table.

Teacher:	Can you work out where your bedroom door is? Do you remember, I kept closing my eyes when I was thinking about my bedroom. You try that.

I was encouraging the children to image; to see their bedrooms in their minds' eyes. As the children were producing their plans I talked to them about the features and where they are positioned.

Nicole:	I can't draw chairs properly.
Teacher:	Imagine you are in the balloon, what would a chair look like?

When the group had all produced plans of their bedrooms I invited them to do the same thing for the bedroom of the mice. This time I provided a 'boot-sole' shape for the bedroom (since the new house was in a large boot). The group were asked to work in pairs.

Teacher:	Think about what the mice need in their bedroom. Remember how we did our bedrooms. Decide where you want everything and you can label things.
Christopher:	I'll do a bunk bed.
Matthew:	We need another one. We'll put it there. (*points*)
Christopher:	I'll make a wardrobe.
Teacher:	You might need to think – is the wardrobe the same size as the bed? The bed looks small to me – look at the size of the one I used on my plan.

Later on Christopher suggested the mice needed a 'cheese fishing rod' which then dominated the pair's discussion. It ended up being placed behind the bed 'in a safe place'. This theme was developed further with the addition of a 'cheese fishing tackle box'. After about fifteen minutes work I asked them to finalise plans before sticking everything down.

Christopher: We could change this. This cupboard is right next to the bed. (*Matthew moves it*)

Matthew: It might go there, this bit can go by the toy box.

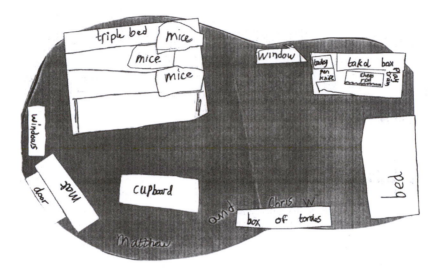

Figure 4.6 A design for a bedroom for mice

The boys then stuck each element down carefully without changing their finalised design (see Figure 4.6). The girls were less careful and took off all the elements prior to sticking them so that their design ended up being different to that 'finalised'.

The review and evaluation was structured by asking each child to write a letter to the mice about their new bedroom. Christopher and Matthew insisted on a joint letter which read, 'We hope you like cheese because we put in some cheese and a cheesing rod. We made a mat for you to wipe your feet on. There is a triple bed for three of you to sleep on.'

The teacher with whom I was working, Betty Buxton, had collected evidence throughout the session. We used this to assess the learning that had resulted for the children. The following was our analysis of Christopher's learning:

He showed an understanding of mapping skills (during the discussion about the teacher's room). He was capable of reasoning (for example, about the best position for the alarm clock). He appropriately described the drawings in the story book as 'plans' and provided the explanation of a 'bird view' to the others. During the activity he provided evidence of identifying needs (such as a torch for lighting, a mat for wiping feet, as well as the 'cheesing rod' and 'tackle box'!); imaging (during the generation of plans about his own bedroom he was capable of 'seeing' his room and describing its features); evaluating his pair's ideas and suggesting changes (such as placing the mat by the door). His creativity was particularly evident in his idea about a 'cheesing rod' which did not feature in the story and the 'tackle box' suggestion demonstrated how he linked this idea with his previous experience. There was limited evidence that he was developing an understanding of scale (in terms of the size of the bed) but he had used accurate specific mathematics' vocabulary (triple bed for three). He cooperated well with Matthew, discussing decisions throughout the paired work and sharing tasks, especially noticeable when it came to sticking down.

The activity was structured to support the children in generating designs. Their lack of experience of plans and limited drawing skills were overcome by the introductory activity on my bedroom and their own. The potential difficulty of drawing plans and not being able to make corrections or changes was addressed through the use of cut-out shapes that could be easily moved around. The evaluation was structured through the letter writing that the children responded to as a purposeful task.

There is general agreement that primary children should be given some kind of formal instruction in drawing, such as one minute sketching, disassembly and annotated drawing activities, scale and orthographic drawing exercises (Anning 1997; Constable 1994 a, b). Further guidance for teachers related to subject knowledge for supporting children's drawing skills is contained within the TTA's needs assessment materials (TTA 1998a, Diagnostic Feedback, pp. 69–74) and DATA's *The Design and Technology Primary Co-ordinator's File* (DATA 1996a, Section 5.3). Alongside drawing skills, children should be taught to exploit the graphics' package used on the school computers to support their designing. More specific programs can also be used during specific projects – for example a net-generating program during an assignment related to packaging, or pattern-creating software to add decorative cladding to a product.

7. Planning

Developing and communicating ideas can also involve planning how to put those ideas into action based upon a clear idea of what has to be done, for example, deciding and listing what materials and tools will be needed, allocating jobs within a team and setting a timetable for different stages. The latter is particularly necessary for projects which are spread over a long time period. Planning should also involve children in suggesting alternative methods of proceeding if things go wrong (DfEE/QCA 1999, Key Stage 2 PoS). Children need to be given time to plan and taught how to do this. The SACLA framework introduced in Chapter 2 can be useful for encouraging systematic planning before children start making. In most of the case studies featured in this book the teachers have asked the children to identify what they will need (materials, tools and help), where they will get it from and how they will use it. Careful planning encourages the children to work more independently and in a more efficient way.

8. Conclusion

This chapter has explored the way in which teachers can foster children's creativity when they are engaging in designing. It has focused upon strategies to help children generate ideas, develop them and communicate those ideas to others, and themselves. It has reinforced the idea that designing does not always involve drawing before making and that a variety of means and media can be used when designing. The interaction between thought and action is at the heart of good designing: cognitive activities such as imaging and concrete modelling are two linked and essential dimensions to this. Children need to be taught the benefits of imaging and offered a variety of ways of developing their imaged possibilities. The contribution of 'evaluation' to designing has not been dealt with in depth at this stage and will be explored further in Chapter 7. Designing should not be seen by teachers or children as a chore to get out of the way before the real job of making can be started. Designing is important, and enjoyable, in its own right and as an essential aspect of design and technology. We all engage in 'designerly activity' throughout our lives and skills learnt in the primary phase can be applied in many everyday situations, including for the teacher, mounting displays, planning school trips, organising a classroom and producing resources.

CHAPTER 5

Making – using construction kits

1. Introduction

Making is the means by which an outcome is produced; it is when plans are put into action, when design ideas become a reality. This chapter and the next discuss children's use of a wide range of materials, tools, equipment and techniques. Although, sometimes, children will be making things simply to practise particular skills, this part of the design and technology process will be most successful when it builds upon effective designing. In other situations, as discussed in the last chapter, making can be an integral and essential element of designing. Making things has been valued as a part of children's primary education for many decades. In the past children have had frequent experiences of using paper, card, clay, fabrics, other everyday materials and construction kits to make things – however, these experiences have not necessarily been in the context of design and technology. Much of the making that went on in primary schools could, more appropriately, be described as a craft, or art and craft activities. In this chapter, and the next, making is seen as more than this, although the skills and techniques that can be practised through art and craft work can make an important contribution to learning in design and technology.

The National Curriculum PoSs (DfEE/QCA 1999) require that pupils are provided with opportunities to work with a range of materials and components. This chapter explores the use of one group of resistant materials: construction kits (commercially produced and packaged sets of components for making models). The following chapter will focus on making, using other materials, including everyday and reclaimed materials, wood, textiles and food. While no longer explicitly referred to in the National Curriculum Orders at Key Stages 1 and 2, as they were in the previous version (DfE/WO 1995), construction kits remain a valuable resource for design and technology.

This chapter begins with a general discussion about assessment of children's learning during the making phase. The sections concerning the use of construction kits deal with aspects of progression and with the teacher's role in supporting children's learning. These sections address issues that apply to the use of other materials. The fact that the use of construction kits is discussed before these others is not intended to suggest that they should be prioritised in this way in the classroom or that there is a progression from kits to other media. Construction kits provide a practical way to organise making activities, but they are are not the only, nor necessarily the best, medium in all situations. Kits can also be used during the designing stage of a project.

2. Opportunities for assessment during the making phase

The making stage of design and technology activities provide numerous opportunities for teachers to assess children's learning. In this book assessment is seen as the way teachers gain insights into children's learning in order to make decisions about what they should do next. Its formative purpose is, for me, the most important: assessment cannot be separated from teaching, they go hand in hand. Therefore the teachers' interventions, discussed in this chapter and illustrated in case studies throughout this book, are the result of judgements teachers have made which are based upon the assessment evidence that they have collected. This evidence may be what the children do, say or produce. Alert teachers are constantly on the lookout, in every classroom activity, for significant evidence of children's learning that can help them make decisions about what to do next. For example, when children are working with construction kits, the talk is likely to be considerable, both amongst the children and with the teacher. Such talk can be revealing about the children's current understanding. Significant utterances could be recorded, perhaps in a floorbook (Ollerenshaw and Ritchie 1997, p. 50) or a notebook. Their model-making and its outcomes can also reveal their current level of skills and understanding, for example, how they go about fixing wheels to their models. Getting children to evaluate and talk about their own outcomes, or to produce some linked written outcome, provide further layers of evidence for the teacher to consider. Assessment in design and technology should have an holistic dimension and not simply be an assessment against specific criteria. It requires a teacher to probe understanding in specific areas and determine the learner's skills and competence at different stages. Tests at the end of a project are certainly not the way to do this. Assessment in design and technology is ongoing throughout the children's work. It requires teachers to develop certain skills among which active listening is possibly the most vital. Teachers have to identify the significant utterances from among all those they hear every day. Judgements based upon this evidence enable teachers to identify pivotal points in learning experiences; the points when interventions will move learners forward in terms of their understanding, their skills or attitudes. Through collecting evidence and making judgements a teacher decides how to 'scaffold' a child's learning and facilitate further learning in the 'zone of proximal development'. A teacher's questions (open and closed), prompts, guidance and demonstration all play a part in this. To assess and facilitate learning in this way the teacher needs an understanding of the processes in which the children are engaging, of the nature of the challenge involved, and some ideas about how the child might tackle the challenge. The latter are not to enable the teacher to direct children to the teacher's preferred solution but to ensure the children can, if necessary, be supported in moving forward if they are unable to generate ideas for themselves.

Throughout this book, the parallels between teaching and design and technology have been addressed. The making phase of design and technology parallels the implementation phase of teaching. Children, when making, are putting into action their designs: teachers are implementing their plans. The children need to be encouraged to look for evidence during making to inform their evaluations of the work, its outcomes and the processes involved. Similarly, teachers should be collecting evidence of children's learning and of how they interact with the children to allow them to evaluate their teaching and to inform future plans.

3. Learning through the use of construction kits

Bricks, blocks and construction kits have been common in early years' classrooms for many years. Their potential for developing children's manipulative and social skills, imaginative powers and attitudes has long been recognised by nursery and infant teachers (Browne, 1991; Gura, 1992). This section considers the potential of the wide variety of commercially produced kits that are now available for developing children's learning throughout Key Stages 1 and 2. The following case study illustrates one way in which an early years' teacher was able to provide children with a learning experience using basic kits.

CASE STUDY

10: Ricky's post office

Karen Patey was teaching a class of Y1 children at Southdown Infants' School, as part of her initial teacher education course. Her topic with the class was 'People who help us' and as part of this work the children had already been involved in helping Karen turn the home corner into a working post office. On the morning that she intended to start the construction kit activity she placed a letter, addressed to the children, prominently on the outside of the post office that they had made. When the children were sitting on the carpet, she read it to them (Figure 5.1).

Ricky,
24 Postie Street,
Greendale,
London,
GR5 7RS.

19th January

Dear Green Class,

Last night I came into your classroom and I saw your wonderful post office. I really wanted to play in it, but when I tried it was much too big.

I am only this tall:

I was wondering if you had any smaller post offices so that I could come back and play again ... that would be really fun.

Yours hopefully,

Ricky   (a small friend of Postman Pat)

xxxxxxxx

Figure 5.1 Ricky's letter

Once she had set the scene with the letter she said to the children, 'Poor Ricky, what shall we do?' 'Aahh, we'll have to help him,' was Samuel's immediate response. Richard added, 'He needs a post office of his own.' Christopher explained, 'Yes, but it would have to be very little.' Samantha wondered whether, 'he'd like a van to get to . . . to give his letters out'. Lisa offered, 'I'll make him a post office and a van.' The children had taken the 'hook' that Karen had offered and were immediately identifying needs that were 'real' to them. The children were asked to think about 'What things will Ricky need in his post office?' and each group's ideas were recorded in a floorbook. These included the following ideas from one group: open and closed sign, doors, windows, post box, toys, sweets, stamps, letters, presents, envelopes, writing paper, weighing machine, cheques, clock, alarm, something to say it's a post office, roof. In the floorbook each comment was ascribed to its originator, giving Karen some valuable assessment evidence about the children's retention of ideas introduced earlier in the topic. She also had ideas to inform her questioning when the children got to the making stage, for example, 'Can you make a post box to go with your post office as you suggested earlier?'

The children drew designs individually while sitting in groups and Karen moved around to each group and asked them what they were going to make. She made notes and helped the children annotate their drawings as they worked. The children were asked to decide which kit to use prior to producing a design. For example, Lisa, decided to make a post office with *Lego*. During planning, Karen noted that she took care to ensure she showed not only brick pattern and windows, but also where her favourite things (crisps and sweets) would go inside. Figure 5.2 shows her finished model. She was pleased with her design because of its coloured brick pattern and opening door. She later added a chimney, 'in case Ricky wanted a fire'. She thought she could improve her design 'by adding a proper roof'.

Figure 5.2   Lisa's post office

Samantha wanted to make a van for Ricky in which he could take a friend 'otherwise he would be lonely'. She chose *Mobilo* because 'it was square and I like the colours'. Evaluating her outcome (Figure 5.3) she decided 'it would be a bit cold outside and I couldn't make a steering wheel'. However, it moved well and she was pleased with the result.

Figure 5.3 Samantha's van

During the making children had various small problems to solve and were good at evaluating their outcomes. For example, Corky had intended to build stairs into his model but could not work out how to do it with *Lego* bricks. His solution was to state, 'Ricky will have to use his ladder to get on to the flat roof.' Jane decided that her *Polydron* post office was too big, when compared to the size of Ricky (shown in the letter) and resolved to try again with a different kit. Shaun made Ricky a scooter which he modified by adding a roof and door 'to keep him dry in the rain, but to let him get his foot out to scoot along'.

Some children were invited to have another attempt the following day, during which improvements were made and in some cases completely new models made.

Karen's planning and support of the children had ensured that learning had resulted from an holistic design and technology project. Her choice of context had also been informed by her understanding of how girls might best be encouraged to use construction kits (Browne 1991; Zarins 1996). The context, with its 'helping' dimension was one which she hoped would, and considered in the event did, motivate and interest the girls and boys alike. She was fortunate to be in a classroom that was reasonably well resourced in terms of construction kits and to be working with a class who had previous experience of using the kits. This allowed her progressively to develop the children's skills, knowledge and understanding of the materials they were using, and the ways in which they could be used.

Construction kit activities can make valuable contributions to children's learning if appropriately planned and implemented by teachers. Unfortunately, the use of construction kits is far less common in Key Stage 2 classes and, even where kits are available, there is still a tendency for the work to be devalued by a teacher, perhaps as something to be done after the 'real' work is finished or even as a time-filler or to occupy children during wet playtimes. Construction kits offer so much more and should be available in every classroom, together with quality time for children to use them. The variety of kits available ensures that there are some which provide sufficient challenge for the most able children (in terms of design and technology). Indeed, kits such as *Fischertechnik* are used in secondary schools and university engineering departments as a means of modelling prior to production using other materials.

There are good reasons for using construction kits in primary schools to fulfil the National Curriculum requirements for design and technology. Construction kits provide a useful ready-made supply of parts that allow children to develop and apply their ideas. In particular they can be an excellent way of providing children with experience of building, modifying, and dismantling structures and mechanisms. Their understanding of how things move can be fostered through experience of wheels, axles, hinges, levers, pivots, gears, pulleys and drive mechanisms. Children can also learn about sources of energy and how they can be controlled through mechanical and electrical means. They can develop manual dexterity and technical competence through handling kits. The use of construction kits can foster children's spatial awareness, which is especially important for girls, since research indicates that this area of learning is more difficult for them than boys (Shuard 1982). They can be very motivating for children, especially more reluctant learners, as the story of Andrew in Chapter 2 illustrated.

Kits have a number of advantages over other materials that can be used for design and technology:

- the parts are generally accurately made and fit together well so that children do not suffer the frustration of not being able to join materials. Their attention can be focused upon solving a problem or meeting a challenge because assembly is relatively straightforward. Moving parts, such as gears, are precise in action;
- the kits provide a good way of making/testing models/mechanisms before going on to use other materials for the final outcome. They can be an aid to design;
- working models can be made relatively quickly and modified easily;
- the kits can make design and technology work more motivating to the children, in that the models made often look more realistic than those made from other materials;
- the kits are usually compact to store, although the most appropriate storage may not be the packaging in which they were purchased.

4. Progression in the use of construction kits

To maximise the potential of construction kits it is important for a teacher to think about progression. This can be considered in terms of the kits themselves (the variety of kits provided and the methods involved in assembling parts), or in terms of the way the children are introduced to and encouraged to use the kits.

When considering the progression, in terms of the range of kits available, we need to consider the variety of shapes and types of components, how they are assembled, the scale and the material involved. Kits can include squares, cubes, A and H shapes, triangles, curves, strips or rods. Components may be small, large or a combination of various sizes and vary from simple building elements to parts with specific uses such as gears and pulleys. They can be made of wood, plastic, metals or a combination of materials. Children generally work from larger to smaller scale kits, from single and simple shapes to a variety of more complex ones, from kits with no specialist components to those with an extensive range allowing much more flexibility in outcome.

The method of connecting components provides a possible means of identifying progression in the way that they can be introduced to children. Most children will have played with stacking bricks or kits such as *Duplo* or *Lego*, involving blocks that push to fix, at home or in playgroups before coming to school. They are easy to use and popular with children. They often lead to static models, but have lots of potential for imaginative play. The next level of challenge comes from kits that allow instant fixing (push to click) of a variety of components (such as *Mobilo*, which includes preassembled push fit axles). These allow children to make models that move. The way in which movement is achieved offers progression within this type of kit. *Masterbuilder*, for example, includes wheels and axles that need assembling. *Reoclick* requires children to use even more parts to make up an axle including spacers and fixings.

Joining components with nuts and bolts, using simple tools, is a skill developed through the use of kits such as *Bauplay*, which has large parts and can be used by young children who do not have fine motor skills. However, often kits of this type have small components which are more difficult to join (*Meccano* or *Plawcotech*).

There is a range of 'framework' kits available, some large scale (for example, *Quadro*) which can be used to make models to play on or in, and others with smaller rods and connectors (*Mini-Quadro, Construct-o-straws, K-Nex* and *Plawcotech Junior*). *Construx* (no longer in production but still used in many schools) provides a more varied set of components for younger children with considerable potential for making moving models based upon structures assembled from plastic girders. Figure 5.4 shows children trying out a desk-top rubbish collector that they had made using *Construx*. *Teko* offers similar potential using wood strips.

Figure 5.4 Desk-top rubbish collector

More sophisticated kits involving a range of components (including gears, pulleys, motors and pneumatic components) are available for older children. *Lego Technic* and *Fischertechnik* are obvious examples. The components join in a variety of ways and offer maximum flexibility for designing and making working models as illustrated by the instructions for a pneumatically operated train signal designed by a Y6 child in Figure 5.5. They also have enormous potential for developing concepts in areas such as geared mechanisms as Bennett's (1996) research into the learning of Y6 children who were using *Lego Technic* showed.

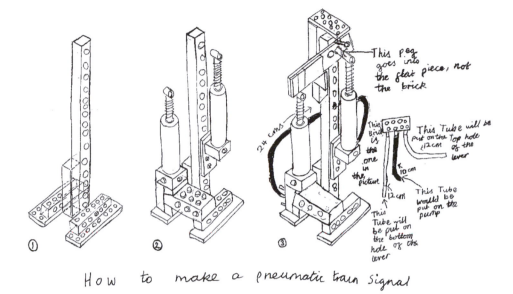

Figure 5.5 Diagrams of a railway signal

Kits like these have potential for children exploring and learning about mechanical, electrical and electronic control. Computer-controlled models made from construction kits provide a good starting point for the activities where the focus is on programming (*Logicator*).

When considering suitable construction kits to use with children, some potential problems need to be considered:

- parts with specific uses and of standard size, shape and colour can lead to unimaginative and 'standard' solutions;
- components from different kits are rarely compatible, which restricts the ways children use them;
- frustration can be caused if children find parts do not fit in the way they wish or if the model falls apart easily (complicated *Lego* models on display in toy shops are usually glued together!);
- finished models cannot be kept and taken home; small parts can get lost; the aesthetic potential of some kits is extremely limited;
- some kits have components which break after regular use or misuse.

An audit of current construction kits in a school and how they are used may be necessary to help teachers identify gaps. Such an audit, and analysis of the results, can inform decisions about the best allocation of kits to different classes (see DATA 1996a – Section 5.5; Bell and Ritchie 1999, Chapter 3 for more guidance on conducting an audit; Cross 1998, p. 191 for a suggested whole-school plan) and best use of future investment.

5. Introducing children to construction kits

When children are meeting any kit for the first time they will need plenty of time for free exploration, finding how components fit together. With more complicated kits (e.g. *Fischertechnik*) they may also need instruction in how to join the parts. Their exploration could include sorting and classifying activities, making basic models with limited types or numbers of components, naming parts and producing identification charts for other children's use. Once the children have had some time for this or as part of the exploratory stage they will start to invent models or perhaps make use of an instruction card/book and try to make those illustrated, as a focused practical task (FPT). At this stage the children will be developing manipulative skills that will contribute to their later learning in design and technology.

Most kits are supplied with instruction material illustrating models that can be made, although the quality of this material is variable in the context of school use. For example, some booklets include a lot of militaristic outcomes or only show boys working on models; these are not acceptable. However, using appropriate illustrative examples can be an important stage for the children in exploring the potential of a particular kit and its components. Making models from illustrations is often far more challenging than teachers imagine (try it for yourself) and such activities can lead to significant learning that extends beyond design and technology. If children work together on these tasks they will be collaborating and cooperating, persevering, discussing and explaining, estimating and measuring, using close observation, developing fine motor skills and predicting. The time taken to complete these models can be longer than sometimes anticipated. Those children who find making a particular model easy can be challenged by the teacher to modify it, to improve it, or convert it to a different purpose (for example, a hand-drill could be modified to make a kitchen whisk).

The next stage, when children have developed confidence and competence in using a particular kit, might be to provide them with a picture or photograph of a product from the made-world that they are then asked to model without further help. The products should be suited to the particular kits (some lend themselves to certain outcomes far better than others) and a bank of these pictures can be built up to use with each kit. This stage is both reinforcing the way in which the made-world can be modelled, and developing children's understanding of the limitations as well as the potential of the kit. At this stage children can be reminded that components from the kit can be combined with everyday materials, such as card for cladding or fabric for a sail. They could also be encouraged to mix and match parts from kits they have previously used (not forgetting to replace them after dismantling!).

A similar type of challenge, to that of modelling something from a picture, can come from a problem set by the teacher. The teacher is more likely than the child at this stage of the work with a new kit to be able to identify appropriate problems to be solved by using it. Therefore the teacher may choose to ask the children to make something, such as a vehicle to carry a particular load or a structure for a particular purpose. These challenges can be contextualised in some way, perhaps linked to a topic or theme that is ongoing, or set as an isolated task with the purpose of providing practise in use of the kit. Such a task will also encourage familiarity with the vocabulary of design and technology; words such as problem, challenge, ingenious and original can become part of the working vocabulary of the classroom.

If children have met a challenge of this sort they can be asked to record their work with drawings, produce annotated diagrams (as illustrated in Figure 5.5, drawn by a Y6 child) or write sequences of instructions to show others how to make them. Children who are not yet writing independently, or others as a means of providing variety, might audio tape the instructions for their peers or, perhaps, younger children to follow. This can be particularly good for fostering sequencing and planning skills; children can be asked to turn on the tape and say what they have done after each part of their models are completed. These diagrams, instruction lists and tapes can provide a bank of non-standard models for others to construct, practising their skills. Offering the children a purpose for such work is vital. A classroom where children are always asked to draw what they have made is not conducive to children making complex models since the consequences can be demotivating. Asking children to produce drawings or to write instructions for making their model is fine if it has a purpose other than simply pleasing teacher or keeping them occupied.

After the children have developed their skills with a particular kit they are ready to make use of it in their design and technology work. They should be able to choose a suitable kit to solve their own or their teacher's challenge within a design and technology context, either during the design stage or as a means of producing the final outcomes.

The following case study, which involved Horton Primary School in South Gloucestershire, illustrates an example of older children who had the relevant experience (although in this case from outside school) to allow them to use a familiar kit in a problem solving situation. It also provides an example of neighbourhood engineers being involved in primary schools and of enterprising teachers who exploited an opportunity for involvement in a regional competition which led to free kits for the school. This is one way of dealing with the lack of construction kits often evident in Key Stage 2.

CASE STUDY

11: Young Engineer Competition

Mrs Garven and Mrs Downes share a mixed Key Stage 2 class in this small rural school. During the Summer term, the pupils had the opportunity to use construction kits as a result of entering a Young Engineer Competition which led to the class receiving the kit *K'Nex*. Several of the children had access to this resource at home and therefore had some experience on which to draw. The competition involved the children going along

Figure 5.6 A solar-powered model

to a local school with a 'friendly' engineer – in their case, the husband of the chair of governors. The pupils were set a challenge to meet in 75 minutes. This was to design and make a futuristic flying machine. They worked in pairs (mainly single sex through pupil choice). The event was thoroughly enjoyed and some interesting outcomes resulted. Tommy (aged 11) and Chris (aged 10) produced a solar-powered vehicle with rotating blades (see Figure 5.6). They started by sorting out the rotating movement of the blades using the motor and then started building on the lower structure. This led to problems of stability at the base and they added additional struts to strengthen the framework to ensure it wasn't too 'wobbly'. Other problems solved during construction concerned the way to fix a free-running wheel on an axle and space it properly. Working cooperatively, they were well able to finish in the time limit. In fact they had time to add a few 'extras' such as a number of observation cameras around the structure and a second set of blades that were shorter and intended to allow the craft to 'float down to Earth under control if the main blades broke'. Both were very pleased with their outcome, especially when they were told that they had come second in the competition (as judged by the engineers present). The potential gender issues implicit in this case study are discussed in Section 7 below.

Some children's familiarity with construction kits at home has both advantages and disadvantages when they use them in school. At home they associate the use of kits with play rather than work. This perception is not helped by the teacher who tells them to 'go and play with the construction kits' in a school context. I always ensure I ask children to go and work with the construction kits. This is to communicate my conviction that such activity is as important as other classroom work. Some children may not be challenged or stimulated by the use of kits in school if they regularly use them at home. They may need to be offered the chance to meet new kits in school and so be challenged to develop their competence further. However, children's skills and confidence, gained at home, should be capitalised on in school.

The role of the teacher in planning the work has already been outlined in the last section. We will now explore the interactions that may occur during the activities. Teachers' questions can add to the children's experience by drawing their attention to ideas about stability, suitability of materials/components, the relationship between shapes and their position, the nature of the mechanisms that allow movement, and means of propulsion. Questions can also help children predict and plan as they make models. They can focus the children on particular aspects of the problem they are solving, supporting the child's learning within the 'zone of proximal development' discussed in Chapter 2. Asking too many questions can be counter-productive. A question should be an appropriate response to what the child is doing or saying. A key purpose of teachers' intervention during this work is to encourage the children to raise their own questions, particularly of an evaluative type. Children can also be encouraged to image their anticipated outcomes and describe these explicitly to their teacher. Some questions can also help develop children's mathematical learning, particularly in the early years, 'How many red blocks are you going to use?', 'Will it be the same on both sides?', 'Can you make it taller, longer, wider?', 'How much will it hold?' Older children can be asked about scale, proportion, gear ratios and symmetry.

The teacher's role in supporting children's use of kits also concerns the variables involved in a particular challenge, and the degree of complexity. For example, a child can be challenged to make a house, to make a house with a door, to make a house with a door that opens. There is obviously a progression here and early experiences should involve problems involving few variables. Others can be added as appropriate. Young children do find it hard to hold in mind more than one or two requirements at a time. The introduction of too many variables too soon can be counter-productive and frustrating for the learner. The progression from simple to complex problems and outcomes does not directly relate to the age of the child; it is related to the development of the individual child as well as to the nature of the particular kit and the task set. An 11-year-old child with limited experience of construction kits will need to progress through stages of development that might have been achieved by another child at a much earlier age.

6. Organising the classroom for construction kit activities

The classroom needs to be organised in a way that makes construction kit activities practical. In many early years classrooms the activities are carried out by children in a carpeted area that is comfortable and provides the necessary space for larger models. However, when using kits with smaller components it can be better for children to sit at a work-surface or table. Components they are using can be stored in trays and there is less chance of bits getting lost. The space needed to test models is also a consideration; for example, a smooth floor area for testing vehicles. Children can work and test models outside if the weather is suitable and the area can be safely monitored. Finished models will normally need to be displayed, at least for a short period, and therefore a suitable surface should be identified for this. Valuing a child's model by displaying it well can make the later dismantling less upsetting. In this context, taking photographs of finished models (ideally using a digital camera, for immediate viewing and integration into follow-up work) is useful. It shows children that their work is valued, it provides a way of displaying the work for a longer period, and it provides assessment evidence for adding to a child's profile or portfolio.

Another approach to help children deal with the need to dismantle a model so that others can use the parts is to provide them with a purpose for the model, which once achieved means dismantling is acceptable. Using the outcome as a prop for retelling a story, or adding a new ending to a story is one possibility. A story and its characters, can provide children with 'a reference point for establishing criteria but it can also be used when making decisions and evaluating the success of the project' (Stables 1992, p. 111).

To return to other organisational issues, storage is a factor in the successful use of kits (and other components/materials). Multi-compartment boxes, that allow for quick sorting, for selection of particular components and for teachers and children to check parts are not missing, makes classroom organisation easier and more efficient for everyone. Children can take responsibility for maintaining the kits, perhaps through a monitor system. Dismantling, sorting components to put away and tidying up offer potential for further learning. Colour-coding and clear labelling of containers helps with this.

Decisions taken about which kits are used in which class should be taken by the whole staff, based upon discussions about progression and continuity. In some schools kits are rotated around classes and in others a central storage system is used. As long as the approach has an educational rationale agreed by staff then it is likely to work. Clearly construction kits are an expensive resource for schools and their use needs to be maximised to justify the expenditure.

7. Classroom management and the use of construction kits

The next consideration is about how best to manage the class for construction kit activities. In most kits there are rarely enough components for more than two or three children to work together. Therefore it is necessary for the class to be organised in a way that allows for pair or small group work. In early years' classes this is usually unproblematic, although on occasions I have seen far too many children, often during so-called 'choosing time', trying to work with an inadequate supply of parts. This can lead to frustration, lack of cooperation, and sometimes disruptive behaviour. It is not always possible to offer the same degree of flexibility in classroom organisation in Key Stage 2 classes as that found in infant classrooms. And yet, construction kit work is not teacher-intensive and therefore is less of a challenge to classroom management than might be imagined. It is also an activity that if organised appropriately rarely leads to control or discipline problems with older children since it is intrinsically appealing to most. One answer is to ensure that a small group of children are working with construction kits whenever possible or appropriate; the organisation requirements of this are similar to those involved in classroom-based computer activities.

Questions of management raise gender issues, which are important ones for every teacher and staff group to address (Zarins 1996). There are various reasons why gender is such a concern with regard to the management of children using construction kits. To begin with, girls are less likely than boys to meet these materials at home, unless they have access to their brothers' toys or their more aware parents hold non-sexist attitudes. Beat (1991) in a small-scale research project also found that even those girls who played with kits at home (usually *Lego*) did not necessarily feel confident about using them in school (p. 90). The stereotypical view of construction kits is that they are 'boys' toys' and manufacturers explicitly target their wares towards boys. This can often mean that packaging and advertising (especially during children's television programmes) project inappropriate images. Browne and Ross (1991) collected evidence to show that stereotypical views about boys' and girls' toys are often well-established in children when they enter school. They asked children to sort toys and both sexes generally grouped doll's, dolls houses and felt pens and paper as suitable for girls; *Lego*, *Mobilo*, wooden bricks and woodwork as suitable for boys; and books, puzzles and sand as suitable for both sexes. The researchers also looked at the way children used kits in infant classes and found that boys tended to use construction materials in more sophisticated ways, making more use of the medium, exploiting its three-dimensional properties. The boys tended to approach the activity as individuals. Girls, by contrast, frequently made simple structures such as houses or lay-outs and used these as a 'foil for social play'. The girls were more interested in the process of social interactions as opposed to the process of making things. Girls generally have less opportunities and encouragement to 'tinker' and take things apart at home. They are therefore less confident with such activities. Add to this the difficulties girls can have with spatial awareness and the lack of experience and confidence of many female (and, of course, some male) teachers with more sophisticated construction kits and the complexity of the issues becomes evident. The solution is not simple. There is undoubtedly a need for positive action in the classroom to ensure opportunities for girls that they may have missed. It may also be appropriate to ensure girls have the chance to work in single-sex groups. There is evidence that in mixed groups, even in the nursery classroom, girls end up servicing the boys' work (for example, fetching and carrying parts) (Ollerenshaw and Ritchie 1997, pp. 181–184). Browne and Ross (1991) found that girls, even when teachers positively encouraged them to use kits, were 'very adept at sabotaging teachers' efforts to ensure that they engaged in an activity they would not normally choose' (p. 46). They also tended to do the minimum required to 'please' teacher, which was often very little. Ironically, those teachers most keen to develop girls' constructional skills were most generous in their praise of such 'minimalist' approaches. On a positive note, their research found that cross-domain play (girls engaging in the use of constructional activity and boys in creative activities) was considerably increased when an adult was involved in the activity. Bennett (1996) in his research on understanding of geared mechanisms found girls performed as well, if not better than boys in a supportive environment. It is necessary for female teachers to provide positive role models for the girls, demonstrating their own confidence with the material and other technological equipment.

Another factor is the nature of the task the children are tackling. Many kits are designed so that vehicles can be made and the standard models illustrated are often lorries, helicopters, tanks and rockets. These have, some would argue, 'male' appeal (which could be offered as a criticism of the theme of the Young Engineers Competition in Case Study 11, where the boys' outcomes were generally more sophisticated and technical than those of the girls). Girls are more likely to respond to tasks with a human dimension; a pushchair, wheelchair, roundabout, ambulance (Harding 1997; Whyte 1993). Boys are often happy to make a model for the sake of it or as a toy to play with themselves; girls may look for different purposes. Girls are likely to use construction kits for imaginative play, building static models such as houses and furniture; boys are inclined to make moving models. These tendencies need to inform a teacher's planning. Ideally, like Zarins (1996 p. 212), I consider that we should be encouraging mixed-sex groups for all classroom work and therefore, although the benefits of single-sex groups for girls have been advocated at the early stages, it is preferable to encourage mixed-sex groups when the girls feel confident enough to work alongside the boys. It is also preferable to begin with activities with which the girls are familiar and confident and then move on to less familiar contexts where they can apply their skills and understanding. Some boys equally need teacher support, but in different areas: to be more sensitive to the needs of others in group situations, to be tolerant of others' views, to recognise others' strengths and contributions, to respond positively to tasks with a human dimension, to be more open-minded about the range of outcomes they can produce.

Use of kits in isolation from other curriculum activities can be one way of building up children's confidence and skills, but if the work can be related to other curriculum activities, topics, or projects it is likely to be relevant, more motivating and more successful. In the context of design and technology, some of the work described above is perhaps best seen as 'design and technology-related' activity. For me, it becomes richer design and technology when the kit becomes the medium a child uses to meet a need through engagement in the whole cycle of activities I have used to describe the design and technology process. Case Study 10 (Ricky's Post Office) illustrated an integrated and holistic approach of this kind.

8. Conclusion

This chapter has looked in detail at the use of construction kits and their potential for contributing to children's learning in design and technology. Construction kits offer one way in which children can be introduced to the use of resistant materials in the classroom.

They provide a suitable resource for the whole primary age range and the variety of kits available and the diverse ways in which they can be used by children mean that they can be used to offer appropriate challenges to children regardless of age or ability. The issues related to the use of construction kits, explored above, also apply to the use of these other materials discussed in the next chapter. Issues of equal opportunity and access for girls have been highlighted and these are also relevant to girls' use of other materials. From their first days in school, all children should be experiencing making activities with a variety of materials; activities that involve construction kits can be planned and organised alongside work with other materials.

CHAPTER 6

Making – using everyday and other materials

1. Introduction

This chapter continues the theme of children's making activities, focusing on the use of a range of materials that require different skills from those needed when using construction kits. In particular, the uses of everyday materials and wood are explored in some detail, as exemplars of the issues involved in children making, with shorter sections on food and textiles. Everyday materials include paper, card and reclaimed materials such as packaging, bottle tops, corks and containers. In some of the literature the latter materials are sometimes termed 'junk'. This label has not been used in this book, since there is a danger that it implies the work produced with such materials is, itself, somehow 'junk'. It is possible to produce outcomes of high quality using reclaimed and everyday materials, as this chapter illustrates.

The National Curriculum (DfEE/QCA 1999) at Key Stage 2 refers to a range of materials, including electrical and mechanical components, food, mouldable materials, stiff and flexible sheet materials and textiles (p. 95). The PoSs list the making skills that were discussed in Chapter 2. These include measuring, marking out, cutting, shaping, joining, combining (for example, in food preparation) and finishing (involving techniques such as cladding and painting).

The case studies in this chapter will illustrate children learning within the National Curriculum framework and, in some cases, going beyond it.

2. Using reclaimed and everyday materials

Design and technology work does not necessarily require the purchase of expensive kits or consumable materials; many projects can be carried out using reclaimed and everyday materials that can be easily collected for classroom use. Reclaimed materials have considerable potential for children's design and make activities. We have already seen such materials used in earlier case studies (e.g. Case Study 1: Our neighbourhood) and the following one provides further insights into how they can be used effectively by young children. It is based upon the work of Angela Andrewes, when she was a student completing her initial teacher education.

CASE STUDY

12: Litter bins

Angela was working with a Y1 class at Sandford Primary School in North Somerset. The task she set the children was to design and make a litter bin. The challenge was contextualised using a story she read the class called *Giant* which is about the need to care for the environment. This led to a lively discussion about rubbish and litter and how it can be disposed of carefully and safely. The challenge of designing a litter bin, to be used next to their tables, was introduced a few days later and Angela reminded the children of the story and their discussion. She showed them some examples of litter bins and asked them to identify the features which contributed to a 'good' design. The children identified the following criteria, which were recorded on a large poster (with the children's names beside their contributions):

You have to have a lid.

It could have a swinging lid.

You need the lid to stop the litter blowing away.

It needs a hole in the top so that rubbish collectors can get the litter out.

You need a handle on the lid to lift it up.

If you've got a big pile of rubbish you wouldn't lift the lid up – you need a hole to post it through.

It needs a hole at the front to see where you put the litter.

It needs to be painted yellow to make it look nice.

It needs a sign to say litter so people know to put their litter in it.

There was a discussion about different types of lids and Angela introduced the word 'hinge', showing the children some examples. They then discussed the resources they would require. The children were amused by the idea of making a litter bin out of materials which could themselves be called litter. The next stage was to draw their ideas, and list what they needed, helped by a simple worksheet divided into two parts. The top half of the sheet was headed *I would like my litter bin to look like this*, and the bottom half, *These are the things I need to make my litter bin*. Prior to drawing their designs the children were invited to select materials from the sorted collection of reclaimed materials that were available in the classroom. The children, individually, drew simple and clear drawings which Angela asked them to label. Two children exploited the fact that they had found boxes with a transparent side, using this as a feature so that 'you can see how full the bin is'.

The following week, Angela organised the making session. This began by reminding them of their designs and the different types of fastenings they had discussed for attaching their lids. They were asked to collect all the resources for themselves using their resource lists. The making proved problematic for some, despite the fact that the designs were uncomplicated and required relatively limited cutting and joining skills. Cutting slots was a challenge, and trial and error using different tapes was necessary to produce working hinges. The major difficulty occurred when some children, who had selected shiny boxes or plastic containers, attempted to paint them as part of the finishing process. Angela brought the class together at one stage to discuss the problem and to draw attention to the properties of materials that were involved.

Once they had completed their models and these had been photographed, they were asked to describe what they had done and how well they thought they had done it. Angela aimed to get them to:

- identify and explain design features in their own outcomes;
- identify problems encountered and how they were overcome;
- recognise the limitations of their bins and suggest modifications;
- identify their preferences – likes and dislikes concerning the bins.

The responses to the discussion about design features were recorded by Angela. Later they were displayed for the children to see and eventually became part of the project class-book. The discussion of design features resulted in comments such as:

I put a label on the front so people would know it was a bin.
You put the litter through the hole in the front and then get it out through the hole at the top.
I painted it to make it look nice.
You pull the handle and then you can put the litter in.
I glued a bottle top to the lid so that you can lift it off.
You put the litter in by folding up the lid.
To get the litter out you lift the lid off.

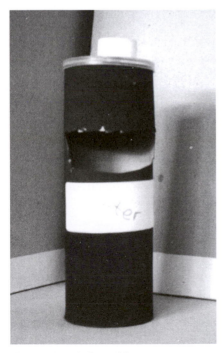

Figure 6.1 A litter bin

The children were referred back to the earlier discussion to remind them of the extent to which their designs and outcomes reflected the features identified at the outset. Figure 6.1 shows a typical outcome from the project. The children were able to identify ways of improving their outcomes. Modifications that were suggested included, 'have a hole in a different place so it's easier to put the litter in'. 'Have a lid that lifts off the top because it would be easier for getting rubbish out'. The children were clear about their 'dislikes' and critical of their own outcomes: 'the words show through the paint', 'the hole I cut was zig-zaggy', 'it hasn't got a hole in the front', 'the lid doesn't work well enough', 'the paint flakes off'. They were also, however, able to identify plenty of positive features, and, overall, Angela considered they had enjoyed the work (which had been spread over three weeks). Her own evaluation of the project makes some interesting points:

The children responded enthusiastically to the task despite having had very little experience of this type of activity. However, although they were able to produce designs and identify the resources they would need with ease, they found it more difficult to make the bins. They were not used to selecting resources for themselves and found it problematic to join materials together. The fact that some of them encountered difficulties when painting highlighted a lack of knowledge. On the previous few occasions they had undertaken junk modelling (sic), they had apparently been provided with boxes already covered in paper for them to paint. During this activity none of the children attempted to cover their boxes, indicating that they had not understood the reason for the covering on previous occasions. This reinforces the need for children to have practical experiences in order to discover things for themselves, and to experience problems in order to recognise the need to overcome them.

There are several issues that arise out of the use of reclaimed and everyday materials. It is important that children have access to a good range, including different shapes, sizes and types of materials. Reclaimed materials can be collected from a variety of sources but getting children to bring them in from home is probably the most obvious way to maintain a supply. Some teachers regularly display a list of current requirements, in a place where parents can see it. It is essential that all materials are appropriate, clean and safe, without jagged edges for example. School and LEA health and safety guidance should be followed with regard to finding materials which meets these requirements. Whatever is obtained needs to be stored, possibly in a central school store area which classes can use to top up their own supplies. In the classroom the materials should be separated and sorted in a organised way to help the children select the most suitable material or item for the purpose required (see Case Study 8: Puppets).

Children need to be taught how to handle reclaimed materials safely and to use tools properly to cut and join them. Some, such as metal cans, should not be cut without close supervision using 'tin snips'. The range of tools available in classrooms should be a decision taken by an individual school staff after consulting any national and LEA policies and guidance available. Appropriate risk assessment exercises should be conducted. It is essential that children are taught how to use tools, such as hacksaws, drills, craft knives or glue-guns, properly and safely. This usually requires a clear teacher demonstration. Children need to know how to maintain a safe working environment: how to hold and pass tools safely and where and how they should be stored. Safety measures, such as the availability of goggles, should be taken where appropriate. Guidance of health and safety issues in design and technology is available from Cross (1998), DATA (1996a – *The Design and Technology Primary Co-ordinator's File* contains a comprehensive section) and NAAIDT (1992 – a *Make it Safe* booklet that should be made available to every teacher). Health and safety is included in the National Curriculum under 'general teaching requirements'. It is worth quoting in full:

When working with tools, equipment and materials, in practical activities and in different environments, including those that are unfamiliar, pupils should be taught:

  a. about hazards, risks and risk control

b. to recognize hazards, assess consequent risks and take steps to control the risks to themselves and others

c. to use information to assess the immediate and cumulative risks

d. to manage the environment to ensure the health and safety of themselves and others

e. to explain the steps they take to control risks.

(DfEE/QCA 1999, p. 40)

In other words, children should be taught to carry out risk assessments, not just their teacher.

To ensure that reclaimed and everyday materials can be used in the most creative ways children should have access to and be taught to use a variety of glues and fixings, for example, paper fasteners, staplers, sewing, various glues and tapes, nails, pins, dress fasteners, poppers, plastic rivets and elastic bands. It may seem surprising to suggest that children need to be taught to use different glues, but it is my experience that frustration over not being able to join materials often results from inappropriate use of the glue. Too often, excess is applied and there is no attempt to remove air trapped between surfaces. Children often act as if more glue will make a stronger joint. With a glue like PVA a thin film of glue is far more successful.

Unlike construction kits, reclaimed materials rarely fit together well and so children's finished products may not look as realistic as those made with kits. However, in other ways, reclaimed materials are more flexible and children can make models which they can keep. It is, of course, possible, and indeed desirable at times, for children to combine reclaimed materials with other materials, including construction kits. Reclaimed materials can also lead to aesthetically pleasing outcomes, particularly when a teacher focuses children's attention on the quality of finish of their models. Figure 6.2 illustrates model houses constructed as part of a topic on the local village by Wendy Dowding's class when she taught at Stoke Lodge Junior School, South Gloucestershire. These have been well finished using cladding techniques, painting and other adornments.

Figure 6.2 Model houses from reclaimed materials

Figure 6.3 Building bridges

Reclaimed materials can be used to make large scale outcomes. Figure 6.3 shows Y5/6 children working on wooden bridges using full-size components. A similar project that I worked on with a teacher a few years ago (British Gas 1986) involved children making working rafts to cross a 'shark-invested' swimming pool at their annual school camp. On another occasion when I had taken my own class of Y4 children on a school camp, one whole day was spent designing and making overnight shelters from materials found locally. Working on projects like this with large-scale components require children to apply skills developed through the use of classroom-based activities. It also requires additional attention by teachers to health and safety concerns. The production of large outcomes places greater emphasis upon collaborative work and the need for good cooperative skills. Following up such projects back in the classroom can provide opportunities for teachers to concentrate upon the knowledge and understanding dimension of the children's learning. The children who made the rafts went back to school and investigated ways of improving the stability of their outcomes by building and testing small-scale models. This helped them develop an understanding of why their original rafts tended to cause them to fall off rather frequently!

Reclaimed and everyday materials can be difficult to use to make anything but very simple mechanisms. It is common, in books for teachers and children, to find suggestions for making gears from cardboard wheels and match or lolly sticks. These can be used to illustrate principles, but rarely work well enough to be built into a working model. If children are to include such mechanisms in their models it is better for them to be able to use components from construction kits or specially manufactured components.

Difficulties in manipulating and joining everyday materials mean that the children's efforts can be consumed by the materials and not by the problems they are seeking to solve. It is necessary for teachers to monitor this possibility and intervene with appropriate advice or support before the children reach the point of giving up. Sometimes encouraging children to work on outcomes using construction kits to sort out mechanisms and structures before attempting to reproduce them using other materials can minimise these difficulties. Making an outcome from reclaimed or everyday materials can be quite time-consuming and demand considerable patience, as children wait for one part to dry before moving on to the next, unless a glue-gun or double-sided tape is used.

Organising the children to use these materials, like organising their use of construction kits, usually requires a teacher to work with groups. This allows appropriate supervision for health and safety reasons, and provides better opportunities for teachers' involvement in the work. However, as we have seen in earlier case studies (Case Study 1: Our neighbourhood, and Case Study 5: Air-raid shelters) some teachers prefer to organise the work as a whole-class activity. This is more demanding on resources and teachers, but allows the work to be fitted in at a time that suits them, perhaps when other help is available.

3. Using wood

Wood is a resistant material with considerable potential for design and make activities. The use of a technique based upon strips of wood easily and accurately cut with a cheap hacksaw and jig or bench-hook, joined with card triangles glued with PVA to make corners (NCET 1989; Williams and Jinks 1985) provides a means of allowing children to explore this potential. The practical and successful use of wood in primary classrooms is possible as the first example of children's work in this book (the model of Tower Bridge in Chapter 1) has illustrated.

Figure 6.4
A wooden sleigh

Children can be introduced to wood as a material for their designing and making as soon as they enter school although it may be more appropriately introduced later in Key Stage 1. As they progress through school the children's use of wood can become more sophisticated as the following examples illustrate: Figure 6.4 shows an outcome from a Y2 child, in Lesley Stone's class at Embleton Infants' School in Bristol, who made a sleigh, in the context of work on 'Icy places'; the car (Figure 6.5) was made by Y5 children in

Figure 6.5 A motorised car

Richard Harrison's class when he was at Luckwell Primary School and is motorised using a simple electric motor; two Y6 children from Blagdon Primary School, North Somerset, who had considerable experience of using wood, designed and made the crane in Figure 6.6 as part of a topic on Bristol Docks (Alan Murphy was their teacher at the time).

Figure 6.6 A crane from Bristol docks

The following case studies of work with one class, show two approaches to the use of wood and other everyday materials.

CASE STUDY

13: A new ship for Columbus

Myra Ginns, technology subject leader/coordinator at Crossways Junior School in Thornbury, was teaching a Y6 class of 33 children. The assignment involved the children in designing and making a model ship. The context for this was a humanities topic during which the class researched the activities of Christopher Columbus. They had used a variety of secondary sources to find out about his life and times and, in particular, about his ships and what life would have been like on board. During a whole-class discussion, Myra asked the children to think about the requirements of a ship used for exploration. She linked this with the children's discovery, from their research, that one of his ships had foundered on rocks. She then said to the class,

> I want you to put yourselves in the position of ship builders during that time. You're going to build a new ship for Columbus to replace the lost one. You're going to make a model of the ship to show him what it would be like.

This provided a purpose for the task and provided a justification for producing a static outcome that would not need to float! She invited them to work in friendship pairings and stressed that they should try and produce several ideas before deciding upon the one to develop further and make. The children had some experience of designing and making in previous classes but limited experience of working with wood. Myra intended to use this project to introduce the children to using wood and to develop their skills in joining wood. She showed them examples of how wood strips could be used to make structures and suggested that they should design a model ship using wood for the hull structure. She reminded them that their designs should include side, front and plan views (orthographic projections).

The children spent several sessions, during group activities over the next two weeks, working on their designs. They were asked to develop one design and produce a working drawing, showing measurements and details of construction. Each pair was also asked to list materials they would need. Figure 6.7 shows one of these working drawings produced by Michael for a ship that he and his partner (another Michael) decided to call *The Santa* (it was just before Christmas!).

When pairs had developed their designs and discussed them with Myra she prepared them for the making phase. This involved a demonstration of techniques for joining wood and a reminder of the safe use of tools involved, especially saws and the glue-gun. In this class the children are allowed to use the glue-gun under close adult supervision. In the classroom there is a large table for practical work and tools (on a board with shadow labelling) and materials are stored nearby. This was where, again during 'group time', children worked in pairs on making their models. They soon learnt to join wood strips successfully, although some early attempts were not very square and intervention from

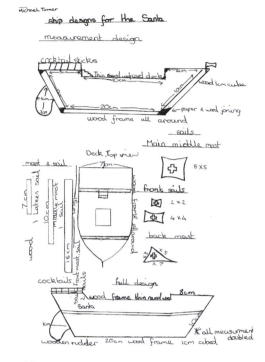

Figure 6.7 A design for a ship

Myra was necessary to draw their attention to the need for accurate measuring and positioning of wood on the card triangles. PVA glue was used to join wood and card but the glue-gun was used where card triangles were not convenient. A jig was available to allow accurate cutting. The jig was also used for the drilling of holes in the centre of wood strips which allowed dowel to be joined to these. The jigs were clamped on to hardboard cutting boards on the work table using G clamps. Myra encouraged the children to clad the wooden structures with coloured sugar paper, rather than painting. The constructions of the hulls went smoothly but several pairs were very dissatisfied with their attempts to use paper to make sails – 'It doesn't look right 'cos it doesn't hang properly.' Myra suggested they might try using fabric and this proved much more suitable although most children chose to staple the seams rather than sew them.

The final outcomes were impressive as Figure 6.8 illustrates. The children were generally very careful during their construction work. They were well-motivated and needed no teacher encouragement to stay on task. Myra was also pleased by the level of cooperation evident in the pairs. The project had provided a good introduction to a construction task using wood. It had led to increased confidence in most children although she did consider that the work had been less motivating for a few of the girls who had not responded as enthusiastically as the others. She wondered whether this was to do with the medium involved or the context of the work. As the next case study (Case Study 14) indicates, the latter seemed to be the most likely reason. The project had also

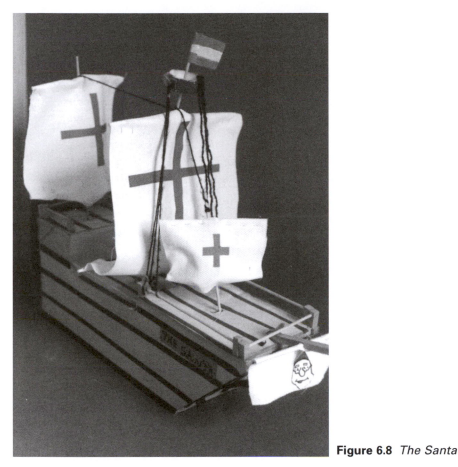

Figure 6.8 *The Santa*

provided a means of extending and enhancing children's learning in history. For example, the common features of fifteenth century ships, researched prior to the project, was more meaningful through the application of this particular historical knowledge in a practical design and make task. The experience of building those features into their outcomes is more likely to lead to this knowledge being retained, since they have strong visual images of those features in their models.

Although these were Y6 children, they had not met the technique for joining wood before and their learning curve was steep. It should be noted that since this case study was produced, Myra's history topic has changed and is now focused on the Tutors. She has adapted this design and technology assignment and now challenges the children to design and model a galleon to fight the Spanish. However, returning to the Y6 class featured above, later in the year, Myra provided an opportunity for them to develop their skills further and integrate their experience with other materials into their design and technology outcomes. Myra's topic on 'Moving toys' was planned before the QCA SoW (QCA/DfEE 1999) was available but fits well within the Unit 5C of that material.

Task: Make a moving toy suitable for a child

1. Make a collection of moving toys to explore and discuss.
2. Make a list of your requirements for a moving toy suitable for a child.
3. Pick a toy from the collection to study and describe.
   a) Draw the toy you have chosen in detail.
   b) Label the drawing carefully.
   c) Write a clear description of your toy – materials, colour, shape, etc.
   d) Describe how it works.
   e) What other special features does it have?
4. Does this toy meet your list of requirements for a moving toy suitable for a child? Explain how it does and does not meet the requirements.
5. Think about a moving toy you would like to make.
   What age child would you make it for?
   What features should your design have?
6. Record several sketches, design ideas, for your moving toy.
7. Pick one of your designs and give reasons for your choice.
8. Draw a series of detailed plans giving information on:
   a) Materials to be used.
   b) Size of model.
   c) Tools needed.
   d) The way materials will be joined.
   e) Mechanisms that will make your toy move.
   f) Colours.
9. Collect all the materials necessary and make your model.
   Make sure you work safely and accurately.
   As you are working review the decisions you have made.
   If you need to make changes record these and reasons for changes.
10. a) When you have completed your model, evaluate how well you have met your original list of requirements.
    b) Did you have any problems? Explain how you solved them.
    c) What knowledge will you use when making another model?

Figure 6.9 Task sheet for 'Moving toys' project

CASE STUDY

14: Moving toys

This project took place during the Spring term and was part of an integrated Energy topic. Myra produced a task sheet for the children (see Figure 6.9).

The task sheet was an attempt to provide a clear structure for the children's work. Myra intended to develop further the children's designing and making skills (particularly in the use of wood), to give them an opportunity to apply their recently gained scientific knowledge of mechanisms and simple electric circuits, to increase their awareness of the process of designing and making, and to encourage rigorous evaluation of their own and other people's outcomes. A strategy Myra used to reinforce the stages involved in the project was to ask the children to keep individual diaries of their work.

The following sections discuss specific children's work during this project. We begin with Kimberley, who was one of the girls who had not been as well motivated by the previous design and technology project (see Case Study 13). This new context generated much more enthusiasm.

Kimberley first decided a toy should be 'safe, colourful, enjoyable and interesting'. She explored in detail a round spinning top and evaluated it as meeting her criteria. When considering a toy she would like to make she produced initial sketches on 12 January of a car, a tortoise and a small horse (all using a small electric motor to make them move). Her diary indicates that working plans of her chosen option, the car, were produced on 17 January. Her entry for 24 January reads,

> I started to make the structure. By the end of the day I had done the base and I was going to put card on the bottom but I didn't because I wouldn't be able to get to the electrical equipment inside.

A disaster occurred on 7 February, 'My model got trodden on. I had repaired it by the end of the lesson, and done a bit extra.' She finished the structure on 14 February. Two weeks later she reports,

> I put in the mechanisms. To start with I wasn't sure how I would attach the motor. I decided where I was going to put it and then worked out how I would do it. In the end I stapled the two pieces of wood together. I didn't have any other problems with the mechanisms.

On 14 March, Kimberley faced another problem, 'I started to think about a switch which would make the car move forwards and backwards. In the end I got an idea from a book.' Her development of a switch had resulted from looking through techniques cards from the STEP material (STEP 1993). Kimberley's research was stimulated by another intervention from Myra when she realised Kimberley had a problem she would find it very hard to solve from her existing experience.

Kimberley had persevered for two months with her project and was extremely proud of her outcome (see Figure 6.10). Her motivation throughout was excellent and her final evaluation positive but self-critical. It included,

> The only problem a young child would have is with the wires. If I did it again I would have a container for the battery and switch and think about a different switch. I was successful in making my car. I managed to get it done in the time I had and managed to get it to work.

Myra was particularly pleased by Kimberley's work and felt that the purpose of the outcome, with a more direct human aspect, may have significantly affected her motivation. Kimberley was also more confident with wood this time, having had experience of it during the earlier project. The diary had proved successful in helping her monitor her own progress over a longer term project.

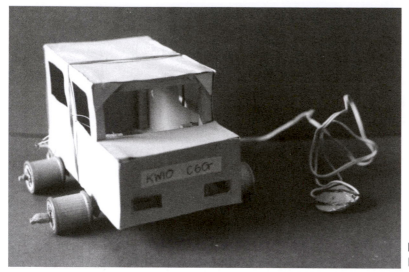

Figure 6.10
Kimberley's car

Matthew was another child whose competence and commitment to this project pleased Myra. Matthew was a child who lacked confidence in more 'academic work' (*sic*). On this occasion he was well-motivated and achieved a very successful outcome. He did some of his making at home which caused his mother to comment that, 'We never manage to get him out of the garage!' His outcome was a 'quad' bike into which he built one of his own *Lego* motors and battery boxes. He showed sound understanding of gears in a discussion with Myra during which he explained,

> When the gears are the same size it goes much too fast. I changed the gears to give a better speed. I needed a small gear on the motor and a big gear on the axle to drive the wheels.

This indicated sound application of work on gears done earlier in the term.

Jennifer worked with Isobel, making a toy lorry, and her evaluation was particularly thoughtful:

> I think overall we should have been a bit more organised. I think most of the problems and changes we had to make were due to lack of organisation and planning . . . At the beginning of the project I made a list of requirements for a toy. I think our model meets these requirements: It must look good – it has been covered in brightly coloured card; It must be safe – the transformer is set on a low voltage or it uses batteries; It must have special features – the fact that it is a TESCO lorry is a feature. We made sure no corners on our model stuck out so it doesn't poke or hurt anyone. We tried our hardest to make sure the motor didn't show much so no-one would put their hand in and fiddle with it which would either break it or they would hurt themselves. The only problem with the quality is the elastic band around the motor which keeps slipping which makes the wheels slip, which makes the model jolt when it moves sometimes. I think it could be improved by adding more mechanisms such as a bulb or a buzzer. It could be slightly bigger and made easier to turn on and off.

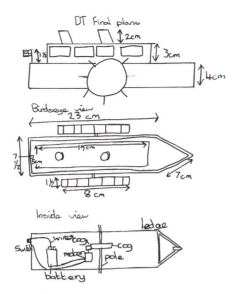

Figure 6.11 Philip's design for a boat

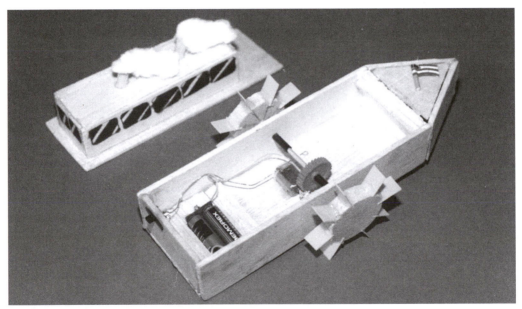

Figure 6.12 Philip's paddle-boat

Philip made a very effective working paddle-boat using balsa wood and plastic paddles. His model illustrates an example of an outcome which was closely matched to his final design (Figure 6.11). This model both looked good (Figure 6.12) and worked well. The battery was firmly secured in the base and a switch fixed into the stern was durable and reliable. It is evidence of how a child with considerable design and technology skills can be challenged to extend those skills.

This assignment provided the children with the opportunity to develop their design and technology competence and moved them on from static models (Case Study 13) to models with moving parts. It required the application of the scientific knowledge and understanding developed as part of the same topic. Summative evaluation played a more explicit part in this work compared to the previous project, and the diary was a practical and useful strategy to which the children responded positively. It facilitated their learning in terms of increasing their awareness of the process in which they were engaging. It also provided valuable assessment evidence for Myra that allowed her to make informed judgements about their understanding of this process, and other aspects of their capability. The children's experiences of wood and techniques for joining it, in the earlier work, were exploited in this project and the children showed increased confidence in working with it. They shared ideas, helped each other and worked in what she described as a 'super' atmosphere that was 'alive with activity'. Like so many teachers featured in this book Myra enjoys her design and technology work with children and shares their enthusiasm, although, as she is the first to admit, she is often learning alongside them.

4. Using other materials

There are other media and materials that children should have experience of using in the context of design and technology (Fulton 1992). These include clay, textiles, food and graphic media. Each requires children to develop particular skills and lends itself to particular types of project.

The next case study illustrates a creative project in which the teacher ended up using a material of which she had limited experience. *Mod Roc* was used by these children to make masks that they had designed.

CASE STUDY

15: Ancient Greek masks

Pippa Tiddy carried out the following work as a student on her initial teacher education course. During a school experience she worked with a Y4/5 class of 28 children, many of whom were on action plans because of their particular educational needs. The work was set in the context of a topic on the Ancient Greeks. Pippa has read the children a story about the Medusa and the children had been asked to perform it for a class assembly. The project concerns the production of masks for that assembly.

The children were posed with the challenge of producing the assembly and a discussion in the early stages of the work considered how the performers could be made to look like Greek gods. Face painting was one option considered. However, the idea of masks, once suggested by Louise, was soon agreed by the whole class. The children then asked questions such as, 'How can we make a mask?', 'Have we got time?', 'What materials can we use?' The latter led to suggestions of paper and cardboard and then one of the children suggested *Mod Roc* (plaster impregnated cloth which is quick drying and readily available from educational suppliers), which they had used the previous year. Pippa was a little daunted by the suggestion since she had very limited experience of using *Mod Roc*. However, she discovered it was available, considered the time available, the possible aesthetic impact of the masks and then decided to go along with the children's decision.

She planned a workshop to demonstrate the necessary skills and a technique to make the basic mask shape. Each child selected a character from the story, which incidentally was not illustrated, for whom to produce a mask. Designs were pictorial and annotated by choice.

One child with learning difficulties did not feel able to design a mask for a character from the story. Together Pippa and the child identified the need for a musician's mask that could be of the child's own personal design. He was very satisfied with his end result and decided to take on the musician's role in the assembly.

Pippa organised the class as teams since it had become evident to her, during the first few weeks of her school experience, that developing collaborative skills was an important aim for her design and technology work. Each team had to agree ground rules and had to have a spokesperson and a scribe. All members of the team had to have a job and decisions had to be discussed and agreed by all. Although the children were working on individual designs they were still able to discuss their designs and help and advise each other. In one group Pippa noted that the same character had been designed by several members of the group. Some had produced fairly simple designs while other designs were more complex. Those children who had produced the simpler designs were impressed by the more complex ones and modified their ideas, after group discussion. Pippa had her reservations about this, thinking it was better for them to stick with their own ideas. However, she was impressed by the patience they demonstrated in developing their skills to produce the more complicated outcomes and felt the outcomes demonstrated a higher standard of work and personal satisfaction than she had expected.

Pippa was pleased by the quality of their designing skills. For example, Darren had designed a mask for the storyteller and intended to use pipe-cleaners to make hair. He evaluated his design and decided it would be too difficult to attach the pipe-cleaners. His second design included sponge for hair that he decided would be easier to attach. However, he was not completely satisfied with his second design and after exploration found a way of attaching the pipe-cleaners, reverting to his first idea, but he decided he preferred the colour of the second and kept that in his final mask. This shows that the process of designing was constructive and creative; contributing to the quality of the eventual outcome.

Partners supported each other in making the masks and the more able practically shared their skills with those who needed help. All of the children achieved success and produced artefacts that were functional, aesthetic and met the original need.

This case study provides a good example of material being used in an appropriate way by the children. The choice of material was theirs and based upon their previous experiences rather than their teacher's experience. It also illustrates the importance of the social context of learning; although the children were working on individual outcomes their participation in group discussion significantly affected their work, and the resulting learning.

5. Using food as a medium for design and technology

Food as a context offers all sorts of opportunities. Elsewhere, I have produced support material outlining these in areas such as packaging, production and processing, storage, healthy eating, equipment, and kitchen design (Ritchie and Smith 1987b). However, food can also be a medium for design and technology work (QCA 1997c, d) and it is this that is an explicit requirement in the National Curriculum (DfEE/QCA 1999). This means more than providing children with opportunities to cook. Although children need to be taught and encouraged to practise skills and techniques related to cooking, the use of food in design and technology goes further. Children should be encouraged to design and make using food. This could be related to food for special occasions, parties, festivals, food for people with special diets or needs (vegetarian, low-fat, babies) or foods for particular purposes (such as camping, packed lunches, long journeys, picnics and mountain climbing). Children can use their knowledge and understanding of food and food preparation to meet challenges such as these. Work with food provides opportunities for teaching children about healthy eating and an understanding of basic nutrition (Health Education Authority 1996). This is an area that links to cultural understanding and citizenship (see Howe *et al.* 2001). Food has particular potential for increasing children's awareness of other cultures, places and times, as illustrated by the 'Roman feast' and 'Italian restaurant' (Case Study 6), featured in Chapter 3. Introducing children to food from other cultures in the context of work on festivals and celebrations is another approach.

The following brief example of food related design and technology comes from Anita Pryor, who taught at Moorlands Junior School in Bath. She was doing a topic on the Ancient Egyptians and asked the children to design and make biscuits that could be sold as souvenirs at shops near the pyramids. The children tried out various recipes for biscuits, evaluated and modified them by adding flavourings and other ingredients and designed shaped biscuits, decorated in appropriate ways. They also designed and made suitable packaging. Food became the medium for their design and technology as they engaged in generating ideas, exploring possibilities, designing, making and evaluating. They used a range of skills including weighing, mixing, cutting and shaping as well as building upon their existing knowledge and understanding, especially in the area of changes caused by cooking, hygiene and food packaging. Food activities can involve a unique range of skills and technical terms such as beating, stirring, whisking, blending, folding, mashing and rubbing in. They can also introduce children to a range of unfamiliar tools including cutters, graters, peelers, rolling pins, moulds, piping equipment and flour sifter (see DATA 1996a for a comprehensive list).

Using food raises particular issues related to organisation and health and safety. Many schools already have food activities rooms or areas used for cooking activities, often enlisting parental help for small group work. Such specialist areas are obviously desirable. However, the approach to food required by design and technology means that it is an activity which will require more teacher input. That is not to say that cookery lessons and the recipe following approach common in primary schools have no place. It is essential that children learn the skills needed to work with food, and such activities are a practical way of introducing and developing those skills (as focused practical tasks – FPTs). The use of food as a medium for design and technology will involve considerable work away from the food preparation area: evaluating existing products, market research, evaluating existing recipes, generating ideas, designing, evaluating. Therefore these projects will require a combination of access to specialist areas and classroom time. If specialist areas are not available, it is still possible to carry out activities in classrooms on suitably protected surfaces (using wipe-clean covers, plastic cutting boards and anti-bacterial sprays), as long as a separate water supply and sets of utensils not used for other purposes are available. The children should also be appropriately dressed and prepared, with wipe-clean plastic aprons, hair tied back and hands thoroughly washed. The National Curriculum PoS at Key Stages 1 and 2 includes a requirement that children should be taught specifically how to follow safe procedures for food safety and hygiene (DfEE/QCA 1999, p. 92). Hygiene and safety are vital and must be observed in terms of food purchases, storage, cooking and reheating, personal cleanliness, the work area, tools and equipment (see DATA 1996a, Section 5.7 for further guidance).

Fears about health and safety should not be a reason for not doing design and technology, but it is vital that teachers are aware of the need for children to be taught safe working practices, whatever medium they are using. Similarly, classroom helpers need to be fully informed about safety issues, as well as briefed about the nature of the activity and what teachers intend the children to gain from it (see DATA 1996b). In some schools, the parents working with children on food activities seem to see the result as a reflection upon their own cooking skills. In the context of design and technology-related activity it is essential to remind parents that the children should be doing, deciding and having ownership of the work.

Planning food activities for design and technology is supported by the QCA SoW (QCA/DfEE 1998) that includes units on: Eat more fruit and vegetables (1C); Sandwich snacks (3B); and Bread (5B). The latter provides particular opportunities for a strong multicultural emphasis – evaluating breads from other cultures.

6. Using textiles

Textiles have, like food, been used in primary classrooms in the past, but not usually as a medium for design and technology activity. Children have often been taught to sew, weave and work textiles in a variety of ways. The use of textiles in the context of design and technology requires a less prescriptive and techniques/skills dominated approach. Textiles can be used in projects related to costumes, puppets, soft toys, masks, furnishings, clothes and uniforms. Children need to be taught to mark, cut out and join textiles in a variety of ways, before they can make use of these techniques in solving problems. They should be introduced to a range of fixings and surface decorations (see NATHE 1998; Lawler and Stables, 1993). These can be introduced in response to need, or planned in a more systematic way as FPTs before children tackle open-ended design and make assignments. Textiles will often be used in outcomes in conjunction with other materials, such as curtains and furnishings in a model or full-size room. The library (Case Study 3) illustrated an example of this. Like food, textiles have considerable scope for introducing children to other cultural influences (ways of joining, types of fabrics used, colouring). Evaluating clothes, such as hats and uniforms, from other places and times, will help children understand the ways in which textiles can be used, and can contribute to their awareness of how people in other times and places have also been aware of and able to engage in design and technology. Textiles will require the use of some specialist tools, and ideally a sewing machine should be available as a central resource for sharing among classes. Textiles are less problematic than food to organise in the classroom and involve less health and safety issues (although the use of sharp and pointed tools, which are essential for cutting and sewing textiles, always requires care). Like food, textile work involves use of a unique set of tools, skills, language and knowledge and understanding (see DATA 1996a, Section 5.6 for further guidance). The QCA SoW units that provide support for teachers planning work with textiles include: Puppets (2B); Joseph's coat (2D); and Slippers (6B). Teachers' subject knowledge with regard to textiles is covered in the TTA needs assessment materials (TTA 1998a).

7. Conclusion

This chapter has featured children using a variety of materials, tools and techniques to make outcomes. The work has varied from the highly structured through to open-ended projects under children's control. It has provided examples of children being taught skills when they needed them and being introduced to new skills through FPTs. In considering the media children can work with it has been apparent that health and safety during the making phase is of considerable importance; teachers need to be conversant with school and LEA policy as well as able to access information from a variety of sources about potential risks and the means of minimising them. Each medium raises particular issues concerning classroom management and in each example teachers have found ways of organising the work to suit their own preferences. A mixture of whole-class, group and individual work is likely to be used in design and technology but group and/or individual work is usually the most practical and safest way of organising the making phase. Progression, through the use of any medium, is concerned with the medium itself, the tools and techniques used to work it, the nature of the context and task set by the teacher. In any situation, the intervention of teachers to move children forward, building upon their existing skills and knowledge and understanding, is the key to providing progressive learning experiences. Judgements made by teachers about these interventions require them to have knowledge and understanding of design and technology as a process, of the materials being used, of the contexts and tasks. It also involves professional knowledge and understanding of the nature of children's learning and strategies that can be used to facilitate that learning. This chapter, and the last, have attempted to contribute to that subject-specific and professional knowledge needed by teachers to supporting children's making.

CHAPTER 7

Evaluation

1. Introduction

Evaluation in design and technology requires children to make value judgements about the worth and quality of their own and other people's approaches and outcomes. In this chapter three aspects of children's evaluation are discussed:

1. the evaluation of other people's outcomes as a starting point for further design and technology work or to inform the design phase of a project;
2. the evaluation of their own outcomes and the processes that led to them;
3. the evaluation of work while a project is in progress.

The first of these has parallels with critical studies in art and these similarities are explored. In the classroom and beyond, evaluation of existing products in the made world (and sometimes evaluation/appreciation of the natural world) is an early stage in design and technology projects. It is a central argument of this chapter that evaluation is much more than something that happens at the end of the making stage. The need to evaluate outcomes produced as a result of design and technology activities is self-evident and examples proliferate in the earlier chapters. Sometimes teachers have structured this into the project, on other occasions the children have evaluated their work more informally. Children naturally evaluate their own work, but the results of such evaluations are not always expressed unless this is prompted by their teacher or their peers. In the best practice children's evaluation of their own outcomes involves reference back to the originally identified needs, agreed criteria for success and, perhaps, a 'design brief'. Evaluation is the process by which those who engage in design and technology decide whether their intentions, or their clients' requirements have been met; has the problem been solved? Clearly, for children, there is a risk to their self-esteem if self-evaluation or comments from others are too negative.

Less obvious, but nonetheless important in design and technology, is the need to evaluate the processes involved: was the approach adopted the most appropriate? This is not as common in primary classrooms, although the use of diaries in Case Study 14 (Moving toys) illustrated one strategy to support this type of evaluation. Formative evaluation, aimed at influencing decisions during a project, is similar to formative assessment in the classroom, and is just as necessary for making informed judgements about what to do next. Again, these evaluations are often informal, but teachers can support children in making them more systematic. This chapter also highlights the assessment opportunities that are linked to evaluation and the way in which the review phase of classroom work can be exploited for assessment purposes.

As well as playing an important part in design and technology, evaluation, of a different nature, is essential to teaching and professional development. Teachers are constantly evaluating their teaching and asking themselves whether their aims have been met by the approaches that they have adopted and the activities they have implemented. Evidence to inform teachers' evaluations comes from the assessment of individual children as well as from their own experiences of particular projects or activities. In most situations this evaluation will be formative in that it will inform decisions about the next phase of a teaching programme. Often such evaluative judgements remain implicit, although increasing collaboration among teachers has meant that these judgements are now more often made explicit and shared with colleagues.

Evaluation of a slightly different kind is used by teachers who choose to engage in classroom enquiries (see Chapter 9) as a means of professional development. These teachers will systematically evaluate the impact of new ways of working and reflecting upon the implications of this for their practice.

2. The nature of evaluating

What do you think of the chair you are sitting in at the moment? Does its form relate to its function? Is it a thing of beauty? Does it achieve its purpose? Such questions are the essence of evaluative judgements in design and technology. The food we eat, the clothes we wear, the environment in which we work, relax, shop and play are all subject to evaluative judgements that we make as part of our daily lives calling upon a complex collection of cognitive and manipulative skills. These judgements are informed, in part, by our personal value systems and beliefs. If children are to make evaluative judgements more effectively, if they are to become aware of what is beautiful and ugly in the world, of what works well and what does not, if they are to become more discerning connoisseurs and consumers of good design, they need to be progressively introduced to the component skills of evaluation. Older children may need to be made aware of issues such as ethical means of production and sustainable development, with links to their citizenship education (Howe *et al.* 2001). All children should have opportunities to practise and develop skills such as close observation, identifying strengths and weaknesses, justifying, prioritising, recognising conflict, testing ideas and communicating. Evaluation may involve investigation; perhaps identifying human factors in design, or thinking about the processes of production. Systematic and rigorous evaluation will be based upon the considered selection of criteria. When children are evaluating their own outcomes or those of others, their criteria should include factors such as the choice and use of materials, the aesthetics of the outcome, the values of the maker and users, quality and function.

To be capable of critical evaluation is an important life skill for children to acquire. We are also interested in teaching children to be designers and makers; the evaluation of other designers' work should help them in developing their own design capabilities. Through looking at products and services in the made world in a critical way, children will begin to form a notion of how to look for good design, how to articulate their own ideas about design, and how to engage in designing themselves. Children will develop an appropriate technical and aesthetic vocabulary along the way, not by chance, but driven by a progressive need to communicate their views and judgements. Children will, through developing a critical appreciation of others' work (their peers as well as adult designers) be better equipped to evaluate their own work and outcomes. The three strands of: children evaluating others' work; evaluating their own outcomes and methods; evaluating their work in progress, are not separate elements but are intertwined aspects of the complex design and technology process.

3. Links with art

The links between design and technology and the art curriculum have already been discussed, both in Chapter 2, where the focus was the contribution of art to children's knowledge and understanding, and in Chapter 4 in relation to designing. Evaluation is another area in which interesting parallels are evident. The National Curriculum for art and design (DfEE/QCA 1999b) establishes a framework in which art is seen as a cycle of evaluating and developing ideas – investigating and making – evaluating and developing work. Critical appreciation and evaluation play an important part in art; the link with design and technology is obvious. Whether children are responding to a painting, a sculpture, a piece of ceramics, furniture or a bicycle, some skills are similar – we are seeking to develop children's visual literacy (Howe 1999). From the study of a single artefact could derive an artistic or technological outcome. Evaluative skills developed in one area will be potentially transferable to the other. The differences are more in terms of the balance between aesthetic and functional considerations although the beauty and effectiveness of a solution should be common to both. That is not to say that the development of aesthetic appreciation and the development of technological understanding are the same; simply that there are important parallels.

Using a critical study approach as a starting point for children's work leads to a potential concern; will children simply copy what they see? Can evaluation of other people's work promote creativity and originality? Tickle (1990) expresses the concern: 'The problem faced by the teacher is how to stimulate and guide without imposing too many preconceptions and stereotypes, and without stifling the child's own creativity and logical thinking and making' (p. 112).

Children are already exposed to an increasing variety of products resulting from design activity. By encouraging them to look critically at these and evaluate a range of possible solutions to a particular need or challenge they will have the opportunity to combine possibilities in a new way. Adult designers usually do not operate in isolation. Designs often evolve from an evaluative process applied to existing solutions, stimulated by a perceived need or opportunity. It is a greater concern that children will not have an opportunity to study and evaluate existing designs. Denying children these opportunities is the surest way of promoting impoverished and stereotypical outcomes. Plagiarism is avoided by careful attention to the selection of a breadth of design alternatives. The framing of the design task, the identification of a novel need or opportunity, is important too. There is no value in asking children to generate a design when they have already been presented with a seemingly 'perfect solution'.

4. Evaluation of the made world

In Chapter 1, the discussion of design and technology began with a description of a major project involving the construction of a bridge; the design of that structure was based upon engineers' evaluations of existing bridges. Examples of classroom work, discussed in early chapters, have also involved the evaluation of existing artefacts as the stimulus for further work (for example, Greetings cards in Case Study 2 and Puppets in Case Study 8).

The following case study is based upon the work of Alan Howe who collaborated with the class teacher, Jo Thornton, at Batheaston Primary School. It was carried out with a group of Y4 children and illustrates a teacher's specific intention of developing children's evaluative skills.

CASE STUDY

16: Musical instruments

The class of Y4/5 children were working on a half-term topic on 'Sound and Music'. In previous activities they had already developed their knowledge and understanding of the nature of sound, and the structure and function of the ear. There was a display of musical instruments in the classroom which had stimulated the children's interest and curiosity. This collection was intended to orientate the children to the work that the teacher had planned. They had been invited to contribute to the collection and had added, among other things, an old violin and a set of pan pipes. Later in the term the teacher intended to ask the children to design and make instruments for a performance of their own compositions to an audience of other children and adults. They had had some previous experience of using a range of musical instruments (in fact they had all benefited from learning to play the violin for a year). They had regularly used the school's tuned and untuned percussion collection during music activities. The children had not, however, evaluated instruments from a technological perspective.

The work was planned within the framework illustrated in Figure 7.1. It began with a whole-class introduction during which they were told that they were going to design and make instruments and that evaluating the instruments in the classroom was intended to help them prepare for this task. Alan then focused his attention on a group of six children using a set of questions and a pupil record sheet to promote examination and evaluation of a few selected instruments. The record sheets, completed by individual children about a particular instrument, asked them to:

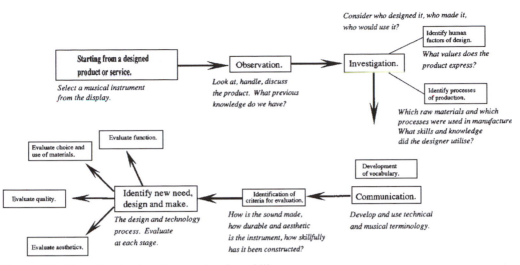

Figure 7.1 Planning to develop evaluation skills

– describe the sounds it makes and how that sound is made;
– list the raw materials used;
– identify the sequence by which the instrument might have been made;
– suggest what information the maker needed to know;
– make a prediction of who might have made it;
– make a prediction of who might use it and when it might be used;
– list their own likes and dislikes about the instrument.

The instruments he selected were intended to be relatively simple in terms of materials and processes used in their construction, ones that would stimulate realistic and attainable ideas from the children. The chosen instruments were:

– a 'slate drum'
– an improvised percussion instrument made from three pieces of slate suspended with string over an open wooden box;
– a thumb piano or 'sansa' of wood and metal construction;
– a shaker woven from plant material and containing seeds;
– a chekere (a rattle made from a hollow gourd encased in a net strung with hard seeds);
– an egg-shaped ceramic whistle;
– a plastic toy whistle in the shape of a bird.

As they worked on the record sheets, Alan instigated a wide-ranging discussion, probing their thinking and encouraging them to reason and speculate. The children completed the record sheets using words and pictures during and after the discussion session. Most children commented enthusiastically on the quality of the sound made, after several noisy minutes of exploration. In asking them 'to describe the sound made', further language development occurred – this time of musical terms, for example, long/short, hard/soft, loud/quiet, high/low. The children had little difficulty in identifying the raw materials used for each instrument although he needed to tell them about gourds and how they grow. They inspected the instruments carefully, identifying wood, metal, plastic, plant material and also the less obvious materials such as paint, varnish and glue. Throughout these initial observations appropriate vocabulary was used by the children, with unfamiliar words being introduced by the more articulate children. Identifying the sequence of production proved more problematic. Jess, for example, was investigating the plastic whistle; initially, he had no ideas as to how the plastic was made and he could not move on. Alan asked him, instead, to consider how the idea or design for the whistle was arrived at. This proved easier, 'someone thought it up, they did a drawing and then made the whistle'. Alan asked, 'Where do you think it was made?' – 'probably in a factory'. 'Did they make any more than this one?' – 'yes . . . probably made loads of them to sell'. The discussion continued with Jess showing that he understood that the designer was probably not the maker, that the whistle was mass produced and probably made on a production line by a machine. Alan explained to the whole group how the plastic was moulded as he discovered most of them thought it had been moulded and fired like clay – a process with which they were familiar.

The sequence of construction for the slate drum seemed straightforward to Amy. Her drawings clearly indicated a sequence of: constructing a wooden box; adding metal eyes as hooks around the top of this box; attaching three pieces of slate using string; decorating the outside of the box. Emily took a more fundamental approach to the gourd shaker, focusing upon the origins of the raw materials, describing how the gourd and seeds were grown, rather than the making process. The processes involved in the production of the string, used in this rattle, were not outlined in such detail; the instrument maker, having grown her own gourd and seeds, was illustrated popping down to the local 'string shop' for her supply. Ellie was able to relate her recent experience of weaving on a loom in an art activity to her deductions about a shaker which was constructed rather like a basket. 'They cut the plant into strips and they weave the plant strips into a shape.'

'What the instrument maker needed to know . . .' needed further amplification and questioning on Alan's part in order to elicit their existing ideas. Some children focused upon the designer, 'he (sic) needed good ideas', 'you need a plan of how to make the instrument'; others focused on the maker, 'needs good skills', 'need a kiln and drill'. Jay studied the ceramic whistle and the plastic whistle and made comparisons. 'They would have to know that you have to put a thin slit where you blow in and a slit on the top where the sound comes out.' Amy identified that the maker of the slate drum knew that 'Different size slates make different notes – the smaller one is the highest, the biggest, the lowest and the middle size makes an in between the highest and lowest note'. This could prove to be a valuable observation in the context of making a similar instrument.

All the children could express some opinion about the instrument they were observing and could express a simple reason for their preferences. This is the stage when the children's critical appreciation skills developed in art were applied. They had, in the past, been encouraged to articulate the reasons for their particular preferences when looking at works of art and were well practised in making these kinds of statements. Similar skills were also used when their teacher asked them to critically review books that they had read. Zoe said of the thumb piano, 'I like the shape of it...it feels nice and it fits into my hand...it is small to take around with you'. This offers Zoe two criteria to work towards when designing her own instrument – portability and aesthetically pleasing form. Jay's opinion of the ceramic whistle was, 'I like it because you can make different sounds with a little thing.'

In the children's drawings of those who they thought had made the instruments, it gave them an opportunity to think about the gender and ethnic origin of the maker. They were well aware that some of the instruments were from cultural groups other than their own. Emily drew an Asian woman with a 'Bindi' mark on her forehead, wearing a sari. It also gave them the opportunity to think about whether the maker and user were one and the same. Generally, there was a realisation that a complex instrument is less likely to have been made and played by the same individual. Many children, in fact, drew themselves as the user, as indeed they were!

Finally, the question of 'When would the instrument be used?' provided interesting responses which highlighted some gaps in the children's own experiences of how music is made and used in other cultures. Often general statements were made, such as 'to dance and sing to' or 'in a band', but they were unable to suggest more specific examples, even when prompted. This provided a reminder to the teacher that the children needed illustrations of music being performed on a range of occasions such as festivals, celebrations and weddings. This lack of experience is likely to be relevant to their design and make project: clarifying the need for and purpose of their own instruments and musical compositions would be enriched by a broader understanding of the potential uses of instruments. This could, of course, lead on to a whole new area of musical activity; critical evaluation of music used on different occasions.

This work began with an evaluation of finished products, although the children had already been informed that they were going to design and make their own outcomes. It involved the children in observing carefully prior to simple investigative work. These investigations were intended to focus their attention on particular aspects of the instruments and inform their evaluative judgements. The teacher's role was to offer an appropriate range of instruments that would give the children the experiences that would be relevant to them as instrument makers, to develop their own ideas through careful questioning and to provide them with essential information.

The activity led to the children establishing criteria that could be used for evaluating their own instruments. Key to these criteria were ideas about 'choice and use of materials', 'the form of the instruments' and 'quality' in terms of fitness for purpose, quality of construction and aesthetics. The quality of construction was difficult for the children to judge in terms of the more professionally manufactured instruments, but in discussion the children came to realise that this would be determined by the appropriateness of their designs, the care with which they constructed their instruments and whether the instruments produced the intended sounds.

This case study also reinforces the importance of children evaluating the outcomes of design and technology from other times, places and cultures. Musical instruments have considerable potential for this (see Kane 1990, for a case study of Key Stage 1 children tackling a similar project). There is a QCA SoW (QCA/DfEE 1998) unit on Musical instruments (5A) which covers similar experiences for children and provides ways of extending the work.

Alan used a series of questions to encourage evaluation as have others featured in earlier case studies. A general framework for such activities might be:

Function	What is it? What does it do? What need or want does it fulfil? How does it work?
Process	How was the design developed? How was it made? What was used to make it? Where were the resources obtained? How long will it last? What will determine its life span? What impact will it have on the environment during manufacture/use/disposal?
Human factors	Who designed/made it? For whom was it designed? Who might have been consulted about the design? Who would use it? How does the design consider the intended user? Does the design discriminate between people?
Aesthetics	Why do you like/dislike it? Why do you consider it beautiful/ugly? How strongly do you feel about it? Would you like to own/use it? If so, what would it say to other people about you?
Future developments	What further information/investigations would enhance the evaluations? How might the product be improved? Can you identify new needs or opportunities based upon this evaluation?
Future evaluation	Can you develop evaluation criteria for your own outcomes based upon this evaluation?

Specific techniques that children can be taught to support their evaluation of products include: choosing; ranking; rating; classifying; testing; fair testing; market research; user feedback; trial and error (Stein and Poole 1997). Garvey and Quinlan (1997) provide evidence (using examples of food activities) of the benefits of children evaluating products made or produced by others as a means of increasing their confidence to evaluating their own outcomes and accepting the critical feedback of others on their work, without it adversely affecting their confidence and self-esteem. They advocate regular, simple and brief whole-class and group teaching sessions that focus on product evaluation. Additionally, attention needs to be given to the issue of progression and continuity in this aspect of learning in design and technology. Younger children, in Key Stage 1, need to be systematically introduced to the skills and techniques to lay the foundations for later 'full' and self-initiated evaluations of their own and others' products.

5. Evaluation during design and technology projects

Evaluation is something children, and adult designers and technologists, engage in throughout projects. Quite often it happens naturally, for example, Abigail (Case Study 1) was concerned about the appearance of her model house; Emma (Case Study 8) reflected overnight on her puppet and came up with changes. However, children often need to be encouraged to look critically at their work and outcomes at each stage. When generating ideas, have they thought about other possibilities? When developing ideas, have they made judgements about the most suitable idea to develop using appropriate criteria? When designing, have they used the most appropriate means of modelling and communicating their ideas? When planning, are they making the best use of human and material resources? When making, have they worked as accurately as necessary? These questions can be addressed by individuals or groups, where collaborative work is involved. Children will need reminders to keep evaluation in mind. This can be achieved through the use of checklists, pro formas, posters around the classroom or the appointment of a designated 'evaluator' within a group. The judgements made during projects should be for a purpose, that is, to improve the work by informing future decisions. The children should be made aware of this formative purpose and not see such judgements, and the discussions leading to them, as a chore that keeps them from the important job of doing or making.

Systematic evaluation during projects can be encouraged through the use of diaries or workbooks in which regular entries are made as work is in progress. Such records can also aid later summative evaluations of the process aspects of projects. An example of this approach to evaluation was evident in Case Study 14. Myra Ginns had asked each child to keep a diary of their work during the 'Moving toys' project. The entries made in these diaries, as the evidence from Kimberley's showed, included regular evaluative comments concerning her successes and disappointments. Diaries or journals provide a means by which learners can record their experiences at the time they take place. They are the medium for supporting reflective thinking, which will potentially lead to more effective work in future. Any design and technology project can be seen as a journey that cannot be mapped with any accuracy at the outset. The diary becomes a way of mapping the landscape covered during the project. Reflection on the route taken is valuable both during the journey and on reaching the destination. On the way, reflection reduces the risk of unnecessarily revisiting places and taking lengthy detours! Reflection at the end should aid future journeys. Diaries do not have to be in a written form: verbal, audio, video, graphic, photographic and computer-based are all possible alternatives. Rogers and Clare (1994) discuss a research project that looked at the use of diaries with Key Stage 2 and 3 children. Overall, the diaries were evaluated as successful in improving the children's learning in design and technology. They found that the younger pupils preferred semi-formal sheets to complete rather than blank sheets of paper. The habit of keeping diaries will grow on children and although the initial stages may require considerable teacher support, this will become less as the diaries become an accepted and natural part of design and technology activities, much as a writing journal has done in some classrooms, where teachers value children's writing and the processes involved. Again, there are issues of progression and continuity to be addressed by the whole staff of schools (see Chapter 8).

Teachers have also found keeping their own diaries or journals a useful means of recording the progress of classroom-based action enquiries. Indeed, throughout the writing of this book, I have maintained a journal to record my developing ideas, plans, field notes during classroom episodes and analysis. This provides a tool for thinking and writing. It has helped me to recognise the process in which I have engaged and to learn from my mistakes. The use of diaries during classroom research activities is thoroughly discussed by Altrichter *et al.* (1993) who describe it as 'the companion to the research process' (p. 10).

6. Evaluation of children's own outcomes

This is the most common form of evaluation found in primary classrooms. Summative evaluation of an outcome is widely recognised by teachers as an important aspect of the work. Indeed the original National Curriculum orders (DES/WO 1990) included evaluation as a separate and final attainment target. Although the Non-statutory Guidance stressed evaluation is not simply something that happens after the children have made something, the separate attainment target rather reinforced this view. The current orders (DfEE/QCA 1999) have a section of the PoSs at each key stage entitled 'evaluating processes and products' (p. 92).

Evaluation at the end of a project should address both the outcome itself and the processes used to produce it. The first strand is the most obvious and one that children will do naturally, but not necessarily systematically. Their natural response to an outcome is likely to be of the 'I like it/don't like it' variety. A more considered view is needed and this will be encouraged if the children are taught evaluation skills. A systematic evaluation of an outcome will be structured: it will involve the use of specified criteria; it will involve individual and group judgements. It may involve systematic testing using investigative skills and fair testing as illustrated in the project on air-raid shelters (Case Study 5). Constable (1994b) reports on a research project which looked at children's design and technology work in several primary schools. She found that when Key Stage 2 children were evaluating their own work they were quite willing to talk about problems they experienced and ways they had modified their designs as they went along. Younger children seemed far more happy with their work and could not recall as many problems along the way. These younger children did not readily establish their own criteria for evaluating work without support from their teachers. The older children were more critical of their own outcomes, expecting more realism. Younger children were happier evaluating their own work as opposed to that of their peers. This finding is supported by evidence in Case Study 1 when Andrew stated, 'I want to tell everyone about mine but I don't really want to listen (to others telling about theirs)!' Encouraging children to evaluate their peers' outcomes needs to be handled sensitively by teachers. It is, however, an important part of evaluation. Garvey and Quinlan (1997) caution about the negative effects that evaluation or exposing children's work to 'the perceived cold, hard light of public scrutiny' (p. 38) can have on children with low self-esteem. They offer a variety of strategies to ensuring children's self-esteem does not suffer, including the use of 'critical friends' within a group context. My own approach has always been to start peer evaluation with at least two or three positive comments about what the evaluator likes or is impressed by. Then, and in the context of those positive comments, I invite them to offer each other constructive criticism. Comments like 'I don't like' must always be followed by 'because...' and suggestions for ways of improving or overcoming identified weaknesses. I also encourage positive and critical comments on the way the outcome was produced, for example a peer evaluator might have been impressed by how tidy the maker kept the work area. Constable (1994b) found children of all ages to be fair and constructive in their opinions of others' work. She did, however, find less able (*sic*) children had some difficulty in considering what they would have done in another person's position (p. 11). The peer evaluator is taking on the role of critical friend, which is not always easy in the social context of the classroom where various power relationships exist between children and adults and between the children themselves. Fostering an atmosphere in which children value and are prepared to listen to the opinion of their peers will improve the children's social skills and attitudes. It is likely to have spin-offs in other areas of the curriculum. Indeed, such evaluation may well already be used in classrooms, in activities such as writing during which peers offer each other comments on draft material.

Evaluation of children's outcomes can be a self-evaluation, evaluation by the teacher, evaluation by a peer, evaluation by a small group, evaluation by the class, or evaluation by other adults. In each of these it can be informal or formal. Obviously, if an outcome was the result of a collaborative activity the group involved are likely to evaluate it collaboratively, although individuals should be expected to evaluate their individual contributions. The various orders of evaluation listed above offer different degrees of 'threat' to the maker. An informal conversation with the teacher is far less threatening than the whole class being invited to comment upon an individual's work. Outsiders may be involved where they have particular expertise or interests (such as a disabled person commenting on children's ideas for making lifting devices).

In many classrooms, plenary sessions or review times are built into the classroom organisation. The literacy and numeracy strategies have made these a common feature of lesson structure. Before these were introduced into schools, the High/Scope approach (Hohmann *et al.* 1979) was common in some areas of the country, especially at Key Stage 1. It is based upon a sequence of plan/do/review and each day is structured to allow children to review with the rest of their class what they have done. The use of such plenary/review sessions can have considerable potential for design and technology learning: it can provide a forum for formal evaluation of children's outcomes; it can encourage individuals to reflect on the processes that they have used and their successes and failures; it can help them to clarify the learning that has resulted – How have their ideas changed? What new skills have they learnt? Plenary/review sessions can be valuable with children of all ages and do not need to be organised as whole-class activities.

7. Evaluation of processes

To reinforce the notion that design and technology involves engaging in processes it is desirable for children to be encouraged to evaluate their way of working, as well as the outcomes they produce. They will not find this easy without practice and support. One way of offering this support is to make explicit to the children, at the time of particular activities, what they are doing, for example, by using terms such as 'designing', 'planning' or 'identifying needs' when setting up an activity or reviewing work with them. Evaluations of children's way of working might address:

- How was the need identified and by whom?
- How were ideas for meeting the need generated?
- How was the decision about which idea to develop taken and by whom?
- Was the necessary information gathered?
- How were designs and plans produced?
- Was the use of materials, tools and techniques appropriate?
- Were health and safety considerations addressed?
- How well did the group work together (during collaborative projects)?
- Were evaluative judgements made at each stage of the work?
- Was the best use made of time and human resources?

The use of diaries (discussed above) and other ways of recording decisions during projects can play an important part in helping children evaluate the process in which they engaged.

8. Self-assessment

The importance of evaluation to design and technology means that work in this area of the curriculum has particular scope for fostering children's self-assessments. Many of the decisions that an individual makes during evaluation of design and technology work are, in effect, self-assessments; judgements about performance, capability, increased knowledge and understanding, evidence of positive attitudes and personal qualities. Self-assessment can play a significant part in learning (Ritchie 1991, pp. 88–108). A teacher who holds a constructivist view of learning recognises the extent to which learners should be encouraged to reflect upon their learning and clarify changes in their understanding and capabilities; self-assessment encourages this. In terms of attitudes and personal qualities, which are so context bound, self-assessment can be particularly important and provide valuable evidence for a teacher to use for planning future learning activities.

Other benefits of encouraging self-assessment are:

- it can help a teacher evaluate whether tasks are well-matched to children's levels;
- it can help motivate children;
- it can improve the relationships between children and their teacher;
- it gives learners responsibility for their learning;
- it can add to the validity of a teacher's assessment;
- it helps children identify progress by comparing past and present achievements;
- it encourages competition with self rather than others.

A key issue in self-assessment concerns the criteria used to make judgements. Teachers who have attempted to develop children's self-assessment skills have often been surprised by the nature of these assessments (Ollerenshaw and Ritchie 1997, p. 141). Children often assess their own work against criteria, such as neatness of presentation or correct spelling, which they perceive to be their teachers' most important criteria, when in fact the teachers' criteria are very different. This is, of course, less likely if teachers and children negotiate criteria for success or targets and make these explicit. In some situations, children may have difficulty in articulating their successes if they do not have the appropriate vocabulary. If a teacher's feedback to children rarely goes beyond simply, 'good work' or 'well done', the children will not have the language to describe their own achievements.

Self-assessment, like other aspects of effective learning, is dependent upon the ethos of the classroom. A classroom atmosphere where children are encouraged to share existing ideas in an unthreatening environment, where they know their opinions and suggestions will be valued and not ridiculed, where mistakes are seen as learning situations, is one which will encourage them to reflect honestly and critically upon their work.

9. Evaluation of teaching

Before ending this chapter, it is appropriate to focus on a different aspect of evaluation – that in which teachers reflect systematically on their own teaching and its impact on children's learning. When teachers evaluate their teaching of design and technology the characteristics identified by OFSTED and listed in Chapter 1 (Section 6) provide a useful framework . Additionally, the following questions might be addressed:

- What did the children learn as a result of the activity/project?
- Was the context appropriate and motivating?
- Was the planning adequate and were learning objectives appropriate?
- Did the children have an opportunity to identify their own needs (where appropriate)?
- Did the children respond enthusiastically to the challenge involved?
- Were adequate and appropriate resources available?
- Did the children have sufficient time to work on the activity/project?
- Were the teacher interventions effective in moving children forward and increasing the learning opportunities available?
- Was appropriate attention given to all aspects of learning (skills, processes, knowledge and understanding, attitudes and values)?
- Were the children encouraged to evaluate throughout the project?

The case studies throughout this book include evidence of teachers critically evaluating their teaching in order to learn from the experience. Evaluation is the means by which teachers identify concerns about their teaching which may become the focus for action enquiries. It is through evaluation that teachers can make judgements about the extent to which their teaching reflects their educational values in action, a theme explored in more detail in Chapter 9.

10. Conclusion

The key themes of this chapter have been:

- the importance of evaluation as something which goes on throughout design and technology projects;
- the value of children evaluating existing outcomes, especially from other times and cultures, to support their own design and technology capability and awareness;
- the need for children to be encouraged to evaluate their own outcomes systematically and critically;
- the significance of children evaluating their way of working as well as the product of their endeavours;
- teachers' own evaluations as an essential and integral part of teaching and classroom enquiries.

Evaluation can take many forms, from an informal chat between teacher and child, a 'show and tell' session through to completion of a detailed questionnaire or thorough testing based upon specific criteria. Whatever the structure, it will involve children and adults making informed and considered judgements based upon the available evidence. These judgements will never be absolutely objective and we should recognise that they will be based upon values that are both cultural and personal. The teacher's task is to encourage children to be aware of the influences upon the judgements they make, helping them to use evaluation as a means of improving the quality of their outcomes and, crucially, the quality of their learning.

CHAPTER 8
Planning for learning

1. Introduction

Teaching, like design and technology, requires forward thinking and planning. This chapter will consider long-term, medium-term and short-term planning. All teachers have to plan for the day to day work of their classes. This planning should take into account the needs of individuals and the needs of the class as a whole. Most primary teachers work with the same group of children over a one -year period. Therefore, planning must involve decisions about how to ensure continuity of experience for those children throughout their time with a particular teacher. This involves issues related to continuity of approach and content, providing breadth and balance within the curriculum, making links between learning experiences for children and avoiding unnecessary overlap. The National Curriculum demands that specified PoSs are covered during each key stage. This requires long-term planning which inevitably leads to whole-school decisions related to the school's policy and scheme of work. Long- and medium-term planning have been made considerably easier in the last couple of years as a result of the publication of a national SoW and related units by the QCA/DfEE (1998). This can be adopted by schools in its entirety or adapted to a school's use – perhaps to supplement an existing scheme of work. It should not, however, be adopted uncritically. Each school will need to decide whether particular units are appropriate in the light of children's experience, resources and teacher expertise.

2. Long-term planning in the context of a school's design and technology policy

Most schools have a policies for specific subjects, which in some schools are linked to a generic teaching and learning policy (see Bell and Ritchie 2000). The design and technology policy for a school should inform the approach taken to long-term planning. The long-term plans of a school should show how that policy is being implemeted.

The QCA/DfEE (1998) advocate that long-term planning for design and technology should be undertaken in the context of the school's overall curriculum plan, which reflects the needs of all children. If we use the analogy of maps, the overall curriculum plan can be considered as a map, perhaps of a country, which shows little detail. This plan will indicate how the whole curriculum will be taught and statutory requirements covered in all subjects. The long-term design and technology plans (often in tabular form, showing what will be covered each term and in each year) can be compared to the map of a county or region – showing part of the overall curriculum map in outline, but still lacking much detail (see Figure 8.1). To produce such a map for design and technology, requires all staff to agree on how parts of the design and technology PoSs will be linked to make coherent, manageable teaching units. The long-term plan shows how these teaching units are distributed across the years of both key stages (in a primary school) in a sequence that promotes curriculum continuity and progression in children's learning. Such a map should provide evidence that *all* of the design and technology programmes PoSs are being covered at some stage during a child's school career. Units may be linked with work in other subjects. It will also indicate the school's approach to the curriculum, showing which aspects are taught as a discrete subject and which will be integrated, perhaps in a topic approach involving a limited number or all subjects. The National Curriculum requires schools to cover curricular themes such as citizenship and this has implications for planning at a whole-school level.

It should be noted that the National Curriculum provides a minimum entitlement for children in all subjects, including design and technology. There is no reason why additional design and technology activities should not be included in a scheme of work. For example, disassembly activities are no longer explicit in the programmes of study, but can be a valuable experience for children. An annual school event, perhaps focused on the creation of 'environments' could be another addition (see Case Study 19), as could activities with a specific citizenship dimension (Howe *et al.* 2001). . As already noted, the QCA/DfEE SoW (1998) offers considerable support for schools by providing an indicative outline plan, showing how design and technology can be taught throughout the school. A case study later in this chapter will illustrate one's school's approach to introducing it. Local evidence would suggest that the majority of schools are now using this QCA framework in some form. The materials are, however, optional and provided as a exemplar of what a design and technology SoW might look like. It is intended to show how design and technology might be taught to groups of children attaining at levels broadly appropriate for their age. It illustrates:

- how a school's work in design and technology can be divided into units to be taught in different years;
- how units can be sequenced across a key stage;
- how investigative and evaluative activities (IEAs), focused practical tasks (FPTs) and design and make assignments (DMAs) are interlinked in a design and technology unit of work;
- ways in which units can build on work that has gone on before and how they link to other units;
- ways in which units can link with and support English, mathematics, information and communications technology (ICT) and other areas of the curriculum.

(based on QCA/DfEE 1998, p. 3)

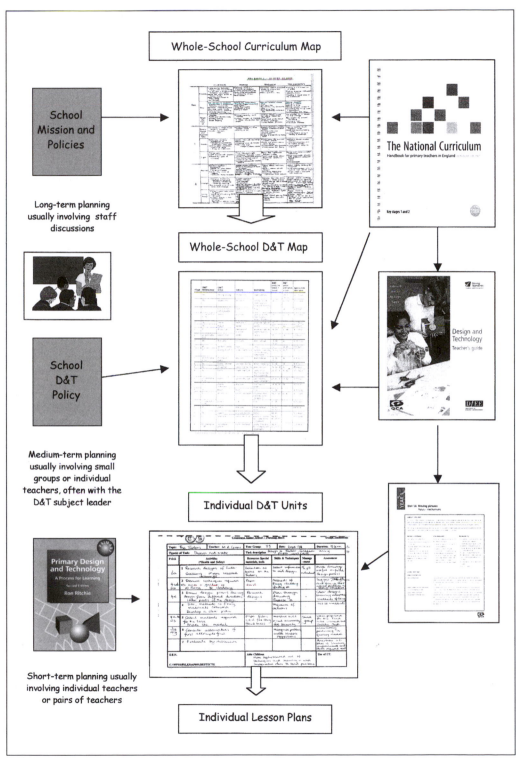

Figure 8.1 Planning for design and technology

At the early stages of developing capability, children should be able to:	As children make progress, they should:	As children make further progress, they should:
• generate and develop ideas through talking about what their design has to do, handling materials and, where appropriate, drawing; • increasingly take account of people's needs and wants; • reflect more on their ideas; • draw what they have made; • recognise and begin to select suitable tools and materials; • apply their previous knowledge and experience; • suggest achievable ways forward and begin to suggest improvements to their own models.	• become more involved in finding out information useful to their designing and use their experience of products and applications as the stimulus for ideas; • use 2D and 3D models to try out and develop ideas as they become more reflective about their designs; • suggest an increasing number of achievable ways forward and develop simple plans which take into account the resources available; • start combining and shaping materials to create products which meet their intentions; • use tools safely and with increasing accuracy.	• use a variety of information sources for their research, and set criteria for their designs, which increasingly take account of the views and preferences of the intended user; • become more familiar with techniques, e.g. brainstorming and product analysis to generate ideas, and have a clearer sense of priorities in their design proposals; • use a range of modelling techniques and be able to justify the decisions they make; • plan and evaluate in a more considered manner, and show a greater awareness of constraints and the implications of their designs; • draw upon a greater range of techniques and skills to create quality products for identified purposes; • become increasingly competent at matching how they work to the materials and the task.

Figure 8.2 Progression in design and technology (based on QCA/DfEE SoW 1998, Appendix 1, p. 21)

It has already be emphasised that a SoW should ensure continuity and progression and the Teacher's Guide to the QCA SoW provides the following three stage model to help teachers understand children's progression as they work through the units or plan their own adaptations of the SoW (see Figure 8.2).

Producing the whole-school plan, or map, for design and technology is the stage at which decisions have to be taken about how much time to allocate to the subject and how to fit it into the crowded timetable. QCA guidance in terms of for time allocation currently suggests that design and technology should receive a minimum of four per cent of the time available in each key stage (about 30 hours per year in Key Stage 1 and 34 hours in Key Stage 2). This suggests one unit of work each term lasting approximately 10 hours each term or several shorter units. Combining design and technology work with other subjects or allocating some of the discretionary time available within the school year to design and technology provide ways of increasing that available. Chapter 3 provided examples of making these links and finding ways of 'fitting it in'. Davies, D. *et al.* (2000) discuss these and other strategies, as well as the role initial teacher training students can have on increasing the amount of design and technology going on in schools. Some teachers increase the time available for design and technology by organising a group to work on design and technology while the rest of the class are focused on another subject area. The emphasis on literacy and numeracy every morning, in many schools, limits the times when design and technology can be taught, unless, of course, creative ways are found to link it with literacy and mathematics work. It has increasingly become a subject taught in the afternoon or at periods of the year when more flexibility is available, for example after SATs (Standard Attainment Tests) or in the run up to Christmas or Easter. This is not wholly desirable but the reality of schools currently.

The following case study focuses on the way in which one subject leader for design and technology set about introducing her colleagues to the use of the QCA SoW. It indicates the difficulties that loss of 'ownership' of planning decisions by individual teachers can cause. Despite the subject leader's endeavours to highlight the benefits of the national SoW she met reluctance among some colleagues to change.

CASE STUDY

17: Introducing the QCA Scheme of Work

Dilys Collins is the design and technology subject leader at Barley Close Primary School in South Gloucestershire. During 1999, her first year in post as subject leader, Dilys agreed with her head teacher that the current school scheme of work needed review with a view to making use of the QCA SoW in adapted form from September 2000. They considered that this would help them address concerns they had about whether design and technology was being taught in a way that fully covered the National Curriculum requirements. They felt the QCA SoW would be a good framework to adopt, but were worried that if only some units were used it would be difficult to ensure continuity and progression. The SoW was also a potential threat to the school's preferred way of using a topic approach for foundation subjects.

The head teacher provided Dilys with some non-contact time. She drew up an action plan showing how she would approach the task and use the non-contact time. This involved four stages, outlined below.

The first stage was an audit of all design and technology teaching planned and implemented during the 'current' academic year. She collected annual and termly plans and analysed these against the school's existing design and technology SoW. She found a good range of design and technology being taught, and in some classes the amount of design and technology exceeded that required by the school SoW. However, other significant issues emerged. In some cases the content included in annual plans was not addressed in termly plans and continuity was not ensured. There was limited evidence of appropriate planning for focused practical tasks (FPTs). The identification of specific skills to be taught were another gap in the planning. She was also concerned by the lack of ICT being used in design and technology. All of these issues could, she felt, be addressed through use of the QCA SoW.

The next stage for Dilys was to compare the existing school scheme of work with the national National Curriculum requirements to see where the gaps were, allowing her to highlight weakness for colleagues, and to inform how the QCA one could be adapted. She identified areas of the PoS which were not well covered in both Key Stage 1 and Key Stage 2. She was now convinced that children were not being provided with their full entitlement to a broad and balanced design and technology curriculum. She was reassured that many of the school's units of work were similar to those in the QCA SoW, although the latter provided more emphasis on FPTs. She felt that colleagues would be able to adopt these relatively easily, although including more ICT might prove more difficult. Dilys then selected QCA units which she decided should be used in the school. She choose those that were most like the existing units in terms of content and those that tied in well with their existing topic approach to teaching. At this stage she reported back to the head teacher about the results of her audit and her decisions with regard to QCA units. He was supportive of her approach.

Stage 3 involved a staff meeting to share her ideas and the draft SoW, including QCA units, with the whole staff. Unfortunately, the head teacher was unable to attend and this made it quite a difficult meeting for Dilys to manage. She shared her findings with colleagues, who accepted them, and she offered a rationale for the changes proposed. The QCA framework and units were introduced and then discussed in key stage groups. This led to some amendments to her proposals as several colleagues were keen to retain some existing units which she had intended to replace with QCA ones. She felt that colleagues' responses to the QCA units were varied – most were enthusiastic, but she felt there was some reluctance to change apparent in a few staff. The meeting left her with more work to do and feeling a little despondent – the adoption of the QCA units was not going to be as extensive as she had hoped.

The fourth stage of her action plan involved rewriting the SoW, including the changes proposed at the meeting. Although she felt the revisions were generally acceptable, she remained concerned about some 'gaps' – for example, no food activities were planned for years 5 and 6.

The school's SoW was ready to be used in the following Autumn term. Ironically, the school underwent significant staff changes before the new SoW could be implemented. A new head teacher and several new teachers were appointed. Dilys shared her actions and ongoing concerns with the new head. She took the decision that the QCA SoW should be more fully implemented than proposed after the previous staff meeting. This led to a new action plan for Dilys, focused on ensuring resources for the QCA units were available, supporting colleagues in short-term planning of the units and identifying explicitly the skill progression involved in those units. Her confidence and enthusiasm was boosted by the support of the new head, but she was left a little disappointed that all the work carried out the previous year had not ended up with the staff commitment that she had sought for adopting QCA units. She had learnt quite a lot about challenges posed by the management of change and felt that the work the previous year had certainly helped prepare her and her colleagues for implementing the QCA SoW.

Much has been written about the leadership and management of change (Bell and Ritchie 1999) and Hopkins *et al.* (1994) reminds us, 'if reform initiatives are to succeed, they need to be reinvented in local settings'. This was what Dilys set out to do and although not wholly successful at first, the school has subsequently made good use of the QCA units and is now confidently adapting some of them to suit their particular needs of the children and the strengths and enthusiasms of individual teachers. Guidance on adapting the QCA SoW to a particular school's needs is provided in the Teacher's Guide (QCA/DfEE 1998). Additional information on devising and reviewing SoW can be found in DATA's useful publication, *Planning into Practice* (1997).

3. Medium-term planning

A medium-term plan identifies learning objectives and outcomes for each unit and suggests activities which will enable these to be achieved. A medium-term plan usually shows a sequence of units which will promote progression. In many schools, all staff are involved in the production of the medium-term plan in collaboration with the design and technology subject leader/coordinator, ensuring that there is consistency within the units and that they promote progression.

The QCA SoW is based on units which are effectively relatively easily adaptable as a teacher's medium-term plan – their map of how this subject will be taught over a period of several weeks of individual lessons or more intensively over a few days (see Figure 8.1). Within the QCA SoW, each unit is set out in the same way and has a reference code, e.g. *Unit 4E Lighting it up: Focus – control: electrical, computer*. The number gives the year group for which it is intended. The letter is provided to give a quick reference and is not intended to imply an order in which the units should be taught during the year. There is an outline of the main content of the unit and contexts for the work. A section, 'prior learning' indicates the knowledge and skills that it is desirable for children to have before they start the unit. Teachers are reminded of the specific design and technology vocabulary that children might meet. Helpfully, there are lists of materials, tools and equipment that are necessary for the activities. 'Expectations' are identified which, in broad terms, indicate what children might be expected to know and do at the end of the unit. They also describe the range of responses which might be achieved by average, more and less able children in the class, providing support for teachers in addressing differentiation and providing a framework for assessing children by grouping their attainment within these three levels. These are followed by explicit 'learning objectives', an outline of 'possible teaching activities' and 'learning outcomes' to inform teachers' assessments of the children. Finally, each unit has a useful list of points to note covering: links with other design and technology units; links with other units in the QCA SoW for all core subjects (including ICT); practical suggestions regarding content; notes about classroom management, health and safety, out of school activities and homework. The units can be downloaded from the QCA website (www.standards.dfee.gov.uk/scheme) into a word-processor and adapted as necessary. Although the SoW was published before the changes to the national National Curriculum introduced in September 2000, few modifications to the SoW were necessary. A Teacher's Guide (update) was provided (QCA/DfEE 2000b) together with one new unit (4E: Lighting up) and three revised units (4D: Alarms, 5A: Musical instruments and 5B: Bread). A welcome inclusion in this new guide is a section promoting the opportunities for design and technology to support Personal, Social and Health Education (PSHE) and citizenship, highlighting examples such as:

- developing children's sense of responsibility in following safe procedures when making things, for example when they learn about food safety and hygiene in Unit 1C 'Eat more fruit and vegetables', Unit 3B 'Sandwich snacks', Unit 5B 'Bread' and Unit 5D 'Biscuits';
- helping children learn how to keep healthy and about what influences health, for example when they learn about a healthy diet in Unit 1C 'Eat more fruit and vegetables', Unit 3B 'Sandwich snacks', Unit 5B 'Bread' and Unit 5D 'Biscuits';
- developing the skills children need to share opinions about things that matter to them, explain their views, listen to other people and work cooperatively, for example in Unit 2B 'Puppets', Unit 3C 'Moving monsters' and Unit 4B 'Storybooks';
- developing children's goal-setting skills, for example when working on a project to meet a specific deadline or improving on an area of weakness after evaluation, such as in Unit 4A 'Money containers';
- letting children apply their understanding to what improves and harms their local, natural and built environments when designing and making, for example in Unit 3A 'Packaging' and Unit 6A 'Shelters';
- letting children apply their understanding to personal hygiene and how disease spreads, for example when working hygienically with food in Unit 1C 'Eat more fruit and vegetables', Unit 3B 'Sandwich snacks', Unit 5B 'Bread' and Unit 5D 'Biscuits'.
  (QCA/DfEE 2000b)

Despite being generally welcomed by schools, and, especially, design and technology subject leaders, the units do not necessarily provide sufficient detail to support the least confident teachers. Fortunately, a range of support materials are available, many linked specifically to particular units. For example, DATA have produced help-sheets (1997, 1999c).

Indeed, it should be noted that DATA played a significant part in the construction of the QCA SoW which that builds on the earlier *Guidance Materials for Design and Technology* (DATA 1995a) that were well received and extensively trialed by teachers. The internet increasingly provides a resource for teachers to draw on to support their planning and teaching of design and technology (see, for example, www.vtcentre.com; www.data.org.uk/; www.technology.org.uk/; www.dtonline.org/; www.ngfl.gov.uk/). If a school is developing it's own units, DATA (1997) provide a planning template and detailed advice on what to include.

Medium-term planning can be the stage at which an individual teacher makes a decision about how to approach the teaching of design and technology if the school framework allows such flexibility. Should she or he plan an ingerated project/topic, link the work to another specific subject(s) or plan the work as a completely separate design and technology activity? The latter is organisationally the most straightforward, but as examples throughout this book have illustrated, it is almost impossible (and in many ways undesirable) to isolate learning in design and technology from that in other areas. Despite criticisms of integrated approaches from HMI and others (OFSTED 2001, para. 30), such approaches can improve children's motivation and enthusiasm for learning by making it more like their everyday experiences – which don't come in subject boxes. It can allow them to apply learning from other subjects or stimulate further learning in those subjects as was discussed in Chapter 3. Case Study 10, Ricky's post office, provides an example of an integrated topic approach to planning. Karen Patey had planned a topic on 'People who help us'. Her initial planning had identified a range of areas of the topic with learning opportunities linked to the whole-school plans provided for her. This offered her a menu from which she could select and plan activities. The particular work covered in the case study was planned to address specific learning needs: introducing the children to simple design-related skills; developing their manipulative skills with construction kits; introducing them to critical self-evaluation of their models. Having decided on the learning outcomes, she turned to her menu of ideas to select an area to develop into a viable classroom activity. Other activities, within the topic could have offered similar potential for learning, but her focus, when selecting a task, was the children's learning, not the activity. Her choice of context for the work was informed by her understanding of issues related to the social aspects of classroom work; that girls are most likely to respond positively to a task with a 'human' dimension. Her choice of trigger for the work (a letter from Ricky) was chosen to increase the children's enthusiasm for the task and motivation. It also offered potential for linking with literacy work.

There is no one single infallible approach to planning design and technology work. Free-standing projects, projects as part of topics, a cross-subject activity (such as book-making or a mathematics game), short-term and long-term projects, activities designed to offer practice in the use of particular materials or specific skills, individual, group and whole-class activities are all appropriate means of supporting children's learning in design and technology.

4. Short-term planning

The way in which teachers develop short-term plans of individual lessons on a day to day basis varies considerably depending on the teacher's experience, the demands of the school, his or her familiarity with the content being covered etc. Most teachers admit that their planning is rarely as detailed as that they did for 'teaching practice' during their initial teacher education courses. Karen Patey's daily plans (Case Study 10) produced as a student were very specific, identifying the learning intentions for each activity, listing the resources she would need, indicating the time to be allocated, noting prompts for questions, and reminding herself about specific children's needs. For experienced teachers it is not necessary to plan in such detail, but the discipline of identifying intended or possible learning can result in more focused teaching and more purposeful interventions. There is evidence of this effect in many of the case studies discussed in earlier chapters (for example, Case Study 2: Greetings cards). However, planning for learning should never become restrictive, nor prevent children from thinking laterally, following their own lines of enquiry and investigation.

Few would claim short-term planning is unnecessary. Developing and evaluating daily plans are part of the professional role of teachers. Using the map analogy, these plans should include the most detail and be of the largest scale – the equivalent of a street map. Such plans should indicate a sub-set of objectives for a lesson drawn from the medium-term plans. They should, ideally, indicate specific strategies for differentiating children's learning and highlight any specific targets for individual children. Short-term plans should be informed by a teacher's understanding of exactly 'where the children are'. They are the tool for using formative assessment to inform the next stage of learning. Crucially, short-term plans, especially for less-experienced teachers, should indicate how a lesson will be structured and paced. Figure 8.3 provides an example from a series of lessons planned to cover QCA Unit 3B: Sandwich snacks, which build on the children's previous experiences of evaluating other products. Further examples of teachers' daily plans linked to QCA units can be found in *Planning into Practice* (DATA 1997). These excellent cases include the teachers' evaluations of how the lessons went and additional practical guidance for those using the plans. The DATA *Journal of Design and Technology Education* is another useful source of examples of teachers' planning. Recent articles including detailing examples of lesson plans and discussion of their implementation include McGee (2000) and McInnes (2000).

Every teacher has a personal approach to planning and it was not my intention to provide a blueprint for how it should be done. The message of this section is that effective learning in design and technology requires forward planning on the part of the teacher. The plans may be a flexible and adaptable framework that allows a teacher to respond to the unexpected, but, like design and technology itself, the teaching should be purposeful, and the purposes should be clarified by the teacher. It is worth noting that teachers' planning is one of the areas which OFSTED inspectors use to judge quality of teaching (see Chapter 1). The generic criteria refer to 'effective planning which sets clear objectives that pupils understand' (OFSTED 1999a). With regard to design and technology they are looking at planning in relation to, 'whether it includes an increasing range of materials, tools and of kits; focused practical tasks as well as "design and make" assignments; tasks that include an element of evaluation of products including their influence on the environment and the quality of life of others' (OFSTED 2000).

Unit: 3B: Sandwich snacks
Class: 24 children, Year 3: Spring Term
Lesson 2: Evaluating sandwiches

Objectives: Children should learn (with references to Key Stage 2 Programmes of Study):

1. that there are a variety of sandwiches (5a)
2. that people have different preferences (1a and 3c)
3. that different combinations of ingredients can affect the appearances, taste and texture of the product (4a and b)
4. appropriate language – such as, ingredients, slices, spread, vegetables, salad, cheeses
5. that a database can be used to store survey information

Timing	Teaching strategy	Activities
10 minutes	Remind children of previous lesson on healthy eating, using poster produced and poster on health foods, link to sandwich ingredients.	Whole-class discussion
10 minutes	Discussion of criteria that could be used to evaluate sandwiches – brainstorm ideas such as appearance, smell, taste, texture and healthiness. Agree a process for evaluating – e.g. look, smell, open and re-look, smell and list ingredients, re-close, cut up for tasting, taste. Remind the children of the difference between tasting and eating.	Whole-class discussion
30 minutes	Reminder of health and safety concerns and need for hygienic handling of food. Supervise pairs evaluating sandwiches and recording results. Assess individual children's responses to task. Focus on stretching Sarah and Tina – get them to predict responses of their mothers and of teenagers, if time. Provide picture prompts for Steven to use for recording.	Work in pairs on tables of 6. Each table has 4 sandwiches. Record results/opinions on pro forma. One person from each table to start entering data into computer database already set up with appropriate fields.
15 minutes	Feedback from each table on initial evaluations. Discussion of how further research on other peoples' views could be done to add to data already collected.	Whole-class discussion

Figure 8.3 Exemplar lesson plan

5. Links between planning, assessment and evaluation

Karen Patey's planning of her day to day work with the children (Case Study 10) was a good example of a teacher's planning being informed by her assessments of children's learning and her evaluation of her own teaching during previous work. The links between planning, assessment and evaluation are illustrated in Figure 8.4, which was generated through discussion with teachers during preparation of a previous publication (Ritchie 1991). Classroom work should never be driven by the fear of assessments that may lie ahead, but planning can profitably be informed by previous assessments made of children's learning, and indeed during planning it is appropriate to think about assessment opportunities that may arise in the planned lesson. Teaching in order to be able to carry specifically planned assessments has significant disadvantages. Teachers should be constantly on the look out for unintended or unexpected outcomes of children's learning since these are often the most fruitful in providing insights into how their learning might be supported. Drummond (1993) reminds us that 'unintended learning is not, in any event, easy to recognise; when it runs counter to the teacher's intentions, it may become virtually invisible' (p. 17). Design and technology work will require teachers to be alert to the significance of children's responses by regularly probing their reasons for action.

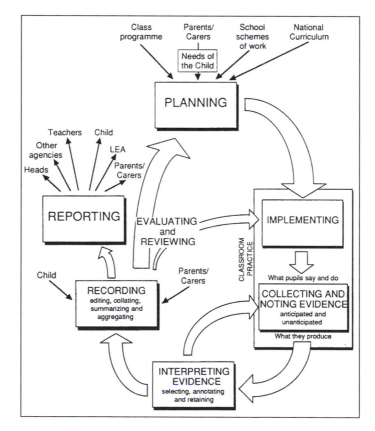

Figure 8.4 The assessment process

Assessment has been referred to in several places in this book and this section attempts to bring some of these ideas together. Effective learning will result from teaching and assessing going hand in hand. This is again an issue for agreement and understanding at the whole-school level. However, assessment can never be precise and straightforward in the way that is implied by the National Curriculum requirements, statutory national testing and regular statements from politicians. As Drummond (1993) states in her excellent treatment of assessment, it is 'essentially provisional, partial, tentative, exploratory and, inevitably, incomplete' (p. 14). My own view of assessment is also very much in tune with that of Christian Schiller (1946) who had the foresight to warn about the dangers of reducing children to ticks in boxes over fifty years ago:

> They say that no one truly sees his own face. This mercy of nature comes from the fact that reflections in a mirror show partial pictures which are flat; they cannot show an object in the round. To see an object in the round it must be observed as a whole in three dimensions. The skills of young children show reflections of their attainment, but they do not show attainment in the round. To see their attainment in the round we must observe it in their way of living.

Design and technology activities provide regular opportunities for observing 'attainment in the round'. The key arguments about assessment in this book have focused upon its formative purposes:

- assessment is an integral part of teaching, the means by which teachers gain insights into children's learning in order to make appropriate interventions and to plan future learning opportunities;
- assessment is ongoing, involving teachers in accumulating evidence of what children say, what they do, what they produce;
- assessment requires teachers to recognise the significance of this evidence and to make judgements based on it;
- self-assessment by children contributes to their learning.

The relationship between assessment, record-keeping and reporting is also illustrated in Figure 8.4. Unfortunately, in the last few years much of the energy that teachers have put into discussions about assessment has been dissipated in the production of often unmanageable and unhelpful record sheets. The really important discussions, about the difficulty of recognising what is significant, and about the quality of teacher judgements, have been less common in design and technology. In some ways, the best record sheet is a blank piece of paper on which a teacher notes significant achievements and insights into a child's learning and needs. My own preference is for a holistic system of recording achievements through a profile (Ritchie 1991) to which child, teacher and parents regularly contribute. Such a profile can be used to build up a rounded picture of the child.

Assessment in design and technology is, it can be argued, less problematic than in other areas of the curriculum, since the emphasis upon ongoing evaluation by children of their own work results in a rich source of assessment evidence for the teacher. The importance of practical work in design and technology means that there are many opportunities for the assessment of skills, as discussed in Chapters 5. The need for children to talk to each other and to their teachers during work ensures a further reservoir of evidence is available for the teacher to tap into when time is available. The level descriptions included in the orders (DfEE/QCA 1999) provide a reasonably straightforward means of assessing the level of pupils in a 'best fit' mode and reporting that to parents. Reporting a child's level in design and technology in isolation is, of course, of limited value to parents and others. Such information needs to be contextualised in terms of the child's response to particular activities and an insight into her or his particular strengths and weaknesses.

Assessment and evaluation are different. Both should be carried out by children and teachers. Children are evaluating as part of the design and technology process; teachers are evaluating the success of their teaching. Teachers are asssessing children's learning and children can, themselves, be engaged in self-assessment – making judgements about what they are good at and what they need to improve. The link is made when assessments of children by teachers contribute to their evaluations of the success of their teaching as was discussed in Chapter 7.

6. Conclusion

This chapter has been based upon the premise that effective teacher planning is necessary for providing quality learning for children. Planning ensures continuity of experience for children in design and technology. Planning helps a teacher to differentiate the learning experiences offered to individual children and so contributes to progression. The chapter has focused upon teachers' planning, as an individual and collaborative task, tackled collaboratively with colleagues. However, it is evident from earlier case studies and the values evident in this book that a teacher holding a constructivist view of learning will also seek to involve children in planning classroom work. Children can be actively involved in planning within a framework that their teacher establishes. The curriculum as a whole is the responsibility of the teacher, but that should not exclude children from making many decisions concerning their own learning. Teachers and children can work together in identifying opportunities for design and technology work within the classroom, they can collaborate on the particular tasks that need doing as part of a project and negotiate the allocation of these tasks. Children can make decisions about the resources they intend to use and take responsibility for collecting these resources from within and outside school. Indeed, progression in design and technology involves children in taking increasingly more responsibility for planning their own activities, becoming more autonomous learners.

One result of the Education Reform Act 1988 (HMSO 1988) has been to encourage far more whole-school planning than before. The collaborative activities that, for example, have produced schemes of work in individual schools throughout England and Wales have had benefits in many curriculum areas including design and technology. Where producing or adapting schemes of work has been approached in a positive and constructive way, as well as generating documents to support individual teachers' planning, the discussions and trying out of activities in classrooms have had considerable spin-offs in terms of professional development.

CHAPTER 9

Professional development

1. Introduction

This book is intended to support teachers who wish to improve the quality of children's learning in design and technology through making changes to their own practice. This chapter offers an approach to professional development that addresses this intention. The previous chapters have discussed the processes of design and technology and the processes of teaching. The similarities between these have been explored and reference has also been made to another process: that of action enquiry as a route for teachers' professional development. The parallels between this and design and technology are discussed in the following sections.

Most primary schools have now got an identified subject leader/coordinator for design and technology. This chapter will consider the roles and responsibilities of this key person in school, particularly those concerned with supporting less confident colleagues and facilitating their professional development.

The latter part of the chapter draws together the key strands of the book and addresses the extent to which design and technology education can meet the needs of children who will face the challenge of adult life in the increasingly technological twenty-first century.

2. Improving the quality of design and technology teaching

Teaching design and technology well is a demanding task, especially for teachers who may have had limited design and technology education themselves, who lack confidence and experience in teaching design and technology, or who lack an adequate knowledge and skills base. Improving the quality of teaching can be achieved through a number of routes. For example, teachers' confidence to teach design and technology may be improved by providing them with practical workshops during which they can develop their own skills and knowledge. Their professional competence may be helped by increasing their understanding of the nature of design and technology and how children learn. Background knowledge and understanding may be increased through the use of distance-learning and other support materials (e.g. TTA 1998a). Some teachers may benefit from observing or talking with more experienced colleagues. Conversely, being observed by a colleague, perhaps in the context of monitoring, and receiving feedback can prove valuable. However, at the end of the day, as established in Chapter 1, individual teachers need to take responsibility for changes to their own practice: they need ownership of those changes. That is why, for me, action enquiries play such an important part in enabling teachers to make effective and manageable changes to their practice. Action enquiry requires teachers to engage in cycles of planning, acting, observing and reflecting as they strive to improve their professional capability and understanding of their practice.

The view of children's learning informing this book is one in which the learner's existing competence and understanding are significant for future learning. Learning involves restructuring existing ideas in the light of new experience, and applying those ideas in new contexts. The same is true for teachers as adult learners. All teachers have existing ideas, about, for example, children's learning, their own role in facilitating learning, and the nature of the subject they are teaching. These ideas are part of the store of professional understanding that informs day-to-day decisions. Underlying this understanding are some deeply held, but rarely examined, values and beliefs. In order to make changes to practice, it helps if teachers make both these ideas and values explicit so that through a process of reflection on what actually goes on in their classrooms they can identify concerns about their work and focus on an area for development. It is often the case that our values regarding teaching and learning are not fully reflected in what we actually do. Everyday, teachers are dealing with dilemmas, sometimes created by forces outside their control, which lead to 'espoused theories' and 'theories in action' being different (Eason 1985) or our values 'being denied in action' (Whitehead 1989). The structuring of existing ideas and clarification of concerns about one's teaching is the first step in carrying out a systematic action enquiry. Sometimes concerns are evident without much searching; in other situations teachers may need to explore their current practice more systematically. This can be achieved through the use of video, audio-taping, field notes, or observation by colleagues to collect evidence of what actually happens during their design and technology teaching. Having clarified a need for change or improvement, the next step is to generate new ways forward. This might be helped by discussion with colleagues, observing colleagues at work, reading, or applying strategies from one situation to another (for example adapting the approach to plenary sessions used in mathematics lessons). Collaboration can be particularly valuable at this stage. Once a specific change has been identified, a plan for its implementation needs to be made. Part of this planning should be a consideration of what evidence might be available to help the individual evaluate the change and make judgements concerning its effectiveness. This evidence may come from a variety of sources. The teacher, as a researcher into his or her own classroom, can make use of the data collection techniques used by educational researchers (see Hopkins 1993), alongside other methods more familiar to them as teachers. Action enquiries involve considered judgements based upon evidence, not impressionistic judgements such as those that often inform informal teacher evaluations.

The plans need to be implemented and evidence collected to allow the teacher, through reflection and perhaps through discussion with colleagues, based upon this evidence, to decide how successful the change has been. The implementation phase might involve a single session or several weeks' work with a class, a group or an individual, depending upon the concern being tackled. What teachers do with the evidence they collect is much more important than what or how much they collect. It is tempting to amass a vast amount of evidence and do little with it. Analysis of data in order to look for significance, patterns or issues that arise can be difficult and time-consuming. The collaborative dimension during this stage of reflection and evaluation allows teachers who are carrying out action enquiries to benefit from the experience and insights of others and to validate their claims: if other professionals consider the evidence available do they agree with the judgements made? The outcomes of this stage are unlikely to be straightforward claims that concerns have been addressed or problems solved! Much more likely are new insights into other factors involved, new concerns or the recognition of a need for a modified approach. In this sense, action enquiries involve a cyclical process – reflection leads to new plans. Although I have described this process as an action enquiry, it has many similarities with action research (McNiff *et al.* 1996; Ollerenshaw and Ritchie 1997, Chapter 8; Ritchie 1993, 1995). It involves teachers researching into their own practice with two key aims: to improve that practice, and to understand that practice better. Action research is essentially action enquiry brought into the public sphere through publication.

Action enquiries have the potential to enable teachers to ensure that their practice reflects more completely their underlying values; that what they think and talk about as their approach to teaching is evident in the way they actually work with children. Action enquiries inevitably lead to changes in practice, and ideally to improvements. However, they require a rigorous and honest approach. They require a teacher to be: open to new perspectives; to value collaboration; to take professional risks; and to be creative in imagining new ways of working.

During an action enquiry, teachers are restructuring their understanding of their practice as well as changing that practice. The model of children's learning, discussed in Chapter 2, features a phase of application; for teachers, application comes when a new strategy or approach investigated through an action enquiry is used in other contexts, and becomes 'embedded' within their professional repertoires.

Many of the case studies featured in this book have resulted from teachers engaging in professional development of this type. The nature of the evidence and its analysis, in these cases, provide examples of how teachers can look closely at their practice and use the insights gained to improve their teaching. For example, Inge Fey (Case Study 1: Our neighbourhood) clearly articulated her values related to the teaching of design and technology which provided her with a framework for evaluating her work with children; Richard Brice (Case Study 5: Air-raid shelters) identified a concern related to his management of children as a result of reflecting upon his practice; Case Study 7: Play areas, was an explicit attempt to gain insights into a specific nature of children's learning. In my work with teachers, concerns that they raise are sometimes related to gender issues: How can they ensure girls have equal access to and opportunities to learn from design and technology activities? For example, Wendy Davey and Neil Tuttiett (Mary Elton Primary School, North Somerset) conducted a fascinating study into the response of girls to different forms of teacher intervention and different types of group composition in the context of design and make tasks (Ollerenshaw and Ritchie 1997, pp. 181–4). Close observation of what was actually going on in their classrooms 'shocked' and 'disturbed' them. In their own words, 'We did not really want to believe that the boys were pushing the girls out of these (practical) types of activities but we were increasingly aware that this was a problem and quite a serious one.' They explored different strategies in an attempt to improve the situation and found much more careful selection of groups proved effective in improving learning opportunities for girls and boys.

The following case study illustrates a teacher engaging in a more limited enquiry, but one also aimed at addressing the question: How can I improve the quality of my design and technology teaching? The teacher involved was Mandy Denning, Design and Technology subject leader/coordinator at Novers Lane Infants' School in south Bristol. She was teaching a class of 25 children aged 4 to 6 years. The account is a shortened version of one she wrote at the time.

CASE STUDY

18: Teaching skills

I feel confident that I can provide children with contextualised or real problems where they can identify needs and opportunities for designing and making. All too often, however, I feel I have put children at a disadvantage as they do not always have all the skills or knowledge and experience of how to use tools necessary to fulfil a task satisfactorily. My teaching of skills is somewhat *ad hoc* and there is a place for this, but I also feel a need to be more organised and specific about the teaching of certain skills. I decided to carry out an enquiry into this aspect of my teaching, with a focus on skills related to ways of joining paper. I often felt that when the children were making models from everyday materials, they did not really consider which glue would be most appropriate to join things, or indeed if there was any other way of fixing them, but instead used what was most readily available.

As an exploratory phase of my enquiry, I decided to compare whether there was a difference in the quality of learning between children who had had a particular skill taught before a design and technology activity and those who had not and were supported in skill development as necessary during the activity. In order to achieve this I worked first with a group of five children, teaching them about joining paper as a focused practical task (FPT), and then got them to tackle a design and make activity. I then repeated the activity, without the specific skill teaching, with a different group of children.

With the first group, I began by brainstorming with the children all the different ways of joining paper and I recorded these on a large sheet of paper using different coloured pens for each child. We then looked at a 'workshop box' that I had put together which contained many different ways of joining, for example different glues, tapes, stapler and paper fasteners. We talked about each one and I demonstrated how they were used to join paper. I then set them the task of joining coloured pieces of paper in various ways to practise the skills introduced.

The following day the children were set a problem relating to a story about a girl who had to carry some apples to her friend's house, but had nothing to take them in – What could the children do to help?

They decided to make a bag for the girl. We examined a variety of bags that I had collected and considered how they had been made. The children looked at the resources available and I asked them to try and use paper to solve the problem. The children then drew designs of the bags they wanted to make and I wrote down the things they said were needed to make their outcomes. Once they were happy with their designs they started to make their bags. I tried to observe as much of what was occurring as possible as field notes. When the children had completed the bags to their own satisfaction we had a brief session reviewing the outcomes.

The second group were not given the skills training, but were asked to tackle the same problem. They had access to the same materials and were given similar teacher support as they designed and made bags.

I analysed the evidence I collected during the activities. The children in the first group were very imaginative during the brainstorming that I organised as part of the skills training; they came up with many alternatives. They had enjoyed joining the pieces of paper in different ways and clearly transferred the skills learnt to the problem solving situation on the following day. The second group produced similar outcomes to the first. However, it was apparent that the children in the first group used the materials more appropriately. They were more confident about what they were doing – they were more skilled. They had more ownership of the product since there was much less help from me during the making phase – the skill input was given the day before.

This first cycle of my enquiry made me aware of the value of teaching skills outside of the context of a specific design and technology assignment. What were the implications of this in other classes?

I discussed my enquiry with my appraiser at a preliminary appraisal interview, held soon after the work had been completed. We agreed that I should be appraised working alongside colleagues, in my curriculum leader's role, further exploring the way that teaching skills improves the quality of children's learning in design and technology.

The work with a colleague began with a discussion of the insights I gained from the first phase of my enquiry. The teacher identified the skill of joining wood as one she felt the children needed and one which she lacked confidence to teach. We decided to work with small groups of children, taking it in turns to teach children the skills involved, as a focused practical task (FPT), and then later posing them a problem in context. We planned the sessions together. The person not actually working with the children was to make observation notes and these observations were to be discussed later. My appraiser was also to observe, make notes and join the evaluation discussion. During the practical part of the lesson we were able to talk and compare observations while the children were working. The teacher felt able to ask about any problems that arose, for example children who found difficulty with sawing, and we were able to tackle these together. It was very much a process of learning together. I had asked my appraiser to look for evidence of whether the skills the children had been taught were used in the follow-up activity. The evaluative discussion proved constructive and added to the insights each of us had gained from the classroom experience.

This second cycle, tackled as a collaborative activity, supported my earlier findings about the importance of teaching skills and how to reinforce them during problems set in a relevant context for the children. It also provided a purpose for my work with a colleague that was of mutual benefit.

Mandy's small-scale enquiry led to changed practice and to improved understanding of that practice. In Mandy's case the enquiry modified her ideas and beliefs about teaching design and technology; before attending a course, which stimulated this enquiry, she had held firmly to the idea that children should be taught skills in the context of a design and make assignment (DMA). Therefore, she approached her enquiry in an open-minded way, demonstrating that she was prepared to try a new approach that she was introduced to on the course. It had a collaborative dimension that led to benefits beyond her own classroom. It also illustrates the way that teacher appraisal, if approached constructively, can contribute to professional development and provide opportunities for subject leaders/coordinators to work with colleagues. Mandy's appraiser supported her enquiry that in turn led to support for a less confident colleague.

Another example of a teacher as learner is Jo Thomas, from Kings Court Primary School in Yate, who had recently started teaching a year 2 class having previously always worked with older children. She taught Unit 2A: Vehicles from the QCA SoW (QCA/DfEE 1998) as part of a broader 'Transport' topic and, as an enquiry, monitored the children's progress and the impact of her teaching, writing up her experiences as an assignment for a subject leader course she was attending. Her summary emphasises the benefits of the process:

> Just as the children had taken part in a learning experiences, I had found out a lot about myself as a teacher and learner. The importance of: flexible planning and organising the stages of the work; ensuring resources and tools needed are readily available; working from the children's ideas and understanding. I became aware of how my comments and interventions could influence children's ideas – sometimes inhibiting and at other times liberating their thinking. This was a particularly steep learning curve for me as I was anxious that I would lead the children's thoughts too much, either over or underestimating their skills of reasoning and creativity, having previously only taught older children. I also increased my own subject knowledge greatly.

Bowen (1996b) reports on a longer-term enquiry into quality teaching in design and technology which involved a number of schools. His findings are useful in helping teachers focus on relevant issues to pursue for their own school-based enquiries. The key lessons from his research include the following:

- the design process should be broken down into manageable steps and taught so that children can assimilate them;
- the development of cognitive knowledge and motor skills need developing in parallel with creative attributes;

- demonstration is an effective technique for teaching skills to children;
- children need to practice working together – use of pupils for mentoring works well;
- children acquire large amounts of conceptual knowledge through activities;
- children do not see knowledge as a tool for realisation of a design, but as an end in itself, however they do use their knowledge effectively when designing and making;
- children use procedural knowledge although little recognition of its importance was evident in his findings;
- imposing structure on the learning situation is essential to ensure that children progress and is powerful in generating creative responses.

Tickle (1996) has edited a number of primary teachers' enquiries focused on design and technology, some of which have already been referred to in previous chapters. Supporting teachers in carrying out classroom action enquiries has been a strategy that I have used on in-service activities for some years (Ollerenshaw and Ritchie 1997; Ritchie 1989, 1993, 1995). I remain convinced that such an approach has the potential to improve the quality of teaching in design and technology, and, therefore, the quality of children's learning in this area.

3. The roles and responsibilities of the design and technology subject leader

A subject leader or coordinator for design and technology has an important and challenging job (Cross 1998): taking a leading role in the development or review of the school policy and scheme of work; being responsible for such things as ordering and maintaining resources; motivating and supporting colleagues in their teaching; keeping abreast of new developments and National Curriculum requirements; arranging school-based staff development and other forms of INSET; talking to parents and governors; coordinating approaches to assessment and record-keeping; monitoring the teaching of design and technology throughout the school; organising whole-school initiatives. The nature of subject leadership is now nationally defined in the *National Standards for Subject Leaders* (NSSL) (TTA 1998b). These standards are generic and cross-phase. They are comprehensive but, in my view, unrealistic for many design and technology subject leaders in the current context, where few have enough time and in particular non-contact time to fulfil their responsibilities. However, they do provide a valuable framework in which subject leaders can audit their current approach and identify priorities. The NSSL stress that the core purpose of subject leadership is 'to provide professional leadership for a subject, to secure high quality teaching and effective use of resources, and to ensure improved standards of achievements for all pupils' (TTA 1998b, p. 3). The subject leader is expected to make a significant contribution to school improvement. The effectiveness of the subject leader should, according to the TTA, be evident through the sustained improvement of all pupils (in their design and technology) knowledge, understanding and skills in relation to prior attainment. Other indicators of a successful subject leader will include a school staff who work together as a team, who are enthusiastic about design and technology and understand its important contribution to pupils' learning. They will have high expectations, but set realistic targets; they will be committed to their own ongoing professional development.

The *National Standards for Subject Leaders* (TTA 1998b) outlines the professional knowledge and understanding (part subject-specific and part generic) that design and technology subject leaders should have, about (for example):

1. the statutory requirements (including assessment, recording and reporting);
2. the relationship of design and technology to the whole curriculum;
3. the characteristics of high quality teaching and strategies for improving standards;
4. relevant research and inspection evidence and pupil achievement data;
5. the contribution design and technology can make to the development of literacy, numeracy and IT skills;
6. the implications of the Code of Practice for Special Educational Needs for teaching and learning design and technology;
7. health and safety requirements in design and technology.

The standards indicate that subject leaders need management and administrative skills, attributes and professional competences to lead and manage people to work as individuals and as a team towards a common goal. These attributes include self-confidence, adaptability, energy and perseverance, reliability, enthusiasm for science and integrity. They need the ability to solve problems and have a range of decision-making skills. Communication is a vital aspect of the role, as is self-management: the ability to plan time efficiently and organise oneself well.

It is beyond the scope of this book to address all aspects of the subject leader's roles and responsibilities. Bell and Ritchie (1999) explore the differences between subject coordination and leadership, stressing that the latter involves a more proactive developmental approach, requiring vision, target and goal setting, action planning, systematic monitoring and evaluation. They stress the importance of subject leaders 'starting from where the school is' and auditing the current situation. An example of this includes the case of a design and technology subject leader, Alison, who had just been appointed to her urban primary school. She had been teaching for three years. She realised through informal conversations with colleagues that there was a considerable variety of construction kits available in the school, but the use being made of this resource was variable, especially in Key Stage 2. She decided to audit exactly what was available and how it was being used. She produced a simple pro forma which invited colleagues to list what they had and give examples of how they were currently using what they had. Based on the responses, she identified several issues: some classes had the same kits, but not enough to be useful; there was no continuity through the school; there was an example of good collaboration in one year group (exchanging kits at different times of the year), but not in others; there was insufficient challenge for pupils at the top end of Key Stage 2; use of construction kits was rarely planned systematically by teachers. Alison developed an action plan. She negotiated with the head teacher the opportunity to take two staff meetings. At the first she asked everyone to bring examples of the kits they had to a meeting. She fedback what she had found through the audit, introduced her ideas about progression and continuity in the use of construction kits (see DATA 1996a) and invited colleagues to consider a more rational means of allocating existing kits around classes and to identify kits that could be shared among more than one class. At the second meeting, staff explored ways of including the use of construction kits into their regular planning. They also identified gaps in their current range of kits and helped Alison formulate a case for asking for some money from the PTA to buy some more 'technical' kits for Key Stage 2 (Bell and Ritchie 1999, p. 42).

Subject leaders should be supporting colleagues' teaching of design and technology, working with individuals and, where possible, the whole staff. The previous two case studies (17 and 18) have already provided examples of this. Bell and Ritchie (1999) provide another case study, illustrating use of a model proposed by Joyce and Showers (1980) which recognised effective professional learning involved the following stages:

1. presentation of new skills;
2. modelling of new skills;
3. practise in simulated settings;
4. feedback on performance in simulated or real settings;
5. coaching/assistance on the job.

Jane is a design and technology coordinator in a rural school of 150 pupils. She was supporting colleagues in introducing new cutting and joining techniques with wood in their classes. She ran a workshop after school and demonstrated the skills involved (1). Colleagues tried out the techniques at their own level, with Jane's support (2). At the end of the session she invited them to reflect and comment on her role as a teacher during the workshop. A few days later, Sally, an older teacher who wanted to improve her design and technology teaching, visited Jane's class for half an hour, while the head took her class for PE. She worked with a small group of children, while Jane worked with the rest on a different activity (3). These children had some experience of using wood, but needed more practice. Sally supported them as they constructed money boxes. At the end of the session Jane and her discussed how it had gone and what lessons Sally had learnt which would help her introduce similar work to her younger class (4). A few weeks later, when Sally had worked with several groups in her own class on the techniques, she invited Jane to pop in and see how the work was progressing. Jane was able to provide positive feedback, but also to remind Sally of some of the health and safety points she had made in the original workshop (5).

(Bell and Ritchie 1999, p. 107)

When supporting colleagues a subject leader can work in a variety of ways. Harland (1990) offers a framework for analysing these, based upon his research into advisory teachers' work. His framework includes the following categories:

- provisionary – when the subject leader provides materials or resources;
- hortative – when the subject leader gives advice and tells colleagues what to do;

- role modelling – when the subject leader shows colleagues how to teach;
- zetetic – a 'let us enquire together' mode, involving the subject leader in asking questions and acting as a critical friend, supporting colleagues' action enquiries or other forms of professional development.

His research indicates that the first two modes, while popular at the time with teachers who received the support, led to limited long-term impact upon practice. Role modelling had more impact, particularly if the teacher involved was expected to take the work started by the subject leader further or try the same work with another group. The zetetic mode was more high-risk, less popular, but potentially that which offered the most likely long-term impact on practice. In reality, support is likely to include aspects of all modes, as was evident in Case Study 18. Perhaps more important is the need for a subject leader to elicit colleagues' needs, generate ideas for meeting those needs, produce an action plan, implement and evaluate the programme of support and from that evaluation set new targets. Again, we meet a process with similarities to design and technology. It is also appropriate to see parallels between the subject leader/coordinator when working with colleagues and the teacher when working with children (see Figure 9.1).

CHILDREN'S LEARNING	TEACHERS' STRATEGY	TEACHERS' LEARNING	SUBJECT LEADER'S ROLE
Engaging with content – being curious and interested	Orientation Unstructured exploration/scene-setting activities	Reflection on current practice and professional understanding	Introducing colleagues to the importance and nature of design and technology and requirements
Structuring existing understanding about the world around them	Elicitation – helping children to find out and clarify what they already think and can do	Structuring existing ideas about teaching and children's learning – identifying concerns	Helping colleagues identify their professional needs and planning ways of meeting those needs
Restructuring ideas by extending, developing or replacing them	Intervention – encouraging children to develop, test out and implement ideas	Trying out new ideas/strategies in the classroom and evaluating them	Supporting colleagues – collaborative planning and evaluation, workshops or in classrooms
Application of what has been learnt to new situations/ everyday life	Application – providing challenges or contexts in which new ideas and capabilities can be tried out	Applying new professional competence and understanding to everyday teaching situations	Supporting application of new teaching competence through whole-school development – schemes of work etc.

Figure 9.1 Parallels between children's and teachers' learning

The ways in which a subject leader might support colleagues' action enquiries include helping them to:

- identify and explore a concern about existing practice;
- focus upon a specific aspect of that concern;
- consider new perspectives;
- set realistic goals;
- generate practical ways forward;
- plan precise action and decide what evidence should be collected to evaluate such action;
- implement the new approach and collect evidence;
- analyse evidence and evaluate action;
- refine or revise original concern.

Whatever form of support is offered it will be most successful when based upon mutual respect between colleagues; when it is flexible and responsive to individual needs; when it is realistic and begins 'from where teachers are' and encourages small manageable steps forward. It is all too easy to highlight colleagues' weaknesses and make them feel incompetent. Teachers are under considerable pressure as a result of current demands – subject leaders should be striving to support colleagues in a constructive and positive manner in dealing with these pressures.

Some design and technology subject leaders have successfully used the stimulus of a whole-school project or event to raise the profile of the subject and support colleagues teaching. Louisa Damer and Paul Brady, who share responsibility for design and technology at Weston All Saints Primary School in Bath, helped organise a whole-school project there during the summer of 1999 linked with a school visit to the Millennium Dome. At a previous INSET day, the staff had agreed that the project should have a curriculum focus on design and technology. All teachers were supported in planning work with their classes over a week-long period during which each class designed and made a 3D display that represented a major historical event to add to a school 'time line'. Louisa and Paul provided ongoing support during the making phase as well. Both were pleased that most displays involved simple electric circuits and pneumatic mechanisms and showed some progression through the school. They reported on a positive response from staff and noted the opportunities it had provided for them to monitor children's achievements in design and technology. Julie Waldren from Raysfield Junior School in Chipping Sodbury also used such an opportunity when she first took over the post of subject leader as a relatively inexperienced teacher.

CASE STUDY

19: Planning a whole-school project

When Julie arrived at the school it was not well-resourced in terms of materials and tools for design and technology. Her head teacher was supportive and keen to see curriculum development in design and technology. One way in which this support manifested itself was in a reasonable budget for her use. She spent a large part of this providing a basic tool kit for each class. Storage and accessing materials was a major problem in the school because of the size of classrooms. Julie got permission to convert a part of a spare classroom into a resource area where children could go to choose the materials they needed for a particular project or task. She was aware, however, that the provision of tools does not, in itself, mean they get used or that design and technology get taught! She talked to colleagues and the headteacher and identified the need to raise the profile of the subject and increase her colleagues' awareness of the nature of design and technology. She felt the design dimension of work was particularly lacking. She wanted to encourage teachers 'to see the ways in which design and technology can encompass the whole curriculum and how important and relevant it is to all walks of life'. She felt staff needed a framework for understanding design and technology on which they could build good educational practice and gain confidence in teaching the subject. Staff perceptions were slightly different: they admitted lacking confidence but more specifically were concerned about children using tools in the classroom. They recognised that their own limited skills and knowledge meant they were unable to teach skills to the children as well as they would like and help them solve practical problems. Colleagues also identified the need for help in generating ideas for contexts and tasks for children. Linked to this, was a concern about how they could help children generate ideas and produce design drawings and plans. It felt to Julie as if there was a lot to do. For a while a solution remained unclear and then her head teacher made a helpful suggestion.

With her class Julie had been working on a project to improve the school's entrance hall, giving it an 'under the sea' theme. The outcome had generated a lot of interest from other children and teachers. Her head teacher suggested that the whole school could tackle a similar project using the space available in the spare classroom. This was proposed at a staff meeting and although colleagues were a little apprehensive they were willing to 'give it a go'. This focused Julie's attention firmly on staff needs and, together with the head teacher, she planned a strategy for supporting colleagues in preparing for the event. The decision to go ahead with a summer term project (after SATs) was taken the previous December, giving Julie plenty of time to prepare. During that period she ran several staff meetings (involving practical workshops), provided in-class support for colleagues, collected resources for the proposed project (through pleas to local businesses, who proved generous) and detailed planning on the two-week event. The event involved the whole school in producing different 'environments'.

The context was set creatively by Julie at an assembly two weeks before the children started work – they were invited to imagine that an alien would be visiting their school for a very short time. They were told that the alien wanted to 'experience' the variety of different environments that can be found on Earth. Teachers worked collaboratively planning how they could support the children. During the event children worked in mixed aged classes and not necessarily with their own teachers. A leaflet was produced outlining the project and listing the learning that was anticipated (to deal with any parental criticism that there might be about the conventional curriculum being partially suspended for a period). This was to be given to helpers and visitors. The work on the evironments was spread over several days and went relatively smoothly (some problems resulted from materials being centrally located and the resources got rather messy).

The results of the children's endeavours were impressive and shared with parents and others during a couple of open afternoons and evenings. The reaction was excellent – it was front page news in the local paper. Hundreds of parents and younger children from the Infants' school experienced the created environments. Many commented on their 'authenticity', especially the common perception of feeling cold when moving from the desert to the icy place (see Figure 9.2). Space and colour had been used to great effect! Children and staff were pleased with their efforts.

Figure 9.2 An icy place

There are, of course, disadvantages to this way of working, identified by Julie: the translation back into ordinary classroom situations is not straightforward and required continuing support from the subject leader; there was a tendency for art and craft activities to dominate the experience of some children; some children ended up tackling tasks without adequate experience of using the tools, techniques and materials available; teachers were not working with their own classes and were not, therefore, always able to build on the existing knowledge of the children. However, it had considerable benefits: it raised the profile of design and technology; it ensured all children had a shared experience of design and technology and allowed the teachers to see that their children could tackle practical design and make activities (DMAs) successfully; it introduced the children and their teachers to a range of tools, materials and mechanisms which they can go on to use in future projects; it increased parental awareness of the learning opportunities available during such work; it enabled the staff to work collaboratively on a project; it increased teachers' awareness of the need for progression and continuity throughout the school and hence the need to ensure that a scheme of work was followed; it provided a focus for the subject leader's work during staff meetings and in colleagues' classrooms; it allowed the head teacher to demonstrate his support for and endorsement of design and technology; it raised the school's profile locally and regionally and established valuable links between the school and local industry.

In many ways, its main achievement was probably to establish a firm foundation for further staff development and provide a stimulus for that development. Whether Raysfield staff decide to repeat a similar project is perhaps less important than the fact that it worked for them at that time and left them with a desire to move forward in terms of design and technology. Not all subject leaders will have such supportive colleagues or head teacher, nor the time or resources to organise a project such as this. However, there are elements of Julie's approach that can be adopted or adapted by any enthusiastic subject leader.

A responsibility of subject leaders which has become more significant in the last few years is monitoring. Monitoring the quality of learning and teaching in design and technology may be difficult if the subject leader does not receive appropriate support from the head teacher. We saw an example in the previous chapter (Case Study 17) of how a subject leader monitored colleagues' planning in order to review and develop the school's scheme of work and above, Louisa and Paul used a whole-school project to monitor children's learning. Other design and technology subject leaders monitor children's learning through examples of work (perhaps by asking colleagues to send children to them when they have been particularly successful or innovative) or by talking to children and looking though books (choosing a sample from different age groups). It can be difficult to build up a school profile of design and technology work because products make up much of the work rather than written work. However, most schools now have digital cameras which mean a record of appropriate outcomes linked to level descriptions in the National Curriculum can be collected and used as the basis for 'moderation' or 'levelling' discussions with colleagues. Class swaps (Bell and Ritchie 1999, p. 148) provide a practical way for a design and technology subject leader being able to assess and evaluate children's learning and attitudes towards the subject. Visiting other classes to observe design and technology teaching and learning (perhaps while supporting colleagues as described above) is clearly desirable, but not always realistic. Where possible, it can provide valuable evidence for subject leaders and an opportunity for proving constructive feedback to colleagues regarding their teaching. Classroom observations can be based on the OFSTED criteria, discussed in Chapter 1, and the feedback can make explicit reference to these. It should be stressed that the purpose of monitoring is to inform future practice – and to help subject leaders prioritise their efforts. Monitoring should lead to evaluation and action. In this way, subject leaders will be making a significant contribution to school self-evaluation (increasingly important within the new inspection framework (OFSTED 1999a)) and school improvement. Another purpose of monitoring, of course, relates to accountability. Systematic monitoring is one way in which subject leaders can help a school prepare for an OFSTED inspection.

All subject leaders have a key role during OFSTED inspections and preparation should start long before the visit. Maintaining a subject leader's file (the DATA Co-ordinator's file (1996a) is an ideal basis for this) is a good way of ensuring the appropriate evidence is available when needed. Such a file might contain some or all of the following (adapted from Bell and Ritchie 1999, p. 153), (grouped as essential and desirable):

Essential
- job description;
- design and technology policy (with reference to other school policies);
- self-evaluation against the National Standards for Subject Leaders (TTA 1998b) (dated and regularly reviewed);
- subject development plans, targets, action plans, review and evaluation sheets;
- task action plans (kept in date order, with the current one at the front);
- scheme of work (overall map of National Curriculum coverage throughout the school (as discussed in Chapter 8), not, necessarily specific units);
- monitoring data and analysis – or index of where such data are available
- health and safety information;

Desirable
- inventory of tools, equipment and resources (central and in classes), including software, television programmes etc.;
- diary of key activities, especially when non-contact time is provided;
- notes of support offered to colleagues, including their action plans and evaluations;
- minutes/notes of meetings – with head teacher (including review meetings/appraisal, with evidence of your effectiveness being evaluated), other subject leaders, colleagues;
- lists of courses attended – subject leader and colleagues, with evaluation sheets;
- information *re* local networks/cluster meetings/links with other schools (including international projects);
- other information *re* external links: community, subject association, governors, OFSTED, LEA.

The kinds of questions that a design and technology subject leader should be prepared to answer, through reference to this file, when interviewed by an inspector during an inspection might include:

What is being achieved in design and technology? How do you know? What opportunities do you have for finding out?

If you have non-contact time how do you use it and why?

What are the priorities for development in design and technology?

How do you contribute to the school development plan? Is there a design and technology development plan? Do you have a subject leader's action plan?

How was the design and technology policy developed? Is it subject to review?

How would you describe your current roles and responsibilities as a coordinator/subject leader? How were you appointed? Do you have subject expertise, or just personal interest in design and technology? How was your job description arrived at? Is it published?

Do you have responsibility for a budget? If so, how do you manage it? What are your priorities for spending at present? What is planned for the future? Are you clear about ordering procedures, budget management and budget monitoring? Have you audited resources recently? Are there any gaps in current resources?

What in-service training have teachers received recently in design and technology? Have you led, or are you planning to lead, any in-service training? How do you support your colleagues?

Have non-teaching staff or parents received any support (training/workshops/talks)?

Has in-service training had any significant impact on the standards of pupils' work in design and technology?

What in-service training have you received as a subject leader and what impact has it had?

How do you assess and keep records of work covered and pupils' achievements? How is this information reported to parents and others?

Are there any specific arrangements to support pupils with special needs in your subject?

Are there any developments in design and technology about which you are particularly pleased? Are there any constraints on developments in design and technology?

(adapted from Bell and Ritchie 1999)

Further advice on preparing for an OFSTED inspection as a design and technology subject leader can be found in Cross (1998), Gadsby and Harrison (1999) and Wesley (1998).

4. Design and technology education for the future

In 1744, as part of a treaty, North American Indians were invited to send their children to college. They declined in the following way:

> We know that you highly esteem the kind of learning taught in those colleges, and that the maintenance of our young men, while with you, would be very expensive to you. We are convinced, that you mean to do us good by your proposal: we thank you heartily. But you, who are wise must know that different nations have different conceptions of things and you will therefore not take it amiss, if our ideas on the kind of education (we desire) happen not to be the same as yours. We have had some experience of it. Several of our young people were formally brought up at the colleges of the Northern Provinces: they were instructed in all your sciences; but when they came back to us, they were bad runners, ignorant of every means of living in the woods...neither fit for hunters, warriors, nor counsellors, they were totally good for nothing.
>
> We are, however, not the less oblig'd by your kind offer, tho' we decline accepting it; and, to show our grateful sense of it, if the gentlemen of Virginia will send us a dozen of their sons, we will take care of their education, instruct them in all we know, and make men of them.

(Quoted in McLuhan 1973, p. 57)

Design and technology education should equip future citizens with relevant, practical and useful skills, knowledge and understanding, attitudes and awareness for life in the twenty-first century. For some this will mean its vocational dimension is of most significance but, for all who are pupils today, capability and technological awareness will be prerequisites of playing a full and fulfilling part as citizens in a democratic society of the future. These are high ideals, and will not easily be achieved. I was reminded of the native American account of inappropriate education, quoted above, when watching a television programme about the apparent failure of modern-day schools and colleges to educate students successfully for scientific and technological understanding. A student from the Massachusetts Institute for Technology (MIT) was interviewed at her graduation and asked to make a small bulb light up using a battery and two wires (a task most five-year-olds, in my experience, can achieve through exploratory play). She was unable to make it work as she tried to use one wire connected to one pole of the cell, and laughing said, 'I'm a mechanical, not electrical engineer!' But what, I thought of the life skills and basic understanding that 15 years of formal education should have provided! The inclusion of design and technology as a subject that all children must study was undoubtedly a step in the right direction for education in this country. However, only continuing effort on the part of teachers will lead to young adults able to cope with the demands of an increasingly technological society.

Technologies can have devastating effects upon people and the environment. Recent years have seen an increasing awareness in society at large of some of the implications of technological developments. However, much remains to be done to educate future citizens to ensure they remain vigilant to the excesses of technology and those who engage in its development. Whether the issue is global pollution or the impact of genetic engineering, if individuals are to make decisions about issues like these, at the ballot box or in other ways, they need to be well informed and able to deal with conflicting evidence and opinions. Some years ago I came across the following from a head teacher's speech to the staff of a school to which he had just been appointed:

> I am a survivor of a concentration camp. My eyes saw what no man should witness: gas chambers built by learned engineers; children poisoned by educated physicians; infants killed by trained nurses; women and babies shot by high-school and college graduates. So I am suspicious of education. My request is: help your students to become human. Your efforts must never produce learned monsters, skilled psychopaths.

These words encapsulate a message we should all hold in mind and reinforces the 'heart' dimension introduced in Chapter 1. Awareness, as much as capability, is an important outcome of design and technology education. The values dimension, should never be neglected: those engaged in design and technology should always question the implications of their activities and the basis of decisions they, and others, are taking. To return to an earlier anecdote about my own life, and the naïve question I asked about Concorde, I hope that in the future, when the aircraft industry considers the viability of a new generation of passenger aircraft, such as the proposed 'super jumbo', there will be others asking similar questions: that our education system will have produced engineers who strive to use their technological capability to meet genuine human needs and enhancing the quality of all our lives, rather than damaging our environment and using up limited resources unnecessarily.

However, I have no desire to suggest that all design and technology should be targeted towards human needs in this way: much of what we value of the made-world is 'decorative' and, as noted earlier in this book, concerned with wants rather than needs. Nor do I wish to over-exaggerate the nature of design and technology in the primary years, simply to remind the reader that such work should be understood in the context of wider issues. For young learners design and technology, as evidenced through the case studies in this book, is concerned with understanding the made environment, with identifying ways in which they affect it and it affects them. Learning in design and technology can lead to children bringing about positive changes for themselves and for others: it can empower them. Design and technology has the potential to enable them to interact with the made-world more effectively; becoming critical consumers and users of technology who can also appreciate, value, enjoy and admire the achievements of others.

Design and technology provides children with the opportunities to learn how to approach problems, how to think creatively, how to work flexibly and collaboratively, how to learn. If they are introduced to design and technology in the nursery or reception class, what they learn, and the way they learn can be built upon and applied throughout their schooling and beyond into the world of work, everyday life and leisure. It is unlikely that the children in our schools today will be in one job all their lives, they may not even have the opportunity to work throughout their lives. Being adaptable, with the ability to transfer skills and understanding from one context to another will be all important. Design and technology offers more potential than any other area of the school curriculum for developing such capability. However, these great expectations will not be realised through design and technology experiences that involve little more than following instructions or reproducing teachers' ideas. These aspirations require teachers to support children in becoming autonomous learners; motivated and curious to identify needs and opportunities, open-minded and creative thinkers prepared to generate a range of ideas for solving a problem, skilled in the use of a range of tools, materials and techniques, capable of working effectively in a group or on their own, knowledgeable and keen to evaluate their work and outcomes critically and rigorously, aware and prepared to consider the implications of their actions and outcomes. Teachers have a responsibility to give children the best opportunities possible to realise their potentials in this vital area of the curriculum. I hope this book has offered some support in helping colleagues fulfil that responsibility so that they can help children prepare for their futures.

Bibliography

ACCAC (Awdurdod Cymwysterav Cwricwlwm ac Aserv Cymru) (1998) *One in Five; Design and Technology and Pupils with SEN*. Birmingham: ACCAC.

ACCAC (2000) *Key Stages 1 and 2 of the National Curriculum in Wales*. Birmingham: ACCAC Publications.

Allison, Y. (1999) 'Product evaluation: Do the values young children attach to packaging affect their sensory evaluation of a food product and impair their objectivity?' *Journal of Design and Technology Education* 4(1) (Spring), 28–31.

Altrichter, H. *et al.* (1993) *Teachers Investigate their Work*. London: Routledge.

Anning, A. (1997) 'Teaching and learning how to design in schools', *Journal of Design and Technology Education* 2(1) (Spring), 50–2.

Assessment of Performance Unit (APU) (1987) *Design and Technological Activity: A framework for assessment*. London: APU/DES.

Assessment of Performance Unit (APU) (1991) *The Assessment of Performance in Design and Technology*. London: School Examinations and Assessment Council (SEAC).

Barnes, R. (1989) *Art, Design and Topic Work*. London: Routledge.

Baynes, K. (1998) *Drawing Papers*. Loughborough: Loughborough College of Art and Loughborough University of Technology.

Beat, K. (1991) 'Design it, build it, use it: girls and construction kits' in Browne, N. (ed.) *Science and Technology in the Early Years*. Milton Keynes: Open University Press.

Bell, D. and Ritchie, R. (1999) *Towards Effective Subject Leadership in the Primary School*. Buckingham: Open University Press.

Bennett, R. (1996) 'An investigation into some Key Stage 2 children's learning of foundation concepts associated with geared mechamisms', *Journal of Design and Technology Education* 1(3) (Autumn), 218–29.

Benson. C. (1992) *Design and Technology at Key Stages 1 and 2*. York: Longman.

Bentley, D. and Watts, M. (1994) *Primary Science and Technology*. Buckingham: Open University Press.

Bishop, J. (1991) 'The relationship of art and design to design and technology in the National Curriculum in the primary school', *Design and Technology Teaching* 24(1), 13–16.

Bold, C. (1999) *Progression in Design and Technology*. London: David Fulton Publishers.

Bowen, P. (1996a) 'Young Engineers in primary schools', *Journal of Design and Technology Education* 1(3) (Autumn) 242–8.

Bowen, R. (1996b) 'Quality teaching in primary school design and technology', *Journal of Design and Technology Education* 1(1) (Spring), 12–23.

British Gas (1986) *A Problem Shared.* (A video.)

Brodie, T. (1994) 'Special Needs and D&T', *Design and Technology Times,* Spring, 14.

Browne, N. (ed.) (1991) *Science and Technology in the Early Years.* Milton Keynes: Open University Press.

Browne, N. and Ross, C. (1991) '"Girls' stuff, boys' stuff": young children talking and playing' in Browne, N. (ed.) *Science and Technology in the Early Years.* Milton Keynes: Open University Press.

Buchanan, M. (1990) 'Design and Technology: issues for implementation and the role of art and design', *Design and Technology Teaching* 23 (1), 5–12.

Carmichael, P. *et al.* (1990) *Research on Students' Conceptions in Science: a bibliography.* Leeds: Centre for Studies in Science and Mathematics Education (CSSME), University of Leeds.

Chalkley, C. and Shield, G. (1996) 'Supermodelling! Developing designing skills at Key Stage 2', *Journal of Design and Technology Education* 1(1) (Spring), 50–3.

Chidgey, J. (1994) 'A critique of the design process', in Banks, F. (ed.) *Teaching Technology.* London: Routledge.

Claxton, G. (1997) *Hare Brain, Tortoise Mind: Why intelligence increases when you think less.* London: Fourth Estate.

CLEAPSS (1988) *Construction Kits: Guide L173.* Brunel: Brunel University, School Science Service.

Constable, H. (1994a) 'The role of drawing within designing and making – a primary perspective', *Primary Data* 3(2), 8–14.

Constable, H. (1994b) 'A study of aspects of design and technology capability at Key Stages 1 and 2' in *IDATER 94: International Conference on Design and Technology Educational Research and Curriculum Development,* 9–14. Loughborough: Loughborough University of Technology.

Cork, L. and Vernon, P. (2000) *Science and Literacy: Developing links between science and language, fiction and non-fiction.* Leicester: AstraZeneca Science Teaching Trust/SCI Centre.

Coulby, D. and Ward, S. (eds) (1990) *The Primary Core Curriculum.* London: Cassell.

County of Avon (1985) *Working Paper 3: A problem solving approach.* Bristol: County of Avon.

Coventry LEA (1983) *An Introduction to Craft, Design and Technology in the Primary Curriculum.* Coventry: Coventry LEA.

Cross, A. (1998) *Coordinating Design and Technology in the Primary School.* London: Falmer Press.

Cullingford Agnew, S. (1996) 'If you go down to the woods today…', *Journal of Design and Technology Education* 1(1) (Spring) 58–65.

Curriculum Council for Wales (1990) *Design and Technology: Non-statutory guidance.* Cardiff: CCW.

Curriculum Council for Wales (1993a) *Design and Technology and Pupils with Special Educational Needs.* Cardiff: CCW.

Curriculum Council of Wales (1993b) *Generating, Developing and Communicating Ideas in Design and Technology.* Cardiff: CCW.

Cushing, S. (1994) 'Investing in inventiveness', *Times Educational Supplement, Technology Extra,* 29 April, p.IV.

DATA (1995a) *Guidance Materials for Design and Technology: Key Stages 1 and 2.* Wellesbourne: DATA.

DATA (1995b) *Design and Technology: A pupil's entitlement to IT at Key Stages 1 and 2.* Wellesbourne: DATA, MAPE, NAAIDT and NCET.

DATA (1995c) *Technical Vocabulary for Key Stages 1 and 2.* Wellesbourne: DATA.

DATA (1996a) *The Design and Technology Primary Co-ordinator's File.* Wellesbourne: DATA.

DATA (1996b) *Design and Technology: A guide for teacher assistants.* Wellesbourne: DATA.

DATA (1997) *Planning into Practice.* Wellesbourne: DATA.

DATA (1998) *Primary School-based INSET Manual for Design and Technology.* Wellesbourne: DATA.

DATA (1999a) *Cross-curricular Links within the Primary Curriculum.* Wellesbourne: DATA.

DATA (1999b) *Developing Language through Design and Technology.* Wellesbourne: DATA.

DATA (1999c) *Help-sheets Linked to the Scheme of Work.* Wellesbourne: DATA.

Davies, D. (1996) 'Professional design and primary children', *International Journal of Technology and Design Education* 6, 45–59.

Davies, D. (1997) 'The relationship between science and technology in the primary curriculum – alternative perspectives', *Journal of Design and Technology Education* 2(2) (Summer) 101–11.

Davies, D. (2000) 'Ten years of universal primary technology education in England and Wales – what have we learnt?' *Journal of Design and Technology Education* 5(1) (Spring) 26–35.

Davies, D. *et al.* (2000) 'Carrying the torch – can student teachers contribute to the survival of design and technogy in the primary curriculum?', *Design and Technology International Millenium Conference Proceedings.* Wellesbourne: DATA.

Davies, L. *et al.* (2000) 'No bits – no nothing', *Journal of Design and Technology Education* 5(1) (Spring) 52–4.

Deacon, H. (1996) 'Mixed ability children and the single open-ended task', in Tickle, L. (ed.) *Understanding Design and Technology in Primary Schools: Cases from teachers' Research.* London: Routledge.

de Bono, E. (1970) *Lateral Thinking.* London: Ward Lock.

Department for Education (DfE)/Welsh Office (WO) (1995) *Technology in the National Curriculum.* London: HMSO.

Department for Education and Employment (DfEE)/Qualifications and Curriculum Authority (QCA) (1999) *National Curriculum: Design and Technology.* London: DfEE.

Department for Education and Employment (DfEE)/QCA (1999b) The *National Curriculum for Art and Design.* London: DfEE.

Department of Education and Science (DES) (1991) *Science at Key Stages 1 and 2: A report by Her Majesty's Inspectorate.* London: HMSO.

Department of Education and Science (DES)/Welsh Office (WO) (1988) *National Curriculum Design and Technology Working Group: Interim report.* London: DES.

Department of Education and Science (DES)/Welsh Office (WO) (1989) *Design and Technology for Ages 5 to 16. Proposals of the Secretary of State for Education.* London: DES.

Department of Education and Science (DES)/Welsh Office (WO) (1990) *Technology in the National Curriculum.* London: HMSO.

Department of Education and Science (DES)/Welsh Office (WO) (1991) *Science in the National Curriculum.* London: HMSO.

Department of Education and Science (DES)/Welsh Office (WO) (1992a) *Art in the National Curriculum.* London: HMSO.

Department of Education and Science (DES)/Welsh Office (WO) (1992b) *Technology for Ages 5 to 16. Proposals of the Secretary of State for Education.* London: DES.

Design and Technology in Education (DATE) Project (1990) *What is design?* Halifax: Design Dimension Educational Trust.

Donaldson, M. (1978) *Children's Minds.* London: Fontanna.

Drummond, M. (1993) *Assessing Children's Learning.* London: David Fulton Publishers.

Duckworth, E. (1987) *The Having of Wonderful Ideas.* New York: Teachers' College Press.

Eason, P. (1985) *Making School-centred INSET Work.* London: The Open University in association with Croom Helm.

Fisher, R. (ed.) (1987) *Problem Solving in Primary Schools.* Oxford: Basil Blackwell.

Fisher, R. (1990) *Teaching Children to Think.* Oxford: Basil Blackwell.

Fulton, J. (1992) *Materials in Primary Design and Technology.* London: Design Council.

Gadsby, P. and Harrison, M. (1999) *The Primary Co-ordinator and OFSTED Re-inspection.* London: Falmer Press.

Gardner, H. (1993) *Multiple Intelligences; The theory in practice.* New York: Basic Books.

Gardner, I. (1996) 'Soap dishes and smelly socks', *Journal of Design and Technology Education* 1(1) (Spring), 54–7.

Garvey, J. and Quinlan, A. (1997) 'Why don't I just throw it in the bin? – evaluation and self-esteem', *Journal of Design and Technology Education* 2(1) (Spring), 38–45.

Glaser, R. (1992) 'Expert knowledge and the process of thinking', in Halpern, D. F. (ed.) *Enhancing Thinking Skills in Sciences and Mathematics.* Hillsdale, NJ: Erlbaum.

Gloucestershire LEA (1991) *Using Nursery Rhymes and Fantasy Stories: Volumes 1, 2 and 3.* Gloucester: Gloucestershire County Council.

Goleman, D. (1996) *Emotional Intelligence – Why it Matters More than IQ.* London: Bloomsbury.

Greenfield, S. (1998) *The Human Brain.* London: Phoenix Press.

Gura, P. (ed.) (1992) *Exploring Learning: Young children and block play.* London: Paul Chapman Publishing.

Hammond, S. (1997) 'From source to sale: developing an education pack', *Journal of Design and Technology Education* 2(1) (Spring), 53–60.

Harding, J. (1997) 'Gender and design and technology education', *Journal of Design and Technology Education* 2(1) (Spring), 20–5.

Hards, A. (1998) 'Ancient Egypt – hands on', *Journal of Design and Technology Education.* 3(1) (Spring), 41–8.

Harland, J. (1990) *The Work and Impact of Advisory Teachers.* Slough: NFER.

Health Education Authority (1996) *A Balance of Good Health Information Pack*. London: HEA.

Hennessy, S. and McCormick, R. (1994) 'The general problem-solving process in technology education', in Banks, F. (ed.) *Teaching Technology*. London: Routledge.

HMI (1991) *The Teaching and Learning of Design and Technology*. London: HMSO.

HMSO (1988) *Education Reform Act 1988*. London: HMSO.

Hohmann, M. *et al.* (1979) *Young Children in Action*. Michigan: The High/Scope Press.

Hope, G. (2000) 'Beyond their capability? Drawing, designing and the young child', *Journal of Design and Technology Education* 5(2) (Summer), 106–14.

Hopkins, D. (1993) *A Teacher's Guide to Classroom Research*, 2nd edn. Buckingham: Open University Press.

Hopkins, D. *et al.* (1994) *School Improvement in an Era of Change*. London: Cassell.

Howe, A. (1999) 'A visual literacy strategy – why not?' *Journal of Design and Technology Education* 4(3) (Autumn), 215–22.

Howe, A. *et al.* (2001) *Primary Design and Technology for the Future: Creativity, culture and citizenship*. London: David Fulton Publishers.

Iredale, N. and Price, J. (eds) (1999) *You Can Make It*. Durham: The Foundation for SME Development, University of Durham.

Jacobs, M. (1994) 'The technology tree – primary schools in partnership with the engineering industry', *Primary Data* 3(2), 14–16.

Johnsey, R. (1986) *Problem Solving in School Science*. London: Macdonald Education.

Johnsey, R. (1995) 'The design process – Does it exist? – a critical review of published models for the design process in England and Wales', *The International Journal of Technology and Design Education* 2.

Johnsey, R. (1998) *Exploring Primary Design and Technology*. London: Cassell.

Joyce, B. and Showers, B. (1980) 'Improving inservice training: the messages of research', *Educational Leadership*, February, 379–85.

Joyce, M. *et al.* (1998) 'What stimulates the creative process?' *Journal of Design and Technology Education* 3(2) (Summer), 113–16.

Kane, T. (1990) 'Making musical instruments at Key Stage 1', *Design and Technology Teaching* 22 (2), 68–73.

Kimbell, R. *et al.* (1991) *Assessment of Performance in Design and Technology*. London: APU/SEAC.

Lawler, T. and Stables, K. (1993) 'Designing and making with textiles', *Primary Data* 3(1) insert.

Layton, D. (1992) 'Values and design and technology', in Budgett-Meakin, C. (ed.) *Make the Future Work*, 36–53. London: Longman.

Layton, D. (1993) *Technology's Challenge to Science Education*. Buckingham: Open University Press.

Lewin, R. (1994) 'Craft, design and technology and the gifted child' in Banks, F. (ed.) *Teaching Technology*. London: Routledge.

Lewisham LEA (1999) *Find that Book: Making links between literacy and the broader curriculum*. London: Lewisham LEA.

Linton, T. (1998) 'An investigation into the interaction of teaching and learning in design and technology, academic ability and classroom behaviour', *Journal of Design and Technology Education* 3(3) (Autumn), 216–22.

MacIntyre, J. (1993) 'Guidelines for School Coordinators', *The Big Paper*, September, 11.

McGee, C. (2000) 'Planning and developing a teaching pack for a unit of work for a primary age group', *Journal of Design and Technology Education* 5(2) (Spring), 145–52.

McInnes, S. (2000) 'Push and pull – a case study', *Journal of Design and Technology Education* 5(1) (Spring), 35–41.

McLuhan, T. C. (1973) *Touch the Earth.* London: Abacus.

McNiff, J. *et al.* (1996) *You and Your Action Research Project.* London: Routledge.

NAAIDT (1992) *Make it Safe!* Chandlers Ford: NAAIDT Publications.

NACCCE (1999) *All Our Futures: Creativity, culture and education.* London: DfEE.

NATHE (1998) *Learning Futures Textiles – a Teacher's Guide to Good Practice in Textiles Technology.* London: NATHE.

NCET (1989) *Primary Technology: The place of computer control.* Coventry: National Council for Educational Technology.

NCET (1993) *Design and Technology in the National Curriculum: Information sheet 1.* Coventry: National Council for Educational Technology.

National Curriculum Council (NCC) (1990) *Curriculum Guidance 3: The whole curriculum.* York: NCC.

National Curriculum Council (NCC) (1991a) *Non-statutory Guidance: Technology.* York: NCC.

National Curriculum Council (NCC) (1991b) *Planning and Implementing Design and Technology at Key Stage 1 and 2.* York: NCC.

Newton, D. and Newton, L. (1991) *Practical Guides Technology.* Leamington Spa: Scholastic.

Novak, J. and Gowin, D. (1984) *Learning How to Learn.* Cambridge: Cambridge University Press.

OFSTED (1993) *Inspection Handbook.* London: DFE.

OFSTED (1999a) *Handbook for Inspecting Primary and Nursery Schools.* London: The Stationery Office.

OFSTED (1999b) *Primary Education: A review of primary schools in England, 1994–1999.* London: The Stationery Office.

OFSTED (2000) *Inspecting Subjects 3–11.* London: The Office of Her Majesty's Chief Inspector of Schools in England.

OFSTED (2001) *1999–2000 Standards and Quality in Education: The annual report of Her Majesty's Chief Inspector of Schools.* London: The Stationery Office.

Ollerenshaw, C. and Ritchie, R. (1989) 'Looking at learning: a classroom research project', *Primary Science Review* 10 (Summer), 22–23.

Ollerenshaw, C. and Ritchie, R. (1997) *Primary Science: Making it work,* 2nd edn. London: David Fulton Publishers.

Piaget, J. (1929) *The Child's Conception of the World.* London: Harcourt Brace.

Pritchard, A. (1997) 'Supporting children's learning in primary design and technology with information technology: some possibilities and some teachers' perceptions', *Journal of Design and Technology Education* 2(1) (Spring), 112–16.

Qualifications and Curriculum Authority (QCA) (1997a) *Expectations in Design and Technology.* London: QCA.

Qualifications and Curriculum Authority (QCA) (1997b) *Use of Language Key Stages 1 and 2: Design and Technology.* London: QCA.

Qualifications and Curriculum Authority (QCA) (1997c) *Food in Schools: Ideas.* London: QCA.

Qualifications and Curriculum Authority (QCA) (1997d) *Food in Schools: Planning a project.* London: QCA.

Qualifications and Curriculum Authority (QCA)/DfEE (1998*) Design and Technology: a Scheme of Work for Key Stages 1 and 2.* London: QCA.

Qualifications and Curriculum Authority (QCA)/DfEE (2000a) *Curriculum Guidance for the Foundation Stage.* London: QCA.

Qualifications and Curriculum Authority (QCA)/DfEE (2000b) *Design and Technology: a Scheme of Work for Key Stages 1 and 2 – Teachers' Guide (update).* London: QCA.

Qualifications and Curriculum Authority (QCA)/DfEE (2000c) *Art and Design: a Scheme of Work for Key Stages 1 and 2.*London: QCA.

Ritchie, R. (1989) 'Using adventures and simulations', *Microscope Special*, Autumn, 18–23.

Ritchie, R. (ed.) (1991) *Profiling in Primary Schools.* London: Cassell.

Ritchie, R. (1993) 'An evaluation of a practitioner's approach to initial and inservice education of teachers in primary science based upon a constructivist view of learning'. Unpublished PhD thesis. Bath: University of Bath.

Ritchie, R. (1994) 'Planning for continuity in primary D&T through the use of environments'. *Primary Data* 4(1), 21–7.

Ritchie, R. (1995) 'Teachers' professional development in design and technology through action research', in Smith, J. S. (ed.) *IDATER 95: International Conference on Design and Technology Educational Research and Curriculum Development* (Conference Proceedings) 111–15. Loughborough: Loughborough University of Technology. ISBN 1 899291 00 8.

Ritchie, R. and Smith, J. (eds) (1987a) *Working Paper 8: Using a Computer to Support Primary Science and Technology.* Bristol: County of Avon.

Ritchie, R. and Smith, J. (eds) (1987b) *Working Paper 7: Science and Technology from Food Activities.* Bristol: County of Avon.

Roden, C. (1997) 'Young children's problem solving in design and technology: towards a taxonomy of strategies', *Journal of Design and Technology Education* 2(1) (Spring), 14–19.

Roden, C. (1999) 'How children's problem solving strategies develop at Key Stage 1', *Journal of Design and Technology Education* 4(1) (Spring), 21–7.

Rogers, M. and Clare, D. (1994) 'The process diary: developing capability within National Curriculum design and technology – some initial findings' in *IDATER 94: International Conference on Design and Technology Educational Research and Curriculum Development*, 22–28. Loughborough: Loughborough University of Technology.

SCAA (1994) *Working with the Current Technology Orders.* London: SCAA.

SCAA/QCA (1997) *Design and Technology and the Use of Language.* London: SCAA.

Schiller, C. (1946) 'The assessment of attainment of young children'. Ministry of Education discussion paper.

Science Working Group (1987) *Interim Report*. London: DES.

SEAC (1993) *Suggested Guidelines for a More Standardised Approach to Design and Technology*. London: SEAC.

Sellwood, P. (1990) 'The national project: problem solving 5–13', *Proceedings of the Third National Conference on Design and Technology Education Research and Curriculum Development*. Loughborough: Loughborough University of Technology.

Shepard, T. (1990) *Education by Design: A guide to technology across the curriculum*. Cheltenham: Stanley Thornes.

Shuard, H. (1982) 'Differences in mathematical performance between girls and boys' in DES *Mathematics Counts*. London: HMSO.

Siraj-Blatchford, J. (1996) *Learning Technology, Science and Social Justice*. Nottingham: Education Now Publishing Co-operative.

Smith, A. (1996) *Accelerated Learning in the Classroom*. Stafford: Network Educational Press.

Smith, H. (1999) *Opportunities for Information and Communications Technology in the Primary School*. Stoke-on-Trent: Trentham Books.

Snow, C. P. (1959) *The Two Cultures: A second look*. Cambridge: Cambridge University Press.

Somerset LEA (1990a) *Primary Design and Technology Guidelines*. Taunton: Somerset LEA.

Somerset LEA (1990b) *Art and Design and Guidelines*. Taunton: Somerset LEA.

Stables, K. (1992) 'The role of fantasy in contextualising and resourcing design and technology activity', in Smith, J. S. (ed.) *IDATER 92: International Conference on Design and Technology Educational Research and Curriculum Development*. Loughborough: Loughborough University of Technology.

Stein, G. and Poole, P. (1997) *A Primary Teacher's Handbook: Design and technology*. Dunstable: Folens.

STEP (1993) *STEP Design and Technology 5–16 Scheme*. Cambridge: Cambridge University Press.

Taylor, C. (1997) 'Introducing technology at Key Stage 2', *Journal of Design and Technology Education* 2(3) (Autumn), 236–41.

Teacher Training Agency (TTA) (1998a) *Assessing your needs in Design and Technology: Diagnostic tasks and diagnostic feedback*. London: TTA.

Teacher Training Agency (TTA) (1998b) *National Standards for Subject Leaders*. London: TTA.

Teacher Training Agency (TTA) (1999) *Using ICT to Meet Teaching Objectives in Design and Technology: Initial teacher education primary*. Paper 37/5/99. London: TTA.

Tickle, L. (ed.) (1990) *Design and Technology in Primary School Classrooms*. Lewes: The Falmer Press.

Tickle, L. (ed.) (1996) *Understanding Design and Technology in Primary Schools: Cases from teachers' research*. London: Routledge.

Times Educational Supplement (1989) *Task Force*. 15 December, p. 20.

Urwin, B. (ed.) (1991) 'Technology special', *Microscope,* Autumn.

von Glaserfeld, E. (1989) 'Learning as a constructive activity', in Murphy, P. and Moon, B. (eds) *Developments in Learning and Assessment*. London: Hodder and Stoughton.

Vygotsky, L. S. (1962) *Thought and Language*. Cambridge, Mass.: Massachusetts Institute for Technology Press.

Watts, M. (1991) *The Science of Problem Solving*. London: Cassell.

Wesley, T. (1998) 'Preparing for a primary school OFSTED inspection', *Journal of Design and Technology Education* 3(2) (Summer), 124–28.

Weston, F. (1991) 'Design and technology: Delivering Attainment Target 2', *Design and Technology Teaching* 23(2), 95–9.

Whitehead, J. (1989) 'How do we improve research-based professionalism in education?', *British Educational Research Journal* 15(1), 3–15.

Whyte, J. (1993) *Beyond the Wendy House: Sex stereotyping in primary schools*. York: Longman for Schools Council.

Williams, J. (1994) 'Learning through puppets: working with children on process and outcome', *Primary Data* 3(2), 5–8.

Williams, P. and Jinks, D. (1985) *Design and Technology 5–12*. London: The Falmer Press.

Willig, J. (1990) *Children's Concepts and the Primary Curriculum*. London: Paul Chapman Publishing.

Wood, D. (1988) *How Children Think and Learn*. Oxford: Basil Blackwell.

Zarins, D. (1996) 'Positive discrimination – Is there a case?', In Tickle, L. (ed.) *Understanding Design and Technology in Primary Schools: Cases from teachers' research*. London: Routledge.

Index

Learning
Resource Centre
Stockton
Riverside College